Other Baseball Books by Peter Golenbock

*Amazin': The Miraculous History of
New York's Most Beloved Baseball Team*

Balls with Graig Nettles

Bats with Davey Johnson

*The Bronx Zoo: The Astonishing Inside Story of the
1978 World Champion New York Yankees*
with Sparky Lyle

Bums: An Oral History of the Brooklyn Dodgers

Dynasty: The New York Yankees 1949–1964

*The Forever Boys: The Bittersweet World of Major League Baseball
As Seen Through the Eyes of the Men Who Played One More Time*

Guidry with Ron Guidry

Idiot: Beating "The Curse" and Enjoying the Game of Life
with Johnny Damon

Number 1 with Billy Martin

Red Sox Nation: An Unexpurgated History of the Red Sox

The Spirit of St. Louis: A History of the St. Louis Cardinals and Browns

Wild, High and Tight: The Life and Death of Billy Martin

Wrigleyville: A Magical History Tour of the Chicago Cubs

7

The
{ MICKEY }
{ MANTLE }
NOVEL

Peter Golenbock

THE LYONS PRESS
Guilford, Connecticut
An imprint of The Globe Pequot Press

This book is a work of fiction. References to real people, events, establishments, organizations, or locales are intended only to provide a sense of authenticity and are used fictitiously. All other characters, and all incidents and dialogue, are drawn from the author's imagination and are not to be construed as real.

7. Copyright © 2007 by Peter Golenbock

The Lyons Press is an imprint of The Globe Pequot Press.

10 9 8 7 6 5 4 3 2 1

Printed in the United States of America

Designed by Kris Tobiassen

ISBN 978-1-59921-270-8

Library of Congress Cataloging-in-Publication Data is available on file.

For Rhonda

INTRODUCTION

When I was a kid Mickey Mantle was my hero. Well, to be honest, he was more like a god. Growing up in Stamford, Connecticut, I would watch him on WPIX, channel 11, the local New York station that broadcast nearly every Yankees game back then. In almost every game, Mickey Mantle would do something spectacular, like make a running catch that took your breath away, hit a long home run, bunt when no one was expecting it, or even steal a base—he was an excellent base stealer, though with those shaky legs of his he made everyone nervous when he did it. Mickey hit in the clutch, and at the end of the day the Yankees inevitably won. I was ten in 1956 when he won the Triple Crown and fifteen in 1961 when he and Roger Maris shocked the world with their assault on Babe Ruth's single-season home run record. What a year! As a fan, I felt privileged every day to have the opportunity to root for Mickey, Roger, Whitey, Yogi, and the rest of those great Yankee players. And in September, when Mickey suffered an infection and had to drop out of the homer race—a race Roger eventually won—he became a martyr to the cause, and we loved Mickey even more.

By 1968, I was a wide-eyed law student at NYU, and Mickey was at the end of his illustrious career. At twenty-two, my life was just beginning. His life, it turned out, was reaching a dead end at age thirty-six. After he took off his spikes, he still had another twenty-five years to figure out what to do. It would have been a tough story to write as a biographer. Perhaps that's why no serious biography has ever been written about him. I mean it—take a look at Mickey's own books. They're all baseball stories, with very little off the field. However, the stories he used to tell, along with those told in smoke-filled bars by teammates and friends with drinks in hand late at night make great reading even if they aren't confirmable journalistically.

It's why I call this an "inventive memoir." Whatever you call it, Mickey's friends swear that the incidents in this book are true. If some of them turn out to be exaggerated or apocryphal, maybe it's because fiction sometimes allows us to get at the greater underlying truths. All I know is that Mickey's friends who have read the manuscript say this is the closest you will ever get to the reality of Mickey's life. So heed this warning: those of you who prefer the myth will hate it. Those of you who would have loved to have sat at the bar and drank with him may be titillated, if not enthralled. Mickey was a worthy heir to Babe Ruth's place in baseball history, both on the field and off. Like the Babe, Mickey was a damaged soul who sought a good time wherever he went. And like the Babe, everyone forgave Mickey's deficiencies and loved him for who he was. Well, almost everyone.

I wish I'd had a chance to talk to Mickey just before he died. It would have been my last chance to express how I felt about him. I imagine it would have gone something like this.

"Hey, man, you were the best. It was because of you that I grew up knowing I would become famous and happy and all those things life promises when you are ten years old and playing home run derby in your backyard pretending to be Mickey Mantle. I remember standing in front of our garage holding the bat just the way you did with my pinky across the bottom of the knob, and my next-door neighbor, a kid named Paulie, was pitching tennis balls to me, and batting right-handed I swung the way you did and I hit one high and deep over the basketball pole in the driveway and over the fir trees at the edge of the property and then I heard a crash as the ball went through the attic window of Paulie's house next door. Paulie's mom was pissed, but I didn't care. I was you, and in my mind I had hit the ball out of Yankee Stadium. It was like I had won the World Series. I never hit a ball so far in my whole life! It was one of the greatest moments of my life. You couldn't know how I felt." After I said it, I felt so stupid.

Mick laughed quietly. He said, "Podner, I think I know how you felt." He asked me, "You said you were sure you'd become famous. Did you? I didn't think sportswriters had it in them to become famous. The writers I knew all wore suits that were a little too big and had food stains on them and drove little Japanese shit boxes. Fucking leeches, those writers. Cheap bastards, most of them, like you." He was laughing. "Jock-sniffing assholes. Never played the fucking game, but they all thought they knew more than we did."

"Hey," I said, "I was the center fielder on my Camp Winaukee baseball team. I even wore number seven."

But Mickey didn't want to hear it. He was on a roll, railing about the reporters.

"Remember Dick Young?" he said. "He wrote a column, so he'd only show up every once in a while. Two-faced bastard. Fucking Dick Young was always writing about morality, dumping on this player or that player. Motherfucker chased puss like a pro. Had a wife and a ton of kids. At one time Young was the biggest. But then he ripped Tom Seaver for not honoring a contract, and right after Seaver left, Young skipped out on his contract at the *Daily News* and went to another paper. When the cocksucker died, nobody even noticed. Like he never existed. Motherfucker got what he deserved.

"So," he asked again, "did you become famous?"

"Not really," I told him. "Writing is a damn hard business. It's kinda like baseball. I've had some big hits, but I've gotten burned real bad, too, so it tends to even out. I've always said the hardest part of being in the writing business is staying in business. I'm happy to say I'm still in business.

"You know, I had the craziest idea. After twenty years of writing serious history, researching, interviewing, plodding along, I ought to write a really raunchy book about you. No one has ever written a book like that before. Women can write about this shit, but men can't. No famous man has ever written a book about chasing women," I said. "Well, except maybe for Wilt Chamberlain."

"That's 'cause no guy in his right mind wants to give away any of his secrets," he said.

"No," I said, "that's because when men talk about sex, it sounds almost pornographic. When women talk about sex, they make a TV series about it. You'd never know it," I said, "but drinking and screwing are very popular in today's society."

"That should be the title of the book," said Mick. "*Drinking and Screwing.*"

"Ahhhh, no," I said. "I don't think that will fly. Let me finish what I've been trying to tell you: what I'm trying to say is that it was because of you I always have had confidence that no matter how bad things looked, they always would turn out well. And I still believe they will. For that, I owe you everything."

"Because of me?" he said.

"Sure," I said. "I remember as a kid listening to the Yankee game on the radio while driving to the Jersey shore to visit my grandparents. The whole family would go to the beach, and I'd sit on a blanket on the sand and listen to my Magnavox transistor radio. My childhood memories are filled with nothing but Yankees' pennants and victory. Except for 1959, the Yankees won the pennant every year for ten years. And you were the Big Guy. I went to games at the stadium in which you hit long, towering home runs from both sides of the plate. I remember you won one game when you beat out a bunt. Another game you made a long running catch to stop a rally. And the whole time you looked like you were having so much fun. When I woke up in the morning, I knew I was going to have a good day because you were in that lineup. When I wake up in the morning today, I still feel that way. I owe you, man, big time."

There was a pause. I could envision a pain-wracked Mickey staring up at the ceiling from his bed in his stark hospital room.

Without emotion, he said, "Funny how you got that from me. I never felt that way ever, not even once."

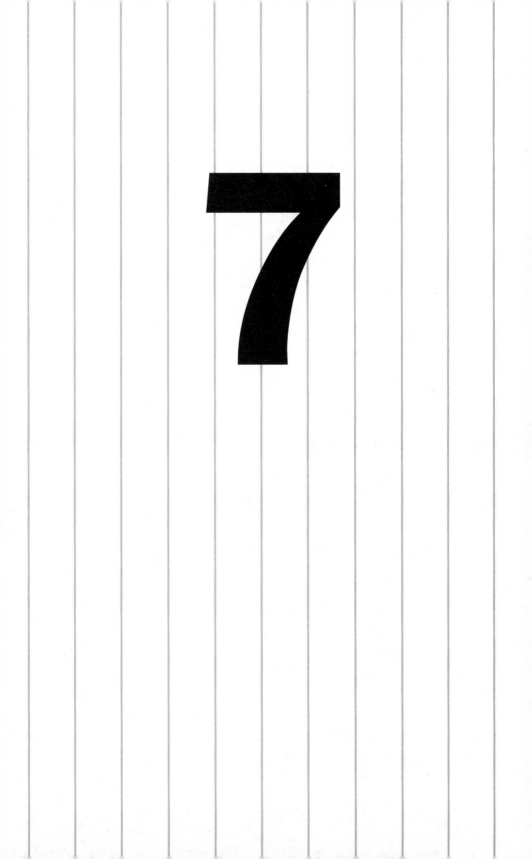

1

The doctors said my cancer was going to kill me, and on August 13, 1995, they turned out to be right. I had termites. I heard that's what the Babe called them when he was dying. They got me, too. Fucking termites ate away my insides, and there wasn't a damn thing anyone could do about it. In my final days I didn't even have the strength to get out of my hospital bed and take a piss.

What really got my goat, I had stopped drinking right after my son Billy died, two years before. The doctors had said my drinking was killing me, so I went to the Betty Ford Clinic and quit cold turkey. I guess I didn't stop soon enough. The cancer hit my liver and spread through my body and ate me up until I looked like a skeleton. I shouldn't kick, though. I certainly had my share of good times.

> Hey, what's the difference between a radial tire and two hundred blow jobs? Ya give up? One's a Goodyear. The other's a great year.

Hey, that's a joke. Get it? I got some real doozies. As I was saying, throughout most of my life, I was a hero to many people. I was as big as Elvis, but what no one ever understood was it never meant squat to me. I never could figure out this hero business. Why people worshipped me never made any sense. Twenty-five years after I put my bat down for the last time, I made more money in a year than I ever made as a ballplayer! Nearly half my life of not doing jack shit, and people were still paying me forty bucks a pop to sign my name to a picture, and I was signing thousands of them! Did you know one of my first baseball cards sold a few years ago for $275,000? That was from 1952, and two hundred seventy-five grand is a hell of a lot more than I made in 1952. You know why they're so rare? Back then kids would mail hundreds of them to me at the stadium to sign. I threw them all out. Fuck 'em, I couldn't be bothered. I never could understand why anyone wanted to save a piece of gum-smelling cheap cardboard with my picture on it. It seems ridiculous, when you think about it. For years those cards had no value whatsoever, but millions of people hung on to them anyway. The ones that exist today are owned by people smart enough *not* to send them to me as kids.

And if card collecting is dopey, autograph collecting is dopier. It's just somebody's name on a piece of paper. What good is it, unless it goes with a phone number and you get it from a really great-looking gal, and she calls you, comes over, and fucks your brains out?

Still and all, I have to admit I am grateful to all the old Yankee fans who would line up and pay me for my autograph. Wasn't for that, I probably would have been on welfare or in the gutter somewhere. If I was frugal, which I wasn't, I suppose I could have made do on my baseball pension. But after I retired, the fans continued to pay big bucks for my fun, and so I tolerated them a lot more than I did when I played. When I was a player the fans were as big a pain in the butt as the pain-in-the-ass newspaper reporters.

It's one of my two big regrets, my not being nicer to the fans. They always were wanting something from me, but I never felt I was deserving, and often I'd punish them for that. I wanted to make them see that they shouldn't be hero-worshipping anyone, especially someone so unworthy as me, that the guy they worshipped was just a regular lunch-pail guy dressed up in a uniform to look like a hero.

We had fountain pens back then, and sometimes I'd deliberately squirt ink on their clothes, or I'd try to slam the bus window on their fingers, or if I didn't want to be bothered, which was most of the time, I'd tell a guy to "fuck off" and then I'd watch as he'd slink away, and I'd wonder who was the bigger asshole, him for asking or me for ruining his afternoon. Looking back, I'm really sorry I acted that way. I wish I could have been nicer. To all of you out there who met me on a day when I was not fit for the company of strangers, please, please forgive me. I wasn't myself. My best self.

If I played today and pulled some of that, I'd get sued, suspended, and probably released. Fans would look at me like I was a real head case. I suppose I was. Maybe that's why it's taken me nearly twelve years since I died to make it up here, to, well, the really big leagues. Took me that long to figure that out.

It wasn't until after I retired that I began to fully understand how important I had been to so many people. It was weird. No sooner had I quit, but it seemed like every week or so someone would mail me a fat scrapbook with clippings about my career. I had a pile of them. I spent hours sitting on the can reading the articles.

I have to say I was astonished that people had spent so much energy and time accumulating that stuff. They collected newspaper and magazine articles and photos about my life, when I figured they would have gotten a hell of a lot more pleasure collecting stuff about their own lives.

That's because I never saw myself as a hero, even when I was playing in the World Series or winning MVP awards. To me, a hero is someone who does something dangerous like the astronauts or someone who makes peace in the world, like Albert Einstein or George H. W. Bush. (I was a friend of Bush's son, George W., the former Texas governor, who at one time owned the Texas Rangers. We used to go out and get wasted together. The man can hold his liquor, let me tell you. The Rangers never won shit when he was the team president, but he was *a lot* of fun to be with. I was surprised he didn't end up commissioner of baseball. Or in rehab.)

A drunk gets on an elevator. He goes up one flight and a beautiful
blonde gets on. He says, "Can I smell your pussy?"

She says, "Why no, what do you think I am?"

He says, "Then it must be your feet."

I was just a guy who played baseball, and most of the time I didn't even
play it all that well. Hard to imagine, but they paid me big bucks to play a
game I'd have played for free. When I hit a home run or made a catch, I
wasn't being heroic. I was just doing what I was getting paid to do. I was
doing the one thing my dad trained me to do. You can't be a hero if you're
doing that.

No one could have known it, but being Mickey Mantle was a curse for
a long, long time. If I'd known back when I was a kid what I know now, I
like to think I would have told my dad to stick his ball bat where the sun
don't shine and leave me the fuck alone, to pick the neighbor's kid and
rest his hopes and dreams on him. Not that dad would have listened to
me. Dads *never* listen to their kids. They have their own agendas. My dad
had a *very* strong will. He had been a ballplayer as a kid, but when the
Depression hit, he had to go to work. When I was born, he decided I was
going to fulfill *his* dreams, and all he ever cared about was my becoming a
professional ballplayer. That's why he made me practice every afternoon
after he came home from the zinc mines. He even named me after a baseball player. Mickey Cochrane. A catcher for Detroit. My name actually is
Mickey; it's not a nickname for Michael. I often wondered why my dad
named me after that guy. Good thing dad didn't like Mel Ott. I'd have
been Melvin Mantle. Would they have called me "The Mel"? If he had
liked Goose Goslin or Heinie Manush, maybe I'd ended up being called
"The Goose," or worse, "The Heinie."

Say, what do you get when you cross a Cabbage Patch doll with the
Pillsbury Doughboy? Give up? An ugly little bitch with a yeast
infection.

I can talk more about my childhood, but I have this burning desire to do it in a book, a *real* book. When I was alive and kicking, I wrote a string of books. Publishers liked me to write them because they knew when I'd go to a bookstore to sign them, people would flock like sheep. Since I usually charged more for my autograph than the store charged for the damn book, the autograph collectors got a bargain, and the publisher got a sale. I suppose a few buyers even read them. Whether they did or not, I ended up making the bestseller list almost every time. Kinda makes a mockery of the book business, don't it? All those great philosophical college-smart writers busting their humps to write about life and death and pain and suffering, and they sell two thousand copies, and all I have to do is talk into a tape recorder for a few hours about my career, sign my name at Barnes & Noble, and bingo, a *New York Times* bestseller. Nothing to it. You would have to say I had led a charmed life.

My first autobiography was called *The Making of a Ballplayer*. Later I did a book all about my playing in the World Series. I did another one about the 1956 season, called *My Favorite Season*. I was going to do one about the 1961 series and call it *The Infection in My Ass that Kept Me from Playing*, but my publisher didn't think that was a good idea.

The thing is, I had too much pride to just let some hack sportswriter take a bunch of clippings and make a book out of my life, like some players do. Any time I wrote a new book, I felt I should write something different, so with each book I was forced to confess something new about my life. Charging for autographs aside, I always believed in earning my money, so you can't keep writing the same shit every time. Not long before I died and ended up here, I went on HBO and admitted to Bob Costas that I had a drinking problem. I told them how I had gone to Betty Ford to dry out. Now, I guess, it's time to write all about it.

I swore in the AA meetings I would look at myself honestly, so I have to tell the whole story. I know there will be people who will ask, *Mickey, does the public really want to know the whole story?* But somehow I ended up in heaven, so how could it hurt? God looks a hell of a lot like Casey Stengel, by the way. Only not as old.

Lies and cover-ups and misinformation is for those who passed and went to the other place where the sportswriters, politicians, and umpires end up. Although not really, it turns out. But I need to find the right guy to write this book with me. Once I find him, I can get started, and not only will I be able to recount some of the best moments of my life, but most important, I might be able to explain myself—to myself—to figure out why I turned out the way I did—to figure out *why* I loved to get rip-roaring drunk and screw the first willing ole gal who walked into the bar. And I know there will be a *wide* audience of guys who will read my stories and nod their heads knowingly, because they do it, too, only they don't do it as much, or as well. I used to live in Texas, and I know a hell of a lot of them because I would meet them almost every night. I also met them in Manhattan, Chicago, Kansas City, and Detroit. In Boston they were the whole city.

Of course, a lot of people *won't* want to read a book like this, people who are deeply religious or who don't like to look at naked gals, or women's libbers who think the word *pussy* is obscene unless you're talking about their cat. And women who suspect their husbands are cheating will not want to read this book. But I'm betting there are enough closet Peeping Toms who want to hear in detail about the great puss I had or read about blow jobs and orgies. I won't write about this stuff because sex sells—there's no money in heaven—but rather I have to write it because this stuff was real. These aren't made-up stories. They happened. It was what my life was all about, and if I'm going to make any sense of my life, I have to find out why I turned out to be the puss hound I ended up being. And maybe then my long-suffering wife, Merlyn, will understand. And maybe I will, too—but to do this I need to find the right sportswriter to work with me on it.

Turns out, not all the sportswriters end up in hell. Up here I found a wide variety of guys to choose from: Grantland Rice, Frank Graham,

Arthur Daley, Red Smith, and Dick Schaap. Rice was before my time, Frank and Arthur loved me, never gave me any trouble. I never saw Red much. He wrote a column. Dick did TV, though he did write a lot of as-told-to books. He was one of the few sportswriters who I actually liked. Dick was smart, but he was one of those mythmakers. All athletes were his heroes. He once wrote a book about George Steinbrenner, and he never wrote one unkind thing about him. That's damn hard to do, and that's *not* what I need. I'm looking for a hard-nosed, skeptical guy who will ask the hard questions and force me to tell my story right.

I thought to myself, *Who did you know who wasn't afraid to offend people?* Then it hit me. The sports book that created the biggest stink when it came out was *Ball Four*, which was written by my big-mouth Yankee teammate Jim Bouton and published just after I retired. Boy, was I pissed when that hit the stands. Funny thing about Bouton: for a couple of years in the sixties he was a real fine pitcher. People forget that. He won eighteen games in 1963 and twenty-one games in 1964. I even gave him the nickname "Bulldog" 'cause he pitched so tough. He'd throw a pitch, his hat would come off, and he'd grunt. He was a competitor, I'll give him that. Then he hurt his arm from jerking off so much. Ha! Bouton was a different kind of duck. He didn't drink much, and he read books and spent a lot of time hanging out with reporters, guys most of us either didn't trust or hated, so none of his teammates trusted him very much.

And we turned out to be right about that. Anyone who liked those scumbags was suspect because few of the writers had any character. All they cared about was beating each other out for stories. They snuck around and wrote shit about you, whether it was their business or not, and what really made us mad, they had the right to give their opinions, whether they knew what they were talking about or not. Some of them were in bed with the owners, and so if a player got in a salary dispute, he would find himself getting reamed out in the papers. Looking back, we were lucky the reporters, as bad as they were, were nothing like reporters today. If players today did some of the stuff we did, the stories would be all over ESPN in a New York minute. It's hard to imagine the players today have much fun living under a microscope.

But the reporters from our day were bad enough. Fuckers ruined my buddy Roger Maris's career in New York. But Bouton liked them anyway, and I guess he was sneaking around like they did, 'cause all those years he kept a diary, and after he left the Yankees, he ended up on the Seattle Pilots, where he pitched for the worst team in baseball. The team was so bad it left Seattle after one year. Bud Selig bought it and moved it to Milwaukee. Guess Bouton figured his career was about over, so he'd make some money writing a book.

During that 1969 season he wrote what became *Ball Four*, in which he wrote that I liked to drink and that a bunch of us—including him— would go on the roof of the Shoreham Hotel in Washington, D.C., with a telescope to peep through high-rise windows at naked stewardesses, which was true, but that didn't mean he should have written about it. This was the sixties, for crying out loud, when nobody told nobody nothing. At first it really pissed me off, because those things weren't the things I wanted anyone to know. Hell, I had a wife and kids. What was he thinking? The worst part about it was after he wrote that, the next time I went back to the Shoreham, the stews, who were no dummies, kept their blinds drawn.

But then after *Ball Four* came out, a funny thing happened. Almost immediately, it seemed like I had become an even greater hero *because* I had done those things. People loved me more, they said, because *Ball Four* made me more human.

And once Bouton told the whole world that I drank, it gave me the courage to talk and write about it a little myself. I even wrote a little bit about some of the shit Billy Martin and I pulled. Not much, but just enough to give people an idea of how much fun Billy and I had together.

People don't remember anymore, but Bouton didn't write that book by himself. He had help. The more I think about it, the more I want *that SOB* to work on this book with me. His name was Leonard Shecter. He wrote for the *New York Post*. A rag, but it had a kick-ass sports section in those days. Shecter had a way of making a dull story exciting, I'll give him that. But he was an aggressive guy, and he scared me, so I avoided him whenever I could. I guess it bothered me that Bouton liked him when I was so afraid of him. But it goes without saying, without Lenny Shecter, there wouldn't have been a *Ball Four*.

I also hated Lenny Shecter when I was a player because of the way he treated my teammates in print. Roger Maris always said there were two kinds of writers, the cheerleaders and the knockers. Lenny was a knocker. He was the guy who called Hector Lopez "What a Pair of Hands Hector." Hector may not have been a great third baseman, but he was a solid hitter, especially in the World Series, and Lenny had no right making fun of Hector like that. And when Roger was on his way to beating Babe Ruth's single-season home run record and his hair started falling out, Lenny told everyone about it in a not very nice way, and I thought Roger was going to kill him. The players were rooting for that. But I give Lenny credit. After blasting him, the next day he showed up and faced Roger. He didn't stay up in the press box until things cooled down like some of them did. Lenny was one tough motherfucker, I'll give him that. No one hated bullshit more than he did.

No one hated Lenny as much as I did. And I suppose he felt the same way about me, so I'm going to have to eat some crow and do some convincing to get him to work with me on this book of mine. He'll do it, though. I know he will, because it kills reporters not to know something, and my real story'll be something he'll want to know. Even now.

If I had ever written my real story, there would have been so much to write about. A true American comedy. Or is that tragedy? I died the first time in 1969, when I retired before the season began. Life became a hell on earth. After I retired there wasn't anything for me in baseball. If I could no longer play, I didn't want to be the guy hanging around. One year Billy and the Yankees wanted me to coach first base, but I couldn't stand it. The inactivity drove me crazy, even though it was a chance to be back on the road again. But I was just there to be seen and draw fans, and since the first-base coach has nothing to do but tell the runner how many outs there are, I got bored with doing that very quickly. I lasted about a month.

I didn't want a manager's job. They told me if I wanted to manage the Yankees, I would have to start managing in the minors, and after going first class all those years, I didn't want to have to ride buses again. And go back to minor league puss? Nah.

Deep down I knew nobody'd hire me to manage anyway. Hell, they said the same dumb thing about me that they said about Babe Ruth: that I couldn't manage myself. Fuck 'em. What did they know about my life? They said I drank too much. Ever heard of Ulysses S. Grant? He was a drunk, and he won the Civil War and he ran the fucking country, didn't he? You try being America's Hero for a week or two, never mind forty-five years. Let's see how well you handle it.

Earlier, I said I had two regrets, and that not treating the fans well was one of them. Well, the other one was not being there for Merlyn and my four sons. I deeply regret I was not a better father. My boys deserved better than what they got. Before I passed, I did let them know how much I loved them. But they were aware I was never the kind of guy to sit at home with his feet up. I needed to be on the go.

As for Merlyn, nothing I can say here would even come close to the depths of my sorrow. You'll see what I mean.

Now excuse me while I track down that piece of shit Lenny Shecter.

When I arrived in heaven, one of God's flunkies asked me where I was happiest during my time on earth. I told him it was in front of my locker in Yankee Stadium. No sooner did I say that than I found myself sitting on my old stool in front of my old locker in my usual spot in the right-hand corner of the clubhouse. The old clubhouse—before the renovation. I was wearing my pinstripes with the number seven on the back. I felt at ease for the first time in years.

Not long afterward, the guy who you could say was God's clubhouse attendant came over to me carrying a big box and two black Sharpies. He asked if I'd do God a favor. Of course, I told him. "Considering the alternative," I said, "I'm so grateful to find myself in heaven that I'll do anything God wishes."

"Would you sign these four dozen baseballs for Him?" God's clubbie asked.

I couldn't believe it. Celebrity never dies, I guess. I couldn't help wonder what He wanted them for. I asked the guy.

"God has the biggest autograph collection in the world," he said. "He has all the guys in the five hundred home run club."

"I'll bet he doesn't have Barry Bonds," I said.

"Not yet," he said. "Barry's a tough signature. But he does have Bobby."

"You think he'll ever get Barry's?" I asked.

"Nothing he's done would keep him out," he said. "So far."

After I opened the box and removed the cap from the pen, I asked him, "Does he want it personalized? Shall I sign '536 home runs' or 'HOF'?"

"No," he said. "Just your name will be fine."

As I was signing the balls, I had a brainstorm.

"Can I ask a favor in return?"

"Anything," the clubbie said.

"Could you arrange for me to meet Lenny Shecter, the sportswriter? He died in the mid-1970s. He was a reporter for the *New York Post*. Can a reporter get into heaven?"

"Why not?"

"Yeah, I guess why not. Would you see if he's around?"

"I'll see what I can do," he said.

I signed the rest of the baseballs, and just as I was signing the last couple, I looked up, and son of a gun, standing there in front of my locker was Lenny Shecter, still wearing black-framed glasses and sporting his Groucho mustache, and he was wearing that same rumpled brown-and-white tweed sports jacket writers prefer. He didn't seem particularly glad to see me.

"Hi, Lenny," I said.

Well, I'll be darned. You're about the last person I expected to see up here. The clubbie said you wanted to see me. What do you want? All those years you were playing, you never said hello to me.

"I'm really sorry about that. I was just a farm boy, and I always felt so insecure around you city guys. It was nothing personal. I didn't mean anything by it."

Weren't you being a bit personal whenever you told me to go fuck myself?

"I'm sorry about that, too. I really am. In fact, I was so sorry about the way I treated you, I became an alcoholic."

I laughed, hoping the joke would put him at ease.

I can't tell you how many people came up to me over the years to tell me stories of the horrible way I had treated them. I cringe every time.

Can I be honest with you, Mick?

"You've never been anything but, Lenny."

I really despised the way you treated people, including me, and I really don't want to have anything to do with you.

He started to walk away.

"Wait, Lenny. Don't go. I need your help. I really do," I said. "I need to tell my story so my wife and kids will understand why I was the way I was."

So your wife and kids will understand?

"Okay, and so I can understand it, too. I have some theories. But please, I can't do it by myself. I don't know the right questions to ask. And if I don't ask myself the right questions, I'll lie to myself. Of all the writers available up here, I need a guy to push me to tell the truth, who won't judge me. And who'll write it all down, no matter how ugly. Please, Lenny. I'm begging you. For old times' sake."

Old times' sake? Too late for that, Mick. Before I died I had left sports. I was sick and tired of you prima donna athletes. My last book was about a cop on the take. I quit sports, and I have no real desire to get back in it. Like I always said, There are two kinds of sportswriters: those with good sense and ability to go on to other things, and those with neither. That's what the great ones did: Westbrook Pegler, Paul Gallico, Damon Runyon. I've moved on. Find someone else. Get one of them.

"I don't know them."

Who do you know, Mick?

"The last writer I had a friendship with was John Drebinger. He wrote for the *Times*."

I knew Drebby. He was a great guy.

"John was great because all he ever wrote about was the game. He knew a lot about the shit Billy, Whitey, and I did, but he was from the old school, where you didn't tell tales out of school. He figured it was none of anyone's business. When he got old, he started wearing a hearing aid, and I used to love to move my mouth like I was talking, only I wasn't really saying anything, and he'd turn up the volume on his hearing aid *way up*, and then I'd shout at him as loud as I could, and you should have seen him jump ten feet in the air! All the guys in the clubhouse would crack up. We all loved Drebby. I really miss him."

I haven't seen him around, but I'm sure he's up here with us. So get Drebby to write your damn book. You don't need me.

"But I do, Lenny. I need someone who will write my story without trying to edit out all the good parts. I promise you, this is a story you will want to hear. Will you be offended hearing about strip clubs?"

No.

"Will you be offended if I use dirty words?"

Nothing offends me but politicians who lie, steal, and cheat.

"Would you be upset if I opened up to you and shared with you all my dirty little secrets?"

I would be upset if you didn't. If you didn't, you'd be Joe DiMaggio.

"Drebby would want me to be Joe D, Lenny. He wouldn't want to know, wouldn't want to tell."

I was desperate to keep Shecter engaged in conversation.

"Can I ask you a couple of questions?"

Ah shit, I suppose so. Not like I don't have plenty of time.

"Then let's get outta here. We need to go someplace where we can get a drink and have some privacy. Can I buy you a drink, Lenny?

Sure, buy me a drink. Where should we go?

"Clubbie!"

Heaven's clubbie came rushing over.

"Can you arrange for us to go to Toots Shor's?" I asked. "Is he in heaven?"

"No problem," said the clubbie.

I changed out of my uniform and put on my street clothes. While I was putting on my pants, I looked down at my legs. It was really strange to see my knees healthy—no surgical stitches anywhere.

We walked out of the stadium. The clubbie had a cab waiting for us—one of those big, comfortable Checkers. Wanna know the way I truly knew I was in heaven? No traffic! It took all of fifteen minutes to get from the Bronx down to Shor's at 51 West Fifty-first Street—all the lights were green! And when we got to Shor's it was like I'd never been away—like the party had never stopped. The big horseshoe bar sat in the middle of the room. Patrons were sitting at the bar, smoking. The room was dark. Toots Shor came over, happy to see me as always. He looked and talked like Henny Youngman, bubbly and friendly, his hair all slicked back. He showed us to the booth usually reserved for Joe D.

"Hiya Mick, what are you drinking?" It was as though I had seen him yesterday.

"I'll have a Coke, Toots. And give Lenny whatever he'd like."

Toots looked surprised to see me with Lenny, but he and Lenny shook hands, and Lenny ordered a scotch on the rocks. After the drinks came, I thought it important to let Lenny know I was interested in his story, and I figured I'd soften him up by giving him a chance to brag a little about himself.

"You were the guy who wrote *Ball Four* with Jim Bouton, right? I was told the book was your idea. That true?"

It was both our ideas. I had been with the New York Post, *and I knew him. I always thought Jim was a smart guy, and I noticed he read a lot, books, not the* Sporting News, *and I thought it might make an interesting book if he would keep a diary of his coming season with Seattle, an expansion team with castoffs and guys just hanging on, and for him to also talk about his years with the Yankees.*

"Jim wanted to do it?"

Oh yeah. He told me he had kept notes through his career, and he turned out to be a terrific storyteller. That year Jim talked into a tape recorder every day.

He sent the tapes to a lady who transcribed them. Jim got a copy, and I got a copy, and we kept the good stuff and threw out the bad. If the book reads like Jim was talking, it's because he was talking. Jim and I were a perfect match. It was amazing how often we agreed on what stayed in and what we cut out.

Jim was fun and he had something to say. He wanted to reveal what it was really like to be a major league ballplayer, something I had been trying to do my whole career. I'd have helped write that book for nothing. And ironically, that's about what we got as an advance after we finished it.

"What do you mean?"

I mean the publishers had no clue what they were reading when my agent sent it to them. All the big publishing houses passed on it. Every single one. It almost didn't see the light of day.

"Wasn't it the biggest-selling sports book of all time?"

Yeah, but editors can be dumber than ballplayers. They all saw the story of a washed-up Seattle Pilot relief pitcher. The only company that decided to take a chance was World Publishing Company, which specialized in religious books. World thought so little of the book that they gave us a grand total of $5,000 to split between us. They figured they'd break even at about thirty-five hundred copies.

"After all that work, it hardly seems worth it," I said.

What choice did we have? Jim and I had invested a full year of our lives working on it. We still thought it was great. It was just the kind of book both of us wanted to read. We were praying Ball Four would find its audience once it hit the bookstores.

"The phones started ringing in my house the minute the press got wind of it. Everyone wanted to know about what I was doing on the roof of the Shoreham with a telescope. I couldn't believe Jim had told on us. He had broken the code of 'What happens on the road stays on the road.' "

It's what actually happened, wasn't it? And the way Jim told it was so incredibly funny, how could we take it out? Every time I thought of you and Jim and the other Yankees standing on the roof peeping into stewardesses' windows, I laughed my ass off.

"Which is exactly why I need you to help me write my book, Lenny. If you do my book, I'll tell you stories that will make that seem tame. Billy and I did things that no one would believe. You have to give me some credit, Lenny. That story about us being on the roof of the Shoreham Hotel sold you a lot of books.

And we had Bowie Kuhn, the tight-ass baseball commissioner, to thank. Someone must have sent him a copy, because Kuhn, a Park Avenue lawyer, railed about the offensive players' language and about the players' childish antics in the book. He didn't particularly like the telescope story, because it made the Yankee players out to be perverts.

"We weren't perverts. We were voyeurs, Lenny, voyeurs. I've always felt that there are two kinds of people in this world, exhibitionists and voyeurs. We were voyeurs. And what I saw in my lifetime just might amaze you if you took the time to sit with me! You have no idea how many men are also voyeurs, but if you do this book with me, you'll find out. Why do you think the telescope story was so popular in *Ball Four?* Because every guy who bought that book wished he was on that hotel roof with us. So you could argue we were just being regular guys doing what guys do.

A lot of people screamed bloody murder over that story.

"Religious fundamentalists. Women's libbers. Prudes. Bowie Kuhn."

Kuhn went on TV and said Ball Four *ought to be banned, and as a result every baseball fan with any imagination ran out and bought it. It was huge, a monster. I'd have made a fortune if World hadn't gone out of business and stiffed us to the tune of a million dollars.*

"Lenny, this book will make *Ball Four* seem like *Rebecca of Sunnybrook Farm.* Jim didn't know a tenth of what we were doing. He was too much of a Goody Two-shoes.

Mick, you've already written ten books. What else is there for you to say? Hell, I'll bet you've written more books than you've read!

I had to laugh. Lenny was always sarcastic, but he rarely was off the mark.

"I'm real sorry I wasn't nice to you, Lenny. But that was then, and this is now. I need you, Lenny, to help me do this."

Why me? Why do you want me? I hated you. You hated me.

"That was before I had therapy, which I needed even more while I was playing than after I'd retired. I hated you because you were the most honest reporter of the bunch. You always wanted the truth. We players felt our careers depended on you *not* finding out the truth. If you had found out we were on the roof of the Shoreham peering in stewardesses' windows, you'd have written that in the fucking *New York Post*, wouldn't you have?

In a heartbeat. It was a great story. But they never would have run it. Not in those days.

"You were a pain in the ass, Lenny. I can't tell you how often we wanted to throw you out of the Yankee clubhouse. Didn't some football coach once get mad at you and throw you out of a press conference?"

Yeah. I once asked Paul Brown if his football team had choked, and he bodily threw me out of the locker room.

"Can't say I blame him. I want to work with you because you can put things in context and make them understandable. And like I said, you won't judge me. Let me ask you, what's the thing you wrote that you're most proud of?"

Ball Four, of course. For the rest of our lives whenever Jim and I got together, all we ever talked about was Ball Four. *This was the best piece of work either of us had ever done. We caught lightning in a bottle with that season, those characters.*

You wrote other books?

I wrote a book called The Jocks. *It was my farewell to sports. I wrote about what I hated about sports, which turned out to be just about everything. I also wrote a book about the '62 Mets. I was the one who called the original Mets "The Amazin's." Casey picked up on that and made it famous. I was also known for being the only writer to pick the Jets to beat the Baltimore Colts in Super Bowl III. I was very proud of that.*

"You were also the bastard who called Hector Lopez 'What a Pair of Hands Hector.' "

I don't regret that. It was apt.

"That was brutal."

It was honest.

"All right, honest. Which is exactly what I need if I'm going to tell my story the way I need to tell it. I don't need some pansy-ass writer censoring my words. I need you to help me explain my life to my family and to my fans, but most important, I need you so I can understand what happened to me. My therapy only went so far. It's far too painful to do without help. I want Merlyn and my sons to understand that I was an alcoholic, that I couldn't help myself. And why. I learned that too late on earth to write about it. I need you to help me do it right."

Sounds to me like you're looking for an excuse to soothe a guilty conscience.

"Maybe I am. Let's bury the hatchet, and I'll let you decide."

I have to be nuts to agree to this. You say you're going to tell me anything I want to know?

That's when I knew I had the smug bastard hooked.

"Everything. Home runs and puss and booze and more puss and booze and puss."

You'll answer every and any question I ask you?

"You have my word. You'll get a lot more out of this than writing about crooked cops."

Where do you want to do this?

"We can do it right here. Toots will keep the green flies away."

I'll be back in a few minutes.

I took a gulp of my Coke and nearly choked on it. I spit it back into the glass and signaled for Toots. He came waddling over.

"What's up, Mick? Another round?"

"God no, Toots. What are you trying to do, kill me?"

We just stared at each other for a moment and then we both started laughing.

"Good one, Mick! Kill me! Ha!" He turned to a passing waiter. "Get a load of this guy. 'What are you trying to do, kill me!' " The waiter blinked, stone faced, and scurried off.

"Toots, I'm sober now. I'm off the sauce. When I asked for a Coke, I meant it."

"Geez, Mick, I'm sorry. I didn't mean nothin' by it. When you said Coke, I figured fill the glass up with rum and splash a little Coke on top for color."

"Toots, you didn't know. No problem. But please, take this away and get me a Coca-Cola—plain."

"Sure thing, Mick. Coming right up." Toots took the glass and waddled back to the bar. In a minute, he returned with a fresh Coke, with ice cubes and a straw, and a small dish with a lemon wedge on it.

"Mick, enjoy. Let me know if you need anything else."

"Thanks, I will."

Then Lenny returned, carrying his Wollensack reel-to-reel tape recorder. He sat back down in the booth, set the tape recorder on the table, and plugged it into a socket in the baseboard. He pushed the record button.

Reporters have no morals. Lenny might have hated my guts, but his getting an exclusive story was more important than how he felt about me. Even in heaven, where he couldn't make a buck off it. Pathetic. It was almost too easy. But since we were now co-conspirators, I was sure by the time we were done he'd understand me better. At least I was hoping for that. It was important for me to gain forgiveness from Merlyn and my boys, and for some reason I also needed to get it from Lenny. I swore to myself that by the time this book was all done, Lenny and I would be friends.

So tell me, did you even like playing baseball?

From the time I was a boy, all I ever wanted to do was play baseball. That, and drink and get puss, of course. Which throughout my life I got a lot of, I'm mighty pleased to say. Pete Rose may have broken Ty Cobb's hit record, but I gotta think I broke Babe Ruth's puss record, and that record was harder to beat, and a hell of a lot more satisfying. If there had been a Baseball Sex Encyclopedia, you could look me up, as Casey used to say.

"Most chicks fucked in a lifetime: me."

"Most chicks fucked in a season: me."

"Most chicks fucked on consecutive days: me."

"Eight Times Most Valuable Fucker: me."

The only person I knew who liked sex as much as I did was Billy Martin, which was one of the reasons we got along so well. Billy comes in second to me only because I was a lot handsomer than he was. Billy was skinny, and he had that big shnozz, but no one could sweet talk a girl like he could. When he turned on that charm, he was irresistible. But when he drank he could get crazy. Some of the girls who knew his reputation were too scared to be alone in a room with him. The ones Billy ended up with in the sack either didn't want to say no, were too young to have heard about him, or were too starstruck to care.

Billy and I didn't just want a woman every night—we needed to have a different woman every night. We used to joke that this legacy was passed down to us by the great Babe Ruth, who always said he got his strength from puss. Babe didn't care whether he ate it or fucked it. He just needed to have it. Joe D was that way. Billy and I were like that, too.

Why do you think you spent so much time chasing women?

What difference does it make why?

You promised to answer my questions. All of my questions. We can stop right here and now if you wish.

Calm down, Lenny. Okay. Okay. Give me a moment to think. It's not an easy question to answer. I actually know why.

You were sexually abused as a child.

How in the world did you know?

Your behavior was consistent with the behavior of child abuse victims. You slept around, and you drank like a fish. So what happened?

Lenny, on this one subject you're going to have to bear with me. I'm too ashamed to talk about it. I'm gonna have to work up to that. After we've come to trust each other more, then I'll talk about it. I'm not being evasive. I just need a little time. Can you do that, Lenny?

Look, I'm not heartless.

I can tell you emotionally why I felt I needed to chase women, beside the great pleasure it gave me. The truth is, all my life I was afraid—afraid to fail, afraid of my father, afraid of growing old, afraid of strangers, afraid to die, afraid to live—but I discovered early on that while I was getting laid, my fears went away. When I was by myself in a strange hotel room waiting for another ball game, I would stare at the ceiling in the middle of the night and worry about what was going to happen to me the next game or what I would do once I stopped playing ball. But if I found a sweet ole gal to spend the night with me, I found that not only was I so distracted that I stopped worrying about myself, but in a way she also made me feel immortal. And if I happened to wake up in the middle of the night in a cold sweat, all I had to do was reach over and grab her in a soft spot, and then I had nothing at all to worry over.

You figured as long as you were having sex, you couldn't die? That certainly didn't work for Nelson Rockefeller. He was porking his secretary when his heart gave out. So was that it?

Something like that, but by the time I found out that sex wasn't going to save me from dying, it was too late to change. Fear is a terrible thing to be feeling all the time. Billy Martin once told me he was just as afraid of things as I was. His mother had left his father while she was still pregnant, and it had scarred him. His old man apparently liked to fool around himself, and his mom caught him, so she threw him out. You'd have thought Billy would try to live a different kind of life than his old man, but he turned out to be exactly the same type of guy. Billy needed women because it was his way of keeping score. The more women he slept with, the better he felt about himself. It was his way of winning in life.

And Billy was a *very* sore loser.

I loved women because I needed them. Billy hated women because he needed them. Billy hated anyone who had control over him. It's why he hated newspaper reporters. It's why he got fired so often. Except for playing for the Yankees, there was nothing more exciting in life for Billy and me than making out with a naked girl for the first time, rubbing your nose against her smooth skin, and having her willingly do whatever you wanted her to do.

Something else I learned about women a long time ago. It's something all seasoned pros know instinctively: it's great to be seen with a good-looking woman, but the homely ones are so grateful they're often better in the sack. And they don't care if you take them to McDonald's instead of a fancy restaurant before you fuck them. And when you're done, you don't feel as guilty kicking them out. Most of them are just happy you paid them some attention.

Billy and I learned that lesson early in our careers one afternoon while

we were playing for the Yankees. We were maybe twenty-three, just kids.
The Yankees were staying at the Muehlebach Hotel in Kansas City. Two
girls who said they went to a Catholic high school came to the ballpark to
ask for our autographs on a coupla baseballs. One was really beautiful,
dark haired with an angelic face and a hot bod I was dying to get my hands
on, and the other one was really homely, kind of a dog, didn't have much
sex appeal at all. Billy could be pretty raunchy. He said to the pretty one,
"We'll sign your balls if you'd come back after the game to our hotel room
and play with ours." I almost died when he said that. I couldn't believe
Billy could be so up front about it. But then I couldn't believe it when the
girls gave us big smiles and showed up that night.

Billy and I were arguing over who would do what with the beautiful
one, when they knocked on the door of our hotel room. We let them in.
The homely girl informed us they would only let us have sex with them if
we'd let them blindfold us first. Billy wasn't sure. He didn't trust anyone,
and he didn't like anyone, especially a girl, to have the upper hand. But if
there was an opportunity for him to have sex, Billy would take the risk.
Any risk. The year before a girl had come into the hotel room of a player
on the Phillies by the name of Eddie Waitkus. Waitkus, who played for
the Philadelphia Phillies, had invited this girl up to his room. Turned out
she was a loony tune. She was obsessed with the idea that she would
become Mrs. Waitkus while Fast Eddie's idea of her was Miss Fuck Me on
Friday Night, or whatever night he was hoping she would give him a tum-
ble in the sack. That night, Waitkus was expecting to get a surprise.

He got one, all right. She pulled out a revolver and shot him right in
the gut. The girl ended up in a psycho ward. As I said, Waitkus was lucky
he didn't end up dead.

Billy asked them, "You're not going to shoot us, are you?" The girls giggled, and after tying black blindfolds on us, they took off all their clothes
and joined us on the beds.

"No touching," one of them said. We were told we had to keep our
hands behind our heads as they undressed us.

We each had sex with one of the girls, and when they were finished, they switched, and we made love to the other one, but of course I had no idea which girl I had sex with first, and you know, both of them were really great. And after they were done with us a second time, they made us keep our blindfolds on until they left. We didn't even know their names.

Which was part of the reason Billy and I never forgot those girls as long as we lived.

After they left, Billy turned to me and said, "Did I have the great looking one first or did you?" I shrugged. I had no idea either. I suppose that was the point of their making us put on those blindfolds.

Billy said, "I'll never kick a girl out of bed again."

I told him, "You got that right, podner."

Are you offended?

Only that it's so impersonal. You didn't even know the names of the girls you had sex with. Weren't you taking advantage of them?

I may seem like a dirty dog to you, but the fact is, a lot of girls, young and old, enjoy sleeping with professional athletes. If you think about it, what's so terrible about giving willing young women a memorable experience? It's no different from what their boyfriends and husbands wanted from me for twenty years while I was playing for the Yankees. I couldn't give half the population a thrill while ignoring the other half. That would make me a sexist, right?

You're not serious.

I lived in Dallas for a long time, and I suppose the Christian Coalition would say that I should be damned. And I was. Damned lucky, if you want to know the truth. You have to realize that all my life I've had time on my hands, hours and hours, in bars waiting for games, waiting for death. If a woman asked for an hour of my time, who was I to refuse her? After all, I played in the House that Ruth Built, not the House that Lou Gehrig Built. Gehrig was a great ballplayer. But he had to be the most boring guy who ever played ball, if you don't count Cal Ripken.

Look up Lou Gehrig and Cal Ripken in that Baseball Sex Encyclopedia I was telling you about. Add both those guys together: "Chicks fucked by Gehrig during a career: one." Mrs. Gehrig.

"Chicks fucked by Ripken during a career: one." Mrs. Ripken.

Maybe if Gehrig had gotten laid more often, he wouldn't have died so young. Who knows?

Does Cal Fucking Ripken even know how to have fun? I mean, the guy lives in Baltimore, for Christ's sake.

I have to admit I was plumb jealous of Ripken when he was playing. After I retired I was envious of any guy who was still playing. Not because of the money they were making. Hell, how much do you think I'd be making today? Twenty million a year, easy. But what would I have done with it? Support every relative I had in a higher style? As it was, I drank the best booze and as much of it as I wanted and hell, most of the time I didn't even have to pay for it. I suppose I could have met a better class of women. But as I told you, I learned a long time ago that puss is puss, and class puss can be such a pain in the butt. You gotta take class puss to a fancy restaurant in a fancy car to make her feel like she's getting something outta you before she lets you take off her clothes. And the funny thing is that half the time when you finally get the classy ones into the bedroom, when the plaid skirt comes off they're not wearing any underwear underneath, because all along what they wanted was to be able to tell their country club girlfriends that they got to fuck little ole me. Do you have any idea how many times after a woman had sex with me she'd get out of bed, go into her handbag, pull out a pen and a baseball or a piece of paper and ask me to sign it? I often wondered whether she took me to bed just so she could get the autograph. If she was special, sometimes I'd sign the ball, "Your puss belongs in the Hall of Fame. The Mick."

There are hundreds of balls like that all over America. I know those women still have them, too, though I doubt if any of those gals ever showed them to anyone.

So, you see, I had all the women I wanted, and if I ever needed money, all I had to do was a sign a few hundred autographs. What would I have needed twenty mil a year for? Besides, it's too late now for doing much of anything but writing about my life, which to a lot of people had been very glamorous, but really I was a sumbitch the whole way through.

My whole life I was angry and scared and pissed off and worried. Everybody knows about the 536 home runs and the .298 batting average and the three MVP awards. What they don't understand is that I retired at age thirty-seven and died at age sixty-one. It had been almost twenty-five years since I had played the game of baseball. Those years after I quit went by in a second, a blur, a faint memory that I was reminded of every day because every day someone showed me my baseball cards or asked for my autograph. I never discussed my life after baseball. Do you know what it's like to wake up in a strange hotel room with a woman you don't know and wonder what city you're in and what you're supposed to do for the rest of the day? Have you ever gotten up in the morning and haven't a clue what to do once you walk out the door and go outside? Ask yourself whether you would have ever wanted to change places with me. I'll tell you the answer, Lenny:

No sir, podner. No sirree.

What's the worst thing about oral sex? The view.

What were your most vivid memories growing up in Oklahoma?

You know how much self-confidence I had when I was growing up as a boy in Commerce, Oklahoma? Zippo. Part of it was that we were real poor, didn't have nothing, and so I never felt the equal of the few rich kids at school. Besides, no matter what I did in school or in sports, it was never good enough for my old man, who, looking back, and I'm gonna be real honest about it, was a real prick, especially after he was drinking.

To give him the benefit of the doubt, he was only nineteen when I was born. Christ, he was a kid himself. When I was born, he took a job to support the family. He did what every young man in Commerce did at that time—went to work in the lead-zinc mines. The only fun he had was playing baseball and getting drunk with his friends, which he did well and often. My dad was the one who taught me to play ball. He also taught me about fear as a motivator.

He had wanted to be a pro ballplayer, but he never got the chance, so I guess he decided that I would live out his dream for him. Happens all the time with failed athletes and their sons. Go watch any Little League game, and you'll always find one asshole father screaming at his kid, "Can't you do any better than that, you pansy-ass?" That was my dad. He was merciless.

If I didn't play well, I had to listen to his sarcasm. How'd you like to perform knowing you weren't allowed to strike out, make an error, or be anything but perfect? Playing in the big leagues later on was a picnic compared to having to play in front of Dad.

Want to know how afraid of him I was? I wet my bed until I was eighteen years old. That's no joke. Only after I started playing pro ball at Independence did it stop. If I had wet my bed at Independence, that would have been the end of my career. Finally getting away from him did the trick, I guess.

I never would have pictured you as a bed wetter. That's a lot to handle.

I can't say he didn't mean well. When I was a little kid he'd pitch to me in the backyard. He wanted me to switch hit, said that one day managers would platoon, said if I learned to switch hit, I'd never have to sit on the bench. I'll say one thing about him: Dad knew his baseball. Dad was a hundred percent right about that. So against Dad, I batted lefty. When my uncle pitched—Pops was a lefty—Dad made me bat righty. I was maybe eight years old, but my dad made me practice like it was an important job. If I missed a pitch, he'd yell at me to concentrate and call me a bum. If I hit a pop-up, he'd accuse me of being a sissy. "Why don't you put on a dress?" he'd say. If I hit a long one, he'd say, "It's about fucking time."

All his adult life my Dad worked in the mines, climbing the ladder till he got to be ground boss, and that's the same hard-nose way he wanted me to approach playing baseball. I suppose his thinking was that the best way to keep me out of the mines was to make me tough enough to succeed as a ballplayer. If I hit a home run and made an error, all he would talk about was the error. Just seeing him in the stands made me queasy and jumpy, but I was too scared of him not to perform the way he wanted me to. The thing is, baseball's a hard enough game to play when you're having fun at it and are all relaxed. I was never allowed to have that fun. Dad didn't allow fun, didn't want me to relax. To him, if you weren't slaving away, you might as well not be playing.

I didn't realize it at the time, but looking back, during those years I hated my old man. Every afternoon I would wait for him with butterflies in my stomach, because I never knew which dad was coming that day. If he came home after drinking, he'd be mad and surly and ready to swing his fists. He was scary when he got like that. I walked on eggshells, hoping I wouldn't do anything to piss him off, praying he wouldn't start screaming things at me most men wouldn't say to a dog.

Did he ever hit you?

I was lucky. Dad only hit me a few times. One time I didn't feel like practicing, just felt like going out with a couple of friends instead. He slapped me around, accused me of being a lazy no-good bum. I suppose I deserved it. I guess I didn't appreciate how much of himself he was investing in me.

No kid deserves to be hit by an adult, especially a parent. That's the worst thing about parental or spousal abuse—it brainwashes the victims, makes them think it's their fault.

What upset me the most was the way Dad treated Ma, who was quite a bit older than Dad. I don't know why Dad ever got married. It seemed to me that to him, Ma was nothing. Her name was Lovell, with the accent on the *vell*, and she gave birth to eight children, two by her first husband, who she divorced. She raised all of us, but as far as Dad was concerned, it seemed like nothing Ma did was ever good enough. I can't remember them ever talking much. He'd come home from the mines all sooty and sweaty, and after he'd call me out to pitch to me or hit me grounders, he'd go inside the house and give her a good yelling cause the beer wasn't cold enough or because dinner wasn't any good, and she'd go to her room, and he'd go off to nearby Baxter Springs, across the Kansas border, to play pool and drink with his mine buddies.

Ma rarely complained. She was a grin-and-bear-it type of person. I can remember one time I was about nine years old. I came home from school. I went inside the house, and she was sitting in the living room watching the twins, who were babies at the time. I could see she was crying. I said, "Mama, you all right?" and after wiping her eyes, she told me that she had been sitting there all day, trying to get up the nerve to move out, but that she couldn't. She said she was more scared of leaving than she was of staying, and besides, she had responsibilities to us kids. That's when she told me how much I meant to her, that she was counting on me, that she would live the rest of her life through me. So you see, when I started playing ball, I wasn't just playing ball for me. I was playing for Dad, but I was also playing for Ma.

That's a lot of weight for a kid to have to put on his shoulders.

I never loved any woman as much as I loved Ma. She was the greatest. Everything I did, I did for her. People always thought I was doing it for Dad, and I suppose on some level I was, because I was scared to let him down, but in my mind I mostly was playing for Ma. I wanted so badly for her to be proud of me. If I'd-a failed, I'd-a let her down something terrible, and I couldn't have lived with that. I owed it to her.

I never met a woman like her. So early on I knew that baseball was going to be my life or that I'd die trying.

Hey, how are fat girls and mopeds alike? They are both fun to ride until your friends find out.

What the hell was that?

Just a little joke, Lenny. You like jokes?

Sure. I enjoy a good joke now and then.

Hey, I never said anything about good!

Tell me about your early baseball career.

Even though I lived in Oklahoma, the first team I got noticed playing for was in Baxter Springs, Kansas, just across the border. They were called the Whiz Kids. I was seventeen. The guy who ran the team owned a funeral home. In my spare time I dug graves for him. He loved baseball, and he hired the best kids in the area to play for his team. We rarely lost. When I joined the team, the manager called me in for a heart-to-heart. I was going to be his shortstop, he said. He said he wanted me to take care of myself, to get to bed on time, to be at my best for the games. He told me, "Stay away from the A & P."

I said, "The what?" I thought he was talking about the grocery store.

He said, "A and P—alcohol and pussy. A couple beers, a girl, and your career is over, kid. Leave the girls alone."

This was the summer after my junior year in high school, and I had left the girls completely alone, mostly because I was incredibly shy. I remember one time I went to a party, and a group of us played spin the bottle. I spun, and the bottle pointed to this one girl, and we were supposed to go into the closet and kiss. Her name was Linda. I said, "Okay, let's go." I hadn't ever even kissed a girl before. Everyone was watching, and we went into the closet, and I said to her, "You better give me a kiss," and I reached over to her and she punched me right in the nose. She bloodied my nose. My nose was bleeding so bad I couldn't come out of the closet for five minutes!

After that, if a girl as much as looked at me, I'd drop my eyes and look at the ground. It wasn't so much that I didn't want another bloody nose. It was because I was a poor kid, wasn't real good in school, and didn't have much else. Didn't seem to me I had much to offer a girl. Like I said, I didn't have much self-confidence, except on the baseball field.

I admit it: I was intimidated by the girls. I didn't know much about them because I wasn't around them much. Everything was football, basketball, or baseball.

There was a small river running behind the outfield fence of our Whiz Kids park, and in right field it was probably five hundred feet from home plate, a hundred feet closer in center. No one had ever hit a ball into the river, but in this one game I hit three home runs over the fence into the river, two righty and one lefty, and after I hit the third one, the fans at the game passed a straw hat, and after I came back to the dugout, they dumped about a hundred bucks in dollar bills and change at my feet. I had never seen so much money in my life! I took it home, but then someone ratted on me, accusing me of being a professional ballplayer because I collected that money. They said I had to give it back if I wanted to play high school ball my senior year. I thought, *This is bullshit. Heck no, I'm not giving all that money back.* So I told everyone I had only gotten twenty-two bucks, and I returned that and kept the rest. And that's when I found out what money could do as far as the quality of puss was concerned. 'Cause before that, I was too shy to ask a girl out. After that, they asked me out.

The better-looking girls wanted to be around the athletes. It gave them status. After I started hitting home runs, I didn't have much trouble getting a girl to go out with me. I was scrawny before I became famous, but I wasn't bad looking, had this dirty blond hair, could smile some. But I was very shy, and I kept my hands to myself because of my coach's warning about "A and P." If the coach as much as saw a player holding hands with a girl, he'd make him run laps in the gym, or run up and down the steps of the football stadium, or threaten to kick him off the team. The guys who had girlfriends had to sneak around. They had to be careful, because whatever the coach said, you had to do it. He was the law.

That's the way it was back in those days.

But after everyone started talking about my three long home runs and the money I had made, for the first time I heard through my friends that this real pretty girl—her name was Sally Cummings—wanted to go out with me. She was blonde, a really beautiful girl with a great figure—she was like a goddess really, like that girl in *The Last Picture Show*, the only contestant running for homecoming queen, and even after my friends told me she wanted to go out with me, I was scared to even meet her 'cause she was so pretty and smart, and I had put her on a pedestal about fifty feet high. But I was flattered and even honored—that's what I was, honored, when they said she wanted to go out with me. I went against my coach's warnings. I told my friends to tell her I was interested. I figured if I stayed away from the A and went after the P, one out of two wouldn't kill me.

A couple days later I happened to run into Sally at the soda shop downtown. It was a Saturday afternoon, and I was sitting on a stool drinking a malt when all of her blondness and charm and perky little nose and those perky, but not-so-little very attractive mounds of allure and danger inside a tight, white knitted sweater walked up to me and introduced herself.

Mounds of allure? Cut it out. This isn't a romance novel.

She had great tits is what I'm saying. All the while I kept wondering why a girl as pretty as Sally was interested in me. We talked about some of the friends we had in common, and I bought her a Nehi with some of the money I had made hitting those three home runs, and even though I had been told she wanted to go with me, it still took me a long time to get around to it, but I finally got the words out, because I so desperately wanted to sit next to those magnetic mounds of sin, er, sorry, her great tits, and that night we went to the movies. Before I picked her up, I snuck into my dad's stash and found some rum. I grabbed two Coke bottles, filled half of them with the rum, and put the bottle caps back on.

I have an idea. Why don't you take us back there.

Can we do that?

No reason why not.

Mickey turned around to call over Toots to settle up the bar bill, but he was gone. So were all the customers. In fact, so was the entire restaurant. Mickey turned back to Lenny, his eyes wide with surprise. Lenny carelessly shrugged a shoulder, so they both turned in their seats to face the balcony of the Roxy Theatre.

It is 1949. The Roxy is the only movie theater in Commerce, but it seems to play the same movie for a month at a time. Mickey and Sally went to that movie even though both of them had seen it already. Mickey paid the twenty cents, then they both ascended the narrow steps to the balcony. They decide to sit in the very last row. Sally starts climbing the balcony stairs, with the very horny seventeen-year-old Mickey right behind her. Her tight, shapely ass is right at his eye level. He can practically kiss it, he's following so close. It's all he can do to climb the stairs without tripping.

Finally, they reach their seats. Mickey reaches into his jacket and pulls out one of the Coke bottles and a church key. He snaps the cap off, takes a swig, and passes it to Sally, who happily takes a drink.

While John Wayne rides around the West on his horse, the heads of Mickey and Sally get closer and closer. Every so often Mickey pulls out the Coke bottle, drinks, and passes it to Sally, until both bottles are emptied.

Lenny, as I started to fall under the spell of the rum, I felt real guilty. I knew I was going to need the A to get the P. I remember thinking to myself, *Tough shit, Coach.*

No one else is around them. Sally is on Mickey's right. They sit there in the darkness. There is an electricity in the air, a feeling of excitement, of expectation. Something is going to happen, but neither says a word. Emboldened by the liquor, Mickey puts his arm around Sally's neck and onto her right shoulder. He waits for her response. He doesn't have to wait long. He was half expecting her to push his arm away, but instead she looks at him and gives him a sweet, tender smile. He pulls her a little closer toward him. Will she resist? No. She nuzzles into him. He can feel her left breast burning a hole into the right side of his body. They stare at each other. Then she parts her moist red lips and gives him a warm kiss.

You enjoying this?

It's a little weird watching myself, I have to admit, but it was a magical afternoon I'll never forget. And it's kind of exciting to see it again as it was, rather than trying to picture it in my head. Man, that first kiss! That's when I knew what lust was.

Sally takes his left hand and places it on her blouse right above her left breast. A look of panic comes over Mickey's face. He obviously has no idea what to do. Then she unsnaps her bra and smiles. He hungrily puts his hand under her blouse. At that point he knows exactly what to do. He reaches in and cups her left breast with his left hand.

Lenny, I was sure my hand was going to catch on fire.
  Shhhh!

After Sally unstraps her bra with a move no man except maybe Harry Houdini could figure out, she puts her mouth about a centimeter from his face and whispers, "Kiss me."

Lenny, she probably wanted me to kiss her lips, but I had never seen a breast before, never mind kissed one. When I held it, I felt as though I had been personally blessed by the Almighty.

Mickey bends over and surrounds her nipple with his mouth. Sally gasps involuntarily, actually making a noise. Mickey's eyes scan the balcony to see if anyone heard it. They're safe. John Wayne was loudly killing Injuns on the screen. Meanwhile, Mickey's whole body starts to tremble.

Remember, Lenny, I was seventeen years old. I had never done this before. And Sally was the best-looking girl in the whole world.

Mickey sits there glowing, red in the face, not knowing what to do next, when Sally reaches across with her right hand and unzips the fly of his jeans. It's obvious that he doesn't have the slightest idea what she is about to do to him. He sits there frozen, trying to concentrate on the posse of cowboys riding across the big screen, when Sally gives Little Mick a flick with her forefinger, causing him to quiver, and it is all he can do to keep from screaming at the top of his lungs. Suddenly his eyes get real big as that feeling of "Oh God" began to swell inside him, and just when he thinks he is going to squirt all his bodily fluids to the ceiling, she bends over, puts his thing in her lovely mouth and swallows it all the way down her throat until he is sure she is going to choke to death. As her tongue licks him, up and down, up and down, he holds his breath until he thinks he is going to pass out, and then he has the most incredible rush as his entire being flows from within him into her mouth and down her throat.

I don't know how she did it, Lenny, but she didn't even cough, never mind choke. To this day the feel of her tonsils down the length of my dick remains one of the warmest memories of my entire life.

It was the first time in my life I understood my own greatness.

And it wasn't after hitting a home run. It was after oral sex from Sally Cummings. Now most of the time I was a pretty wishy-washy person. I didn't usually know things for sure. In fact, I was only positive about one thing in my life. After that first blow job, I was *positive* I was going to do that again.

When Sally is finished, she stuffs Mickey back into his undies, zips up the fly of his jeans, and they sit there holding hands watching the rest of the movie.

Right then, Len, I knew how I wanted to spend the rest of my life: having sex as often as I could. All I had to do was figure out how to do that, which, at the time, was only a pipe dream. How could I know that in a few short years my wildest dreams would come true?

The movie is over. The house lights come on. Sally is wearing her bra, her blouse is buttoned, and she looks as untouched as she had been when they walked in. They descend the balcony stairs, a knowing smile playing on Sally's face, a look of worry on Mickey's.

I always wondered if anyone in the theater could tell what we'd done.

After that, all my thoughts were of Sally. Every time I thought of her, I got hard, and I would need relief. Even when I was on the ballfield, she was all I could think of. I even spoke of marrying her, but talk like that would make Dad furious. He wanted me to become a ballplayer and, like my high school coach, he didn't want a piece of ass to get in the way.

Whenever we were together Sally and I'd hunt for places for her to relieve my inner tension, an act which apparently gave her a great deal of pleasure, though for the life of me I couldn't figure out why. In fact, to this day I still wonder why any girl would give a guy a blow job. What's in it for her?

It's one of life's grander mysteries.

I didn't have to work hard to get Sally to go with me into the storage closet in the hardware store or the girl's bathroom of the soda shop or the corner of the third-base dugout of the high school ballfield at night, and she always seemed to know exactly what was on my mind. She'd unzip my fly and take Little Mick out, and each time she'd try some new method or coat me with something she'd never used before. One time it was butterscotch syrup, which was all sticky. Sally'd say to me, "How does this feel?" I probably should not be talking about this but it meant so much to me at the time. I told her it felt sticky and that there was no way she was going to be able to lick it off, but she did, praise the Lord. One time she licked my balls. Another time she took the head of my dick in her mouth and made a circular motion with her tongue. I thought I would faint. But all that time she wouldn't let me take off her clothes, wouldn't let me do much with her except feel her up with her clothes on. I didn't mind because what she was doing to me was so amazing. I often wondered where she had learned to do those things. Is this what girls talked about with each other? I know my daddy and mama sure never told me about any of this. My coach only told me never to do it.

I thought to myself, *Coach warned us against A & P. The P is turning out to be pretty incredible.*

A couple times Sally and I packed a picnic basket and we went semi-skinny-dipping out by the Blue Goose mine in one of the hundreds of deep sinkholes that dot that whole area of northeastern Oklahoma. Sally made me promise her I wouldn't go near her when we were unclothed. She said she was afraid of getting pregnant.

I never did. Before she went into the water and before she came out, she made me turn around while she was taking her clothes off.

Once I made the mistake of bragging to the other guys that Sally and I had gone skinny-dipping. Remember, Sally was the town goddess, and my buddies let me know in no uncertain terms that I owed it to them to tell them the next time exactly when and where Sally and I were supposed to go. For years they all had had their own fantasies about Sally, and they were dying to see Sally's puss for themselves to see whether it was really blonde. All the guys asked me the same question, "Is she or isn't she?" Remember that line in the Clairol commercial about whether a girl dyed her hair or not?

The truth is that I was so bashful and shy I couldn't have told them. My friend Tommy once begged me to let him come along. He said all he wanted to do was "watch her breasts move up and down when she walks." He pleaded with me. "If I can do that, I can die happy," he said. When you're a kid, life's pleasures sure are simple. But I was afraid Sally would see him, and we'd be finished, so I told him no.

Tommy and the other guys even offered to pay me ten bucks each to watch, and I really wouldn't have minded that, could have used the money, but see, I was very private about myself when I was a kid. I was so bashful I always wore my jeans when I swam, because I was scared to death someone might come along and see me standing bare-assed in knee-deep water with my dick at attention. I'd have been so embarrassed I'd never have lived it down. So I never did give them a chance to watch Sally swim naked. Sorry, guys.

But I can tell you that it was because of Sally I stopped wearing underwear. Once you know your girl wants to get in your pants, it only makes sense to simplify things by leaving the undies at home. This is when time counts. Once she got her hands on my zipper, I wanted her to find me as fast as possible.

From that time on, there was nothing in life I wanted more. Playing baseball never made me feel as good. When she was "doing it," all was right with the world. When I fell under the spell of her fingers, there was no poverty, no zinc mines, no Dad screaming at me or Mom, no fear, no bad feelings. When she was making circles with her tongue, I was the happiest I ever was in all my life, and that includes how I felt after I hit the home run that beat the Cardinals in Game 3 of the '64 Series. I was seventeen, the prettiest girl in the state of Oklahoma was giving me her undivided attention, and my whole life was ahead of me. What more could I have asked for?

So what happened? Obviously, you didn't marry her.

I was terribly naive. I was my entire life. I thought we had a great relationship, that it would last forever. Everyone knew we were going steady, even though we really never discussed it. I was sure we were going to get married. I was so ecstatic to be with Sally, it never occurred to me that she didn't feel the same way about me. It never crossed my mind. One day Sally informed me that she was getting married to some other guy.

"Married?" I said. It was the last thing I expected. Really, I couldn't believe it.

Turned out the man who owned the general store, his wife had died a couple years earlier in childbirth, and he asked Sally to marry him right after our high school graduation. He was ancient, maybe forty. She was eighteen.

And she said yes! I couldn't believe she had accepted the old goober's marriage proposal. I pleaded with her not to do it. I asked her, "What am I supposed to do if you marry that guy?" She said, "That won't change what we have together, Mick. Not one bit." But of course it did.

She was so beautiful. And she had always been so hot for me. I asked her if the old guy was as much fun as I was. She said, "No."

"Then why are you marrying him?" I asked.

She laughed at me. " 'Cause he's rich and he's promised to take good care of me. Besides . . ." I'll never forget what she said. "You can always drop over and visit me." Not long after she got married, I called to see if I could drop over to "visit," and she said, "I don't think that would be such a great idea."

I felt like crying. Maybe it was because Sally got married. But also because I couldn't face the idea of life without a good blow job. Let me tell you, to an eighteen year old there's *nothing* better than a good blow job, unless it's a *great* blow job. But once Sally married that guy, she no longer showed any interest in me at all.

How did the breakup affect you?

Her behavior made me wonder whether people of the female persuasion somehow saw the world different from the way we guys did. One day we were going to get married. The next day she was marrying someone else. Why? How? I knew it would be a long time before I ever trusted another girl—even if she liked giving me blow jobs.

She used me, I guess. She was pretty sophisticated about sex and life, and I didn't know squat. She knew what she wanted. I thought I did, too. I didn't know a gal could use a guy that way—for sex, I mean. Never occurred to me. Not that I'm complaining. But I learned the hard way.

Every time I saw Sally, I hurt so badly inside I knew I had to leave Oklahoma. I told myself, It's time to leave the local puss behind.

Two guys are drinking at a bar. The first guy says, "Do you ever start thinking about something, and then say what you don't mean?" The second guy says, "Yeah, I was at the airport buying tickets, and the chick behind the counter had huge tits, and instead of asking for two tickets to Pittsburgh, I asked for two pickets to Titsburgh."

The first guy says, "Yeah, well I was having breakfast with my wife last week, and instead of saying, 'Honey, pass the sugar,' I said, 'You've ruined my life, you fucking bitch.' "

It was around that time that I signed with the New York Yankees, which, like most things with me, was just dumb luck. When I signed, I knew nothing about Yankee tradition, of the House that Ruth Built. Hell, I couldn't even point to New York on a map. I was so dumb that I don't think I knew that Harry Truman was president or that Oklahoma City was the capital of Oklahoma. I knew two things: from my summer job, I knew how to swing a big mallet in the zinc mines, and I knew how to hit a baseball.

If things had worked out the way they should have, I'd have ended up a St. Louis Cardinal or a St. Louis Brown. They were the two teams closest to Oklahoma. My Dad had contacted the Browns, at the time the worst organization in baseball. They were not interested in kid shortstops. The Browns organization was run by morons and jerks. The Cardinals weren't much better, but at least they had Marty Marion, the best shortstop in baseball. In high school, I was five-ten, about 165 pounds, and even though I hit long home runs, the Cardinals said they weren't interested in signing me unless I grew some more.

Meanwhile, a Yankee scout by the name of Tom Greenwade came to one of my Whiz Kid games, and I hit two long home runs, one left-handed that went four hundred feet, and another righty that went almost as far, and he promised to sign me as soon as school let out that spring. I told him thanks, then forgot about it, because I didn't really believe him, but Greenwade kept his word, and he became famous for being the guy who signed me. His first offer was a crummy $400 for the season. My dad told him I could work in the mines for that. The next day he came back and said he was authorized to give me a $1,100 bonus in addition to my salary. This time Dad said okay. Compared to the $75 a week my dad was making, it wasn't bad. But if you compare it to the $100,000 a rag-armed pitcher named Paul Pettit got for signing with the Pirates, I didn't get shit.

Here's how naive Dad and I were: Mr. Greenwade patted me on the shoulder and confided that he couldn't give us any more money because I was a terrible fielder and probably wouldn't make it. And I believed him.

Then when my signing made the local papers, Greenwade was quoted as saying I was the "greatest prospect he had ever seen." That's got to tell you something about my business ability.

Where did they send you?

Independence, Kansas, Class D. The lowest level they have today is Class A. And this was three levels below that! The biggest problem was that in Class D ball we got Class D puss. I remember my first road trip. We were playing Bartlesville, in Oklahoma, and when we got off the bus, this pimply, chubby girl wearing a short dress came up to me and a couple of the guys and said to us, "If one of you doesn't fuck me right now, I'm going to kill myself." One of my teammates standing next to me pointed behind him to the bus and said, "Bobby Herman'll fuck you. Ask for him." And we kept walking. A group of us got on the elevator and went up to our room on the fourth floor. When Herman, who was famous for fucking absolutely anything wearing a skirt, came into our room, my teammate said to him, "Bobby, aren't you going to fuck that chubby little gal?"

"Nah, too early in the afternoon," Bobby said.

About ten minutes later we could hear the wail of sirens. We looked out our hotel window, and we could see the girl lying dead on the sidewalk below and an ambulance parked next to her body. When no one had agreed to fuck that poor girl, she jumped off the roof of the hotel to her death, just as she said she would.

I felt really horrible. She had died because she had asked me to fuck her, and I had been too selfish to accept. Never mind that the rest of the guys on the team had, too. As a man you have to take responsibility for your actions. I vowed that in the future whenever a girl asked me to fuck her, I would. And for the rest of my life, I pretty well kept that vow.

Is that a true story?

Cross my heart.

So what did you learn at Independence? How to turn the double play?

The most important lesson I had to learn was that in order to make it in pro ball, a player must stay as far away from the manager's puss as possible. I had a teammate named Lou who was a real character. He was a handsome guy with a broad smile, and he acted like he was real religious. He would go to church to scout out girls! He always carried a thin silver cross about ten inches long in his back pocket, even when we were playing. Trouble was, Lou drove the manager crazy. He refused to slide, because he was afraid he'd impale that cross in his ass.

One day Lou and I were standing outside the soda shop in Independence, Missouri, when Lou saw this doll of a woman walk by. She was no high school chick. She was classy, looked about twenty-five. Lou asked her if she had a passport. "A passport?" she wanted to know. "Yeah," said Lou. "You appear to be lost. And I'm here to be your guide." Lou always knew exactly what to say to women.

He had lines for every occasion. When he wanted to be suave, he'd say to a girl, "Baby, you must be a broom, because you have swept me off my feet." Or if he wanted to be sexy, he'd ask, "Do you have a mirror in your pocket?" The girl would ask why. " 'Cause I can see myself in your pants." Or if he wanted to be crude and rude, he might ask her, "Do you know the difference between a hamburger and a blow job?" She'd say no, and he'd say, "Well, do you want to have lunch?"

Turns out this gal was in town to see our manager, who had a woman waiting for him in each of the six cow towns we played in. But Lou sweet-talked her into letting him take her to the movies and then going home to spend the night with him. The next day the manager made a long speech about loyalty to your manager and about being stupid. He glared at Lou the whole time. Lou never did make it to the Yankees. I can just see the manager's report at the end of the season: *The SOB can't be trusted. Release him. He's poison.* Of course, the manager left out the line *The guy snaked my date.*

That was pretty much the extent of my baseball education in Class D.

What happened when you returned home after the season?

One night I went with my friend Glenn to a football game. Glenn was dating a majorette, and she had a friend who was also a majorette and who was a knockout. They were wearing their tight-fitting sweaters and those little short skirts, where if you're horny enough and close enough and bold enough, you can reach under there real quick and grab her crotch and then duck before she slaps you across the face. I got my friend to fix me up with the knockout majorette, and that night we went on a double date.

We weren't getting along too well, and I saw that Glenn and his girl were squabbling. My date had dark hair, and his was a blonde, like Sally. I said to him, "I really like your girlfriend."

And he said, "I really like yours."

I whispered, "Let's switch."

"Okay."

Just like that. So I said to his girlfriend, "I'm going to go out with you," and Glenn said to her friend, "I'm going to start going out with you." And they shrugged their shoulders as only eighteen-year-old girls can and said, "Sounds good to us." And to jump ahead of the story, this was the girl I ended up marrying. Since I ended up marrying her, out of respect I won't say anything more about our dates, except that we had a good time, that she made me feel comfortable, and it made me happy to have someone pretty and fun to go out with whenever I wanted. And unlike Sally, Merlyn wasn't looking for an older guy or a secure future. She was just happy to be with me, which was a good reason for me to like her, and after several months of going together, it didn't even bother me that she told everyone we were "going steady," 'cause she was helping me to get through the off-season, and we were great friends, so what the hell?

How'd you feel about her when you had to go back to playing ball?

When the time came to go back to my baseball life, I can't say I was sorry about it. I could be with the guys again without having to account for my time, and if I spent the night with one of the roller dolls at the burger stand or messed around with one of the female fans, well, so be it. I had no one to answer to, and I liked that a whole lot. I had liked being independent in Independence.

Where did you go next?

I jumped to Joplin in Class C to start off the '50 season. The highlight of that year was my introduction to topless bars by a teammate named Steve, an older player who had been in the organization four or five years and who knew his way around the league. On our very first road trip he made it his business to show me and some of the other young guys the ropes. It's like when you go into the service and go to basic training, there's always a private with one stripe, and everyone calls him "sir." Steve was the same type, mouthy, on top of things. He was going to show us the ropes, and so the first thing he did was take us to a topless bar. Being from Oklahoma, I had never been to a topless bar. We didn't even have booze in Oklahoma. We had to cross the border to even drink beer.

I couldn't believe this place. For two bucks, I could sit and watch buck-naked girls bounce around all day! Big, juicy ones, little perky ones. Young ones, old ones, white ones, black ones, and every once in a while an Indian or a Chinese gal would get up and perform, and that would drive me crazy, because I'd heard from my high school football coach that Chinese girls had straight pubic hair, not curly like white girls, and the one time a Chinese girl came out to dance I moved up front staring, trying to see behind her G-string to see if it was true or not.

Come on.

That's the thing about baseball: with so much time to kill during the season, things can get real perverted, real quick. I'm here to tell you that this is the truth about being a young baseball player. It can really change your down-home values and fast.

The first time we went to this topless bar, I didn't have a lot of money on me, couldn't even order a drink because I was only eighteen. I never had a drink before, except maybe to sip a beer, which I didn't like all that much. Or that rum and Coke on the first date with Sally. I always preferred root beer or sarsaparilla. So we were setting in this topless place, and I'm talking to this girl. She was kind of cute. Wasn't coyote ugly.

What's coyote ugly?

You don't know what coyote ugly is? It's when you wake up with someone, and she's so ugly and she's laying on your arm, and you want to chew your arm off so you can get away from her and up out of bed.

After I told her I was a ballplayer, she agreed to go with me to my hotel room. When we got up to the room, my roommate was in the other bed reading *The Sporting News*. This was the exact moment when I lost my reluctance about other guys watching me. I guess it was because in this situation you really don't have much choice. If you were going to pick up these gals, the only place to have sex with them where you didn't have to spend any money was back in your hotel room.

"You mind if he's here?" I asked her.

"Not if you don't," she said.

My roommate pretended that he was still reading but you can be sure he was watching everything we were doing. Getting puss is great, but so is watching your roommate getting puss. And, of course, the very best is when he gives her over to you after he's done.

Anyway, this girl and I were in bed, and I had taken off all her clothes, and we were starting to get into it, and all of a sudden there was a rapping at the door. I froze. I was new on the team, wasn't aware that our manager was in the habit of coming by and checking everyone's room at eleven. I said, "Who's there?"

The manager growled, "Room check. Open your door."

I said, "Open my door?"

He said, "Yeah, room check. We want to make sure you're in the room by yourself."

This girl, who was lying naked in bed beside me, ran into the bathroom and got into the empty tub. I threw all her clothes on top of her and then covered her with towels and one of my blankets. I was scared to death. If the manager caught me, I was afraid I was going to be sent home and I'd never make it to the big leagues.

The manager walked in, looked around the room and said, "Okay, you guys go to bed."

Thank God, he never looked in the bathroom. I was afraid the manager would come back. Right there in the bathtub, she agreed to give me a short workout, and then I made her get dressed and leave.

That year I got laid enough times to appreciate what it meant to be a professional ballplayer. I also hit .400 and hit some of the longest home runs ever seen in that league.

People don't remember this, but I actually spent the last two weeks of the 1950 season sitting on the bench with the New York Yankees in the major leagues. I was eighteen years old. Never got in a game. That's when I first got to watch Joe DiMaggio, who even at that time was rated the greatest living ballplayer. In his day Joe was as big as Barry Bonds is today. I can't say I had much to do with him, or him with me. Joe would walk into the clubhouse, staring straight ahead. He rarely talked to anyone. You know how people say the Italians are so demonstrative, high-strung, and emotional? You'd never know it from being around Joe. Joe wouldn't have shouted or cheered even if he had gotten a blow job from Rita Hayworth.

No, he was more the Mafia Dago type, a goomba who wore fancy suits and kept his mouth shut. Joe always wore a tie, always looked like he was going to a fancy nightclub affair. Something else I noticed about him: he never laughed, never even smiled except when he was trying to get some gorgeous girl to go back to his hotel room with him, and he was *very, very* good at that. Joe wasn't real handsome, but he was the most famous and highest-paid athlete in America at the time, and it was a lesson for me. I wanted Joe's class of women, and I vowed to become as big a star as Joe to get them. And whatever bullshit you want to fire at me about how I never reached my potential or how if it hadn't been for injuries I'd have been even better, I can tell you with great pride that I fulfilled that vow to myself: it wasn't long before I became as big a star as Joe had been and got just as many great-looking girls as he did, and maybe more.

Forty-some-odd years after Joe and I first met I can honestly say if there was one man more unhappy with his life than I have been at times, that man was Joe DiMaggio. After all, Joe got to learn what life was like away from baseball almost twenty years before I did. Joe quit at the end of the 1951 season, and he spent the rest of his long life reminding people how great he had been. Old Timers' Day was the highlight of his life every year for him. Billy Martin adored him. I thought he was pathetic.

Joe got lucky in the 1990s when he started getting two hundred bucks apiece for signing his name to a picture or a ball. Before that, Joe spent his days taking chump change for appearing at sports banquet after sports banquet, shaking hands with people he loathed meeting, going to towns he didn't want to go to. When he was home in San Francisco living with his sister he was miserable, so he spent much of his time on the road. He lived out of a suitcase. Joe went to so many functions, he became known as "America's guest."

We never talked about it, but I'm sure it had to have been humiliating for him to do that. I know it was for me. I'd go to Schenectady or Akron or some other shithole, pocket five grand, get as drunk as I could as fast as I could, wave to the kids, insult a few of the adults, piss on the center divider of Main Street, and split.

There is no dignity in being a former ballplayer, and it doesn't matter how big you once were. The irony is that you're probably better off being mediocre rather than great. Then when you quit, people don't think of you as something special, and you don't think of yourself as something special, and it's a lot easier to take a shit job selling insurance or real estate or taking a few bucks to shill for some local used car dealer if you're not actually selling the cars.

When I quit playing I had no desire to do anything but drink and fuck. Those were the only two things available to me from my playing career. Joe didn't even drink that much. He was stuck with having to live with himself sober. As for fucking, Joe was more of a perfectionist than I was. He liked quality over quantity. But Joe was no different from the rest of us—even if the girl was pretty, after fucking her he didn't necessarily want her lying there next to him in the morning. And Joe was a little like Billy. If she pissed him off, Joe wasn't above whacking her around a little.

And when I ended up going before that SOB, that really pissed me off. I thought Joe would never die. He was too damn mean and crochety and crazy. The worst thing he ever pulled, we were together at an Old Timers' Day event, and the Yankees announced all the different players—Roger, Yogi, Whitey, Ellie, Bobby, and Pepi—and then they announced his name and everyone cheered him. But my name came last, and I got a louder ovation than he did, which I usually did, because most of his fans were in a home or dead.

Joe was so pissed off he cussed out the Yankee officials and told them he'd never go to another Old Timers' Day. The great Mr. Coffee couldn't stand being shown up. In order for him to come back, the Yankees had to promise him they'd announce his name last from then on. They asked me about it, massaged me by telling me I was more important, said they'd only agree if it was okay with me. They didn't have to worry. I didn't give a shit one way or the other. I knew who had more fans, who was more popular. I didn't care if they didn't announce my name at all.

But that's the kind of guy Joe was. Moody and crackers.

Even back during those last two weeks in '50 and the part of the '51 season when I was with him on the Yankees, Joe was a mess. He was hanging on. Every part of him was hurting, and he couldn't hit the ball like he once could. He'd swing, and balls that he once pulled for home runs became dinky flies to right field. That year he hit two sixty something and hit maybe a dozen home runs. He was a shell of himself. I never saw a man with moods so black. We would travel on the trains, and the guys would show him respect by not disturbing his privacy. Joe would sit on the train by himself, with no one next to him or opposite him, smoking a cigarette and staring sullenly out the window for hours. He wouldn't talk to anyone. The players whispered that Joe and his first wife, Dorothy, had been dating, trying to get back together, but that they had gotten in a big fight, and Dorothy broke it off and announced she was going to marry some other guy. Joe was worried about how that would affect his relationship with his son, who he loved but never saw. I know what that's all about. Joe even got his own hotel room when we went on the road, which was fine with everyone. Who would want to room with a guy like that?

Who did you room with?

I wasn't as lucky as Joe when it came to roommates—at first. My first roommate was a veteran pitcher who I won't name because he was married at the time. He's dead now, but I don't know how his wife would feel finding out about this. We arrived in Philadelphia to play the A's, and we all went out to the hotel bar for a beer. When I returned to my room, it was about eleven at night and the door was locked. I knocked. My roomie said, "Who is it?" Like he didn't know who it was. I told him it was me. He said, "Sorry, you can't come in now. I'm busy. Wait an hour, and I'll be finished."

I thought, Well okay. I was a kid, not even on the roster, and he was this veteran player. I figured it wouldn't kill me to wait outside the room sitting up in the hallway.

When the hour was up, I knocked on my door. "Who is it?"

"It's me, Mickey."

"What do you want?"

"I want to go to sleep."

"You're going to have to wait a little longer. I'm not finished yet."

By three in the morning I was pissed. I said, "Let me in—right now. I want to go to sleep." And I told him if he didn't let me in, I would take the fire axe and chop down the door.

"Well, okay, just a minute."

A few minutes later he opened the door, and this girl came out. She had a big scar on her face. She had a decent body, but I remember the scar. What a mullion! I looked at her and I thought, *I can't believe I had to wait in the hall this whole time for her.* I thought, *If this is big league life, I don't know if I want it.*

I told my roomie how angry I was. He said, "You're going to have to do this for me sometimes, because I have a lot of friends around the league, and I need some time by myself."

I said, "You can have all the time by yourself you want, because I'm not rooming with you anymore." Turned out, it was hard for this guy to keep roommates. None of the veterans would room with him so they had put me in there with him.

The next day the pissed-off traveling secretary put me in with another of the veteran pitchers, also long dead, another guy who really didn't want a roommate, but who was better able to cope with having one. I'll call him Bob, but that wasn't his real name. He too had a wife. That day we beat the A's, and this time when I went back to my room, thankfully it was empty. At around midnight I turned off the radio, got under the covers ready to go to sleep when Bob came in with this gorgeous girl about my age. I was lying on my right side, pretending to be asleep, but when I opened my eyelids a crack I recognized her as the left field line ball girl at Connie Mack Stadium. She was so pretty I had even noticed her at the game. I remember while I was sitting on the bench I was wondering what her big breasts felt like under her wooly A's uniform. This was before I started drinking, so I was too shy to talk with her. She was real cute, with dark hair, a great body, and when she came into the hotel room with my roomie she was wearing a tight skirt to her calves, and she had on high-heels that showed off her great legs. As I watched this dream girl standing there smiling at him, I wondered whether my new roomie was going to ask me to get out like the last one. I was hoping my sleeping act was fooling them.

Without saying a word, Bob switched off the lamp, but there was still enough light from the hotel window for me to see more than just shadows. On the other side of Bob's bed, I could see him taking off his clothes, which alerted me that it would be to my advantage to change my angle of sight, and so I stirred like I was turning in my sleep, and moved my head until I could see that in the space between his bed and mine this girl was standing so close to me I could reach out and touch her with my nose. I lay there and watched.

First she reached down and took off her shoes. She then unbuttoned and took off her blouse, which she folded, then unhooked and took off her skirt, which she folded, and under that she took off a taut, elastic garment which turned out to be a girdle, an item I had never seen before. Then she went for her bra, pulling down first the left strap, then the right, and after that magical twist of the wrist, she liberated herself so that in the moonlight I could see the supple curves of her upper body, and while I lay still staring hypnotized from a distance of maybe two feet at her athletic legs, she grabbed the top of her panties with both hands and, bending over, yanked them forcefully down to the floor, revealing her tight little ass. When she rose back up, she turned and stretched with her arms over her head, allowing me to note that her breasts were not only full but pointy, the kind you can play with and nibble on without having to hold up with your hands. And the other thing I didn't mention, when she stretched, she pushed her pelvic muscles forward so that her fabulous bush was about six inches from my face, and it was all I could do to just lay there. God, I wanted to edge forward and nuzzle this girl so badly. Wouldn't she have been surprised? But since I wasn't even on the Yankees roster, and because I knew it was important to be a loyal teammate, I didn't want to spoil the mood for my roomie. I lay there stock still.

Also, if this was all I was going to get, it was still as good a show as I had ever had in my short life, and so I kept my mouth shut and feigned sleep with my right eye open. I watched Bob hold open the covers for her, and she crawled into his bed, and they started giggling and talking. All of a sudden I could hear him yelling at her. He said, "If that's the way you're going to be, just go get in bed with him." I was laying there with my undershorts on, thinking, what does he mean by, *Go get in bed with him?* Who's him? Me?

My heart was beating so hard I thought it would come out of my chest.

She said, "Are you sure that's what you want?"

Bob said, "I'm positive." As I lay there on my stomach motionless, I watched her leave Bob's bed, saw her sculpted naked form step toward me, and I could feel her getting into bed next to me.

I didn't know what to do. I knew she was naked, but I also knew she was Bob's date. She slapped me on the shoulder roughly and said, "Hey, you. Are you awake?"

"Now I am," I said.

She said, "He told me to do whatever you want to do with me."

I yelled over to him, "Did you mean that?"

"I don't give a shit," he said. "Do whatever you want to do with her."

She was lying on her back next to me under the covers, and I got on my hands and knees and positioned myself right on top of her. I started kissing her mouth, and then moved down to all those wonderful parts I had seen while she was undressing. I had my fair share of her, and after I had enough, we fucked right then and there. I fell asleep holding her, delirious to be on the same team with big leaguers like this guy. Just before I dozed off, I thought to myself, *What a difference a new roommate makes.*

The next morning when I woke up, the ball girl was back in bed with my roomie. Neither of them ever again brought up the subject of what happened. Though he was married, he found ways to see her in different cities for the next year or so until he retired. At the time I didn't know what to make of what happened that night. As best as I could figure out they'd been drinking, and she said something that pissed him off, and he just got mad at her, and I guess she didn't really care all that much who she was having sex with, as long as he was young and a Yankee. And so when he ordered her to get in bed with me, she went over and did it, didn't mind doing it, in fact seemed happy to do it. To please him? To please herself? To have something to talk about with her girlfriends in the morning?

It was wild. Really wild. That was the thing about meeting women when I was young: they didn't seem any more interested in a relationship than I was. They were horny and passionate and wanted a great roll in the sack just like I did. They talk about the sexual revolution in the sixties, but plenty of women were not as repressed and prudish in the fifties as people think. There was plenty of sex—you just didn't see it on TV or in the movies, and no one ever talked about it. There were gals who wanted you to hold them and kiss them and fuck them and let them go home. Which was what I wanted, too. I wasn't even on the Yankees roster, and I was enjoying the first stage of being a major league ballplayer, learning what was available to you if you said please and thank you and weren't a total prick.

Everything.

After the 1950 season I went back home. I resumed dating Merlyn, but I also had sex more than a few times with this other girl who I knew, who had big ones, a great ass, a sex maniac who loved for me to lie down on the floor facing up on the backseat of my car while she squatted down over me, fit me into her, and humped away while she howled like a timber wolf. She was exciting, and she knew just how to drive me crazy by slapping her nipples back and forth across my face as we made love. But boy, I got the shit scared out of me one day when her father showed up at the mine where my dad was working to say his little girl was pregnant, that I was the father, and that he wanted me to do right by her.

I told her I'd do right by her, all right. I told her I'd drive her to Missouri to see this nurse a teammate told me about who performed abortions, which weren't legal back then. I was more afraid of *my* father than I was of *her* father and I had no intention of marrying her, or anyone else, and screwing up my baseball career. I was leaving for New York, and she wasn't going to be part of the journey, baby or no baby. I told her, "It's your kid. You take care of it." It's pretty much what I told all the girls over the years who said they were pregnant. If any girl agreed to go to bed with me, I figured that if she got pregnant, it was her tough luck and that she better leave me the fuck alone.

Mick, that's a pretty shitty, chauvinistic attitude.

It was the same attitude every other ballplayer I knew—every other guy I knew—had. Besides, it turned out I wasn't the father after all, or at least after I said I wouldn't marry her, she said I wasn't. She had also been fucking some other guy, and she ended up marrying him instead. I always wondered about girls who were happy to marry some other guy if you wouldn't marry them. How much could they have loved that other guy? In this case, I couldn't help wonder whether the other guy had any more luck than I had catching her nipples in his mouth. Lucky guy. He'd be getting a lot more chances. As for Merlyn, we saw each other off and on, but I really had no plans to marry her either. Casey Stengel, the Yankees manager, had told me I was going to New York to play in '51, and I didn't see any reason to be married. After all, I had discovered for myself the year before that New York had the classiest puss in the whole wide world.

What was spring training like when you got there in '51?

For me the highlight of spring training was getting to know Billy Martin. Billy was a real ballbuster. He was the only guy on the team who dared give Joe DiMaggio shit. Billy liked to imitate how Joe walked, how he took his coffee, how he got dressed. Joe would just glare at him, even though you just knew he was loving it inside. One time Billy spilled blue ink down Joe's white shirt, and I thought Joe was going to kill him, until Billy was able to get Joe to shut up long enough to tell him it was invisible ink, that it was all a joke. Even though Billy was just a kid, he even talked back to Casey Stengel.

Billy had played for Casey in the minors back in Oakland, and it was because of Casey that Billy became a Yankee at all. The Yankees had an image that all the guys were like DiMaggio, Tommy Henrich, and Hank Bauer: stern, serious classy guys. Billy was a bully from the streets of Berkeley, California. He drank hard liquor and liked to fight. What no one understood was that Billy was the spitting image of the Old Man, only a lot younger. Casey loved Billy *because* he liked to drink and fight. Casey demanded respect and would slice you up with his tongue if he saw something you did that he didn't like, but Casey would take Billy's shit and just shake his head. I couldn't believe some of the things Billy said to him.

One time during a game our second baseman, Jerry Coleman, who was one of the niftiest fielders in the American League, made an error, and Billy got mad and said to the Old Man, "What the fuck are you playing that bum at second for? You know that guy can't hold my jock. Are you trying to lose the pennant on purpose or are you just senile?" Billy knew how badly Casey wanted to win, and to accuse him of throwing a game was about the worst thing Billy could have accused Casey of, except maybe being senile.

Casey put his hands on his hips and harrumphed that he'd play "whoever the fuck I want." The two just glared at each other.

Then Casey turned around, where Billy couldn't see him, and he started laughing.

Baseball managers don't usually become attached to their players, because if you do that, it's too hard emotionally to get rid of a guy you like when he no longer can play, and that happens in baseball all the time. But Casey couldn't seem to help himself. The Old Man loved Billy, no question about it. I guess I did, too. Billy was a scrawny little guy, didn't weigh more than a hundred fifty pounds, but Billy was the type of guy who was as tough as a four-hundred-pound gorilla. He thought he was the star of the team, even when he was playing on the same team as Joe D and even though he wasn't starting. Some of the veterans resented Billy's attitude, but Billy didn't give a shit. He knew he could take any of them in a fight, except maybe Hank Bauer, who had fought at Guadalcanal during World War II, and they knew it, too. So nobody gave Billy any lip. Besides, Bauer and Gene Woodling told me the Old Man had talked about Billy all through the 1950 season, so they knew going in that Billy could do no wrong in Casey's eyes, knew that they'd better lay off the kid if they didn't want any trouble from the Old Man.

Casey wanted Billy on the Yankees so bad that during spring training in '51 he told the general manager, George Weiss, who hated Billy even before he arrived, that if he didn't put Billy on the roster, he'd quit right then and there. Weiss, who was a son of a bitch in a different way, had this thing about his Yankees being gentlemen and family men and all that bullshit. Even though Billy was what we called a juvenile delinquent back then, Weiss knew Casey was heart-attack serious about what he said, and so Weiss kept Billy, despite his being horrified that a zoot-suited son of a bitch like Billy was a Yankee.

Weiss had sent private detectives out to Berkeley, where Billy lived, and Weiss learned that Billy had been the head of a gang of toughs that went from bar to bar at night beating up people for the fun of it. Billy and his sadistic gang would hang around the University of California and beat up the college kids, and he'd hang around the movie theaters where he loved to beat up servicemen. He'd even beat up one of his friends if the guy said something that rubbed Billy the wrong way. Billy was barely twenty, but even then he drank hard, and he had a lot of anger in him, and he loved, really *loved*, to punch guys out when they weren't looking.

As I told you, Billy also was a sex hound. Once he got the smell of puss in his nostrils, nothing else mattered. He didn't care who he was fucking, didn't care if they were sixteen years old, sometimes didn't even care that they didn't want to do it. If the girl was crazy enough to get in a car with him, he'd drive her to a deserted spot, and once they started making out, if she wasn't strong enough or fast enough to stop Billy from pulling down her pants, Billy would nail her. The only way she could get him to stop was to promise him a blow job instead. And Weiss knew all this, so he hated Billy, because he was afraid that one day Billy would end up a big headline in the papers, accused of rape, or murder, or rape and murder.

Weiss told this to Casey, but the Old Man didn't give a shit whether or not Billy was a serial killer. He had seen firsthand what Billy could do for a ball club, that he was the one guy who could intimidate the other team, and Casey respected the power of intimidation. If Casey needed someone to spike a guy or punch him out, he knew Billy was psycho enough to do it for him. The thing about Casey: he was an old guy and talked funny, so the press and everyone wrote about him like he was some kind of clown, and I suppose that looking at that creased mug of his with the big jug ears and hearing the way he talked, using five-minute sentences and always changing the subject, it was easy to do. But looking back, I can see now that Casey was a true genius. He knew how to play the game, and he knew how to teach it. And on the Yankees he had the horses, and Casey led us to ten pennants. Casey always said that the role of the manager was not to screw up, that most managers get hired because they are friends of the general manager, not because they know what they're doing, and over the years I could see that he was right. Casey not only never lost ball games, but he was one of the few managers who actually won ball games.

Later, Billy was that way, too. Casey always knew who to play, knew when to pull a pitcher, knew when to pinch hit. He knew the game. Christ, he'd been playing since the 1910s, and then he played under John McGraw, who Casey said was the worst cocksucker he ever knew. Hated him, Casey told me. McGraw second-guessed the players all the time, cussing you up and down even when you made a good play, he said. Took all the credit for the players' success. Case said the Giants players would get together and plot ways to kill him. Usually in jest, Casey told me, but he said this one time he and a small group of teammates were so tired of McGraw's bullshit that they plotted to ride with McGraw to the Polo Grounds on the subway and when they arrived push him to his death off the platform outside the ballpark. The plan, he said, called for them to blame it on the Negroes who lived up there in Harlem. Casey said the only reason they didn't do it was when they arrived, a uniformed cop was standing right there on the platform. He said that one of the players, a first baseman named George Kelly—a Hall of Famer, by the way—told McGraw of their plans, and for the rest of the year McGraw took cabs and watched his back. At the end of the year he traded Casey away, even though Casey hit two homers in the World Series, including the first World Series homer in Yankee Stadium.

What did Casey teach you?

Casey had started his playing career with the Brooklyn Dodgers, even before Ebbets Field was built. Before we were to play the Dodgers in the World Series in '52, he walked me out to right field and tried to show me how to play the concrete wall in Ebbets Field, which was hard because it was built in a million sections, and where the ball hit determined which way it would bounce. But standing with him I didn't see how that old geezer could ever have been a ballplayer, and so I refused to listen to him. You saw him. He was short and had white hair and had this gimpy walk. I was just a kid. I didn't know. It just didn't register that Casey could have been a ballplayer. For the rest of his life, Casey never did stop telling that story.

But since then I learned that Casey was one tough son of a bitch who played a lot like Ty Cobb, that if you got in his way, he'd just as soon spike you down to the bone as look at you. And that was the Casey Stengel I knew. To me, Casey was no clown. Mostly, he was a son of a bitch who hated to lose, who would do absolutely anything to win, including sending me out with orders to hit a home run or sending Billy out to hurt somebody.

With Casey, the better we played, the worse he treated us. If we lost a couple games, he never said a word. But if we were on a winning streak, Casey would get on our ass and never let up. And Billy was the same way. Like I said, Billy was a psycho son of a bitch. And I admired the hell out of him, too. One thing Casey had in common with Billy was that they were never boring. You never knew what goofy idea or prank Billy'd come up with. Sometimes Billy didn't realize how dangerous it would be, but I found out early that whatever crazy fucking idea Billy came up with, it was going to be exciting, or fun, or both. And Billy admired me, because anything he wanted to do, I was happy to go along with.

What could have been so dangerous?

We roomed together my rookie season in '51, and during this one series in St. Louis our room was on the eighth floor of the Chase Hotel. The Chase was one of the fanciest hotels in America at that time, and it drew the cream of the puss crop. Billy liked to roam the lobby to scope out who was staying at the hotel. He noticed that a really cute blonde had checked in, and Billy got the room number from the desk clerk, after offering him two tickets to our game against the Brownies. Turned out she was staying in a room on our floor at the end of the hall to the left. After he walked down the hall to her door to determine the actual location of the room, Billy said to me, "We're going to watch her take a shower." I thought he was nuts.

I said, "How we gonna do that? We don't have a key."

He said, "Easy. There's a ledge outside our room that goes all around the building. We'll walk around the ledge outside and watch her from the bathroom window."

I said, "Billy, we're eight stories up."

He said, "Don't worry. It isn't dangerous. The ledge'll hold us. And besides, it'll be worth it."

I said, "Are you crazy? What if we fall and die?"

He said, "We're too young to die. And besides, we're Yankees. Yankees don't die."

I followed Billy out our window and onto the ledge, which was maybe three feet wide. In the dark I could hear the traffic on the street below. With our backs to the wall we inched our way around the building until we got to what we thought was the right room. I didn't look down, but if I had, those wouldn't have been ants but cars that looked like ants.

As I slunked about with my back to the wall of the hotel, I could picture myself slipping and falling to my death. I was so scared I could barely move my feet. Billy, he wasn't fazed at all. I had gone out first, and he kept urging me, "Mick, hurry up," like maybe I should run to get to that girl's window. Billy's mind was concentrating on one thing: seeing that girl naked taking a shower.

After what seemed like hours, we finally reached the corner of the building. We had to be careful not to let the woman see us as we inched past her bathroom window. I stood with my back to the wall, petrified. I turned my head to the right to watch Billy, who had turned around 180 degrees with no apparent difficulty, his face pressed against the small bathroom window.

"Anything?" I whispered.

"Not yet," Billy said.

"How do you know she's even going to take a shower?" I asked.

"She's gonna have to take a shower eventually," he said.

"How long we gonna wait?"

"As long as it takes."

I always said that Billy was always one of the luckiest sons of bitches alive, because it wasn't but a few minutes later when I heard the shower go on.

"Big ones, Mick. Ya don't know what you're missing," Billy said.

But I was too petrified to move.

"Ya gotta see her, Mick. She's everything I'd hoped she would be." I knew someone was in that shower, but to this day I have no idea whether it was that girl or just some hotel guest or whether Billy had made up the whole thing. All I could think about was inching my way back around the ledge and going back into my room. But Billy was standing there, peeping into that tiny window, blocking my way, and I couldn't bring myself to go back to my room the long way. I suppose I could have knocked on the woman's bedroom window for her to let me in, but I was afraid of the headlines in the paper the next day. So I just stood there, eight floors up, thinking for sure I was going to die.

Billy, meanwhile, continued to gape into the corner of the tiny window and give the Mel Allen play-by-play of what he was seeing.

"She's soaping up her pussy," he said. "Sorry you can't see this, Mick. Her legs are spread, and she's rubbing it with soap. Oh, I wish I was holding that bar of soap," he said.

"Now she's moving the soap up her body, and hold on, she's rubbing the soap on her tits. And they're beauties. With big round nipples. She's rubbing them, holding them. Oh, Lordy."

You have no idea how much I wanted to turn around and watch. I had a hard-on in my pants that you could have hung a flag on. But I was just too petrified to turn around and take my place at that window. I was so afraid I'd lose my balance and fall to my death, I thought of my mother back home in Oklahoma. It's the only thing that saved my life.

Finally, I heard the water go off. Billy was cooing, "Oh, Mick, I wish I was that towel. Look what she's doing with that towel." For the next three months all Billy could talk about was how exciting it was to watch the girl with the great bod soap herself up in the shower eight stories up. After that, watching girls soap up became like a religious ritual with Billy. We'd be on the road, and I'd be in my room listening to Hank Williams, and Billy would come in with a girl. The first thing he wanted her to do was take off all her clothes, get in the shower, and let us watch her soap herself. In fact, it got so crazy that watching her soap herself sometimes was all Billy wanted a girl to do. Before the blow job, of course.

That's what it took to be Billy's friend. You had to go along with him even if what Billy wanted to do looked like it was going to kill you. You did it anyway, 'cause if you didn't die, you got to watch a hell of a lot of girls get naked and rub soap all over their bodies. I'm only sorry camcorders didn't exist way back then. We'd-a made a fortune.

Billy liked to drink.

Len, Billy didn't trust anybody who didn't drink. Casey was the same way. "Milk drinker" was what Casey called guys who didn't drink, and he didn't say that kindly. We didn't have many of them. Many of the guys on our great Yankee teams ended up being full-blown alcoholics. Myself included. If we'd all stayed in New York after our playing days, and ever owned up to being drunks, we could have had some rousing all-Yankee AA meetings. But the truth was that we loved to drink. Drinking was not only great fun when you were killing time, but it was a great way to ease the pressure. At least, that's what I thought back then. Because there was a lot of pressure on us to succeed playing on the Yankees, not like it was with a lot of teams. I started with the Yankees in '51, and in the next fourteen years, we won twelve pennants and eight world championships. As far as New Yorkers were concerned, we were *expected* to win. To Dan Topping and Del Webb, the team owners, and to George Weiss, our general manager, and to Casey, second place was no better than finishing last.

Why did you start drinking?

I discovered a third reason to drink. I'll get to that in a minute. Once I joined the Yankees, I was ready and willing to learn how to drink. My old man was a drinker, and Billy was a drinker, and Casey wanted his players to be drinkers—and being a fast learner, it didn't take me long to find out how much more fun you could have when you were drinking. If you were feeling bad about something, you could down a few Seagram's VOs, and the guilt would go away. If you were feeling blue, same thing. Many times Billy told me the story of how his mom had left his dad before he was born, and how angry and upset that made him feel, and that drinking always made him feel better. From what I saw, what made Billy feel the best was when he could beat the snot out of some poor guy who made the mistake of trying to cozy up to him at the bar to talk baseball or to argue with him or to challenge him in some way.

One time we were sitting at a bar in Chicago, and this fan came up to Billy and told him he thought Nellie Fox was the best second baseman in baseball. The guy was big, probably weighed two hundred pounds. Now, if you knew Billy, the worst thing you could have said to him was that somebody was better than him. It's what the marshmallow salesman did when Billy was the manager. That guy told Billy he thought Earl Weaver was the best manager in baseball. The guy barely made it out the door when Billy coldcocked him.

In Billy's mind, he was the best and everyone else was lousy. Billy said to the Nellie Fox fan, "Have you ever been run over by a dump truck?" The guy, who had also been drinking, shook his head no, then raised his glass over his head, like he was going to deliver a toast. And when he did, Billy belted him in the face so hard, I thought Billy's fist would come out the other side of his head. The guy crumpled in a heap to the floor.

Billy said to him, "Now you have," and we walked out of the bar. Billy told me, "When that asshole raised his glass, I figured he was going to hit me." I said, "Billy, it looked to me that he was going to deliver a toast."

"Same difference," Billy said, and we began to laugh.

Mickey, that isn't funny. Billy was a danger to society.

Only when he was drinking and someone offended him.

Which happened what—every night? Do you know why Billy drank so much?

Billy started his serious drinking in high school. He could give you a hundred reasons why he drank. He would say he had to drink because he was having trouble with a girlfriend or one of his wives, or it was because he wasn't hitting or because George Weiss hated him or because he was skinny and had a big nose or because he didn't get the respect he deserved from the press and the Yankees fans. The truth of the matter was, Billy just flat-out loved to drink. Drinking was as much a part of Billy as breathing. He said it made him mellow, and it did, so long as no one came along to disturb his mood and make him violent—which happened about once a month. Then he became Rocky Fucking Marciano. And very often, the other guys who were with him would have to rush some poor slob out of the bar before Billy busted up his face.

Had Billy not been a baseball player, he would have had other excuses to drink: "My boss hates me." "It's too hot out." "It's too cold in." "The Russians are coming." "I'm worried about somebody dropping an A-bomb." "There's a hit out on me." "I'm worried about world peace."

I began drinking because Billy loved to drink, and because I enjoyed hanging out with him so much. Early in my career Billy came to visit me in Oklahoma after the season, and he showed me why drinking was so much fun. I remember one night, we were sitting at the bar of this Kansas joint where we liked to go, and these two girls were sitting at a nearby table. They were about our age—Billy was twenty-two, I was twenty—and they were very cute.

"Let's go sit with them," Billy said.

"Oh no, I couldn't do that," I said. "We don't even know them."

Billy signaled to the bartender and I instantly had three bourbons sitting in front of me. "You'll sit here and drink these down until you can," Billy said.

Billy went over and said something to the girls. I downed one drink, then another, then another, and about five minutes after that I looked over at the girls, and I couldn't believe how much sexier they looked and how much more I wanted them. And suddenly, I remembered that I was a professional baseball player and that they sure would be the lucky ones to spend some time with me.

I noticed that one of the girls was wearing white boots, that she had on a tight blouse and that her body was struggling to be seen through it.

"I think I'm ready to talk to those girls," I said to Billy.

" 'Bout time, podner," he said.

I had another drink, and one of those little ole gals started to look better and better until all I could think about was putting myself into her tight little body so deep I wouldn't be found 'til spring.

I went up to the girl and I said to her, "I want to fuck you so badly my whole body aches." Billy almost fell off his barstool, he was laughing so hard. I couldn't believe I had been so forward and crude. It wasn't like me at all.

"I thought you'd never ask," she said. I was so drunk it took me a couple of days to register what she said. *Nothing ventured, nothing fucked,* I thought to myself.

I was such a rube.

"Where can we go?" I asked Billy.

"We're in the bar of a hotel," he said. "Go to the front desk and rent two rooms for the night." That night I learned that as long as I was sufficiently liquored, no one was a stranger. I needed only to ask and anything was possible.

A girl is lying on the beach with no arms or legs. A guy walks up, and she starts to cry. He asks why she's crying. She says, "I've never been kissed before. So he kisses her. She starts crying again. He asks why she's crying. She says she's never been screwed. He picks her up and throws her in the water.

"There," he says, "now you're screwed."

Once I started drinking, a bigger, wider world opened up for me. When I drank, I was no longer a shy Okie. I became a handsome prince.

Drinking opened my eyes to unlimited puss possibilities. Once you start drinking, you can walk up to any woman, look her in the eyes, and ask if she wants to go to bed with you. Or there are all sorts of lines that seem to work just as well: "*How about you sit on my lap and we'll talk about the first thing that pops up.*"

Every once in a while, you'll run across a woman who is offended because you haven't said "please" or who turns you down because she just flew into town from France and is offended because you forgot to say "*merci.*" Or she'll say no because she doesn't drink, and to her you are acting like a jerk. So you tend to stay away from sober women, which is not hard to do if you're out prowling bars.

A few times I got slapped because after enough drinks you not only lose inhibitions but you lose the language of common courtesy. I got laid a hell of a lot of times, though. One other thing, if it's late at night and some girl comes on to you, even if she's coyote ugly, when you've drunk enough and you're packing a hard-on, puss is puss. It's the most important lesson Billy ever taught me. You don't turn down a woman even if she weighs three hundred pounds, 'cause Little Mick is talking and he's who you're listening to. Just make the fat ones lie facedown and get on their haunches. Honest Injun, paleface.

By the end of the '51 season Billy and I had become like brothers. Billy loved me because I had so much talent. He also loved me because he knew I looked up to him. And he loved me because I could drink like he could and could fuck like he could, and I'm here to tell you, that's saying a whole lot. And I never told him this, but I loved him, too. He was my best friend through most of my life, and when his last wife did everything she could to keep us apart, I really missed him.

For many years Billy and I were inseparable. George Weiss always said that Billy was a bad influence on me, but Weiss was an arrogant prick who should have appreciated how important Billy was to the Yankees and to me. In 1950 Billy roomed with Phil Rizzuto. That year Phil was the American League's Most Valuable Player. In 1953 he roomed with Yogi, and Yogi was AL MVP. In 1956 and 1957 he roomed with me when I was the Most Valuable Player. How bad an influence could he have been, for Christ sake?

Nineteen fifty-one was also the year I met Holly Brooke. She was a real-live model, a sophisticated dark-haired beauty. She was so gorgeous, I could barely speak. Like I said, I was such a rube. In fact, after dinner, my first words to her were, "I like you. Let's be buddies." I can't imagine what she was thinking. But we spent a lot of time together. She went with me to the stadium; to Central Park, where we played tackle football; and to bed, as often as possible. I was sharing an apartment with Hank Bauer and Joe Collins over the Stage Delicatessen on Seventh Avenue between Fifty-third and Fifty-fourth Streets in Manhattan. Holly and I had many breakfasts at the Stage. We went to nightclubs or we'd sit in her car by the piers on the West Side and watch the sun rise.

During one of these nights she revealed that she actually owned twenty-five percent of my contract. My personal agent, a real scumbag who also represented her, had made her a deal. She would loan him $1,500 cash for a few months, and if he didn't pay her back by January of 1952, he would give her a twenty-five percent stake in me! It was months before I even knew about it. Did I care? Not at all. I loved her, even asked her to marry me. She would smile, and I'd say, "No, I guess not. You'd never be happy in a little town like Commerce."

Why did you feel the need to go back to Oklahoma after the season was over? Why didn't you just stay in New York?

I was still an Oklahoma boy who pictured himself living in Oklahoma. I was spending half the year in New York City, but I wasn't ready emotionally to leave my roots. I continued to live at home with my parents.

What happened to the agent and the girl?

It took a couple years before the Yankees threatened the guy before I could get out of the contract. Though Holly went to Hollywood, it didn't stop me from seeing her for a half dozen more years. By 1957 Holly had not collected a dime on her $1,500 investment, and she was mad. So she sold her story to *Confidential* magazine. I'm right there on the cover of the March issue with Lana Turner, Ava Gardner, and Tony Curtis. For twenty-five cents, you could have read all about us.

Didn't you start the 1951 season in right field?

I did. Joe DiMaggio was in center, his final season. I had a great spring, hit over .400, hit home runs up and down the West Coast that people still talk about to this day. George Weiss kept insisting that at age twenty I was still too young, but Casey insisted I stay on the team because he didn't want some half-assed minor league manager ruining me. Casey bragged I was going to be his Mel Ott, one of those guys I'm glad my dad didn't name me after.

But when we got to New York to start the season, turns out Weiss was right. I wasn't ready. The opening-day crowd was fifty thousand people. There weren't that many people in the entire state of Oklahoma. When I walked out onto that field, I was scared to death.

Once the season began the pitchers saw I had trouble hitting the fast-ball up, and before I knew it, I was getting nothing but high pitches out of the strike zone, which I told myself I better stop swinging at but couldn't because I was so overanxious. I was so overmatched I felt like I was living a nightmare. I felt so sorry for myself that I even fantasized about killing myself. I had never been to the top of the Empire State Building, but I kept imagining taking the elevator to the top, climbing the fence, and jumping off. I pictured the newspapers the next day, with my body sprawled out on the hood of a car below, and when I thought of all those fans who were booing me, I would think, *How do you feel, now?* Like this was some kind of revenge I would be taking out on them. And Casey made it worse when he started calling me names in the papers, said I was a baby, said I didn't belong in the big leagues.

The day before he sent me down, I struck out three times in the first game of a doubleheader and twice more in the second, and the next time up Casey said to Cliff Mapes, one of our veteran outfielders, "Get in there and hit for him. We need someone who can hit the ball." That day I really hated that old, bandy-legged motherfucker. I wanted to do to him what he said he always had wanted to do to John McGraw—kill him.

In mid-July, Casey sent me down to the minor leagues, back to Kansas City, Triple A. He told me that as soon as I regained my confidence, he'd bring me back to New York, but I didn't believe him. I was sure this was his way of getting rid of me forever. I felt like a total failure. I figured my next stop would be back in my old spot in the mines.

Shit, I was twenty. I wasn't ready. But I was too young to know that was the reason I wasn't ready. Instead, I just figured I wasn't good enough.

How did you handle getting sent down to Kansas City?

When I arrived in Kansas City, I was unbearably lonely, even though Holly would hop a plane and meet me in Columbus for a few days or in Kansas City. But I could only spend a precious few days with her. In desperation I started writing long letters to Merlyn back home to tell her I wished we could be together. I liked her well enough. I liked being with her. I did. She was the face from home I missed the most, and I was feeling so alone.

After striking out time after time in Kansas City, I figured it would be good to have someone at my funeral, that having her there was as good as anyone, so when she would write, I kept writing back. I really was convinced I couldn't play anymore, that I might as well quit baseball, go home, get married to her, and go work in the mines with my dad and uncle.

That's when my dad came to see me in Kansas City.

I'd like to see that. Let's go there.

Ahh, Lenny, I'd rather not have to relive this. It was bad enough the first time.

Fine, Mickey. Then I'm outta here. Hey, would you do me a favor and unplug the recorder for me?

Oh, all right. Don't get your tit in the wringer. We'll go there.

•　•　•

They turned around in their seats and, once again, Toots Shor's had faded into the darkness. Now they see Mickey's twenty-year-old alter ego sitting forlornly in a small, shabby motel room. His eyes are rimmed with red. There's a knock on the door, and Elvin Mantle, a lean, hard man known as Mutt, wearing blue jeans and a work shirt, enters the room. The jeans seem to be falling off his narrow hips, and the shirt seems two sizes too large.

"Hi, Mickey." Mutt looks around the small room, shakes his head, and closes the door behind him. "So what's this shit I hear 'bout you wantin' to quit? Is that what I did—raise a quitter?"

"I'm not good enough, Dad," Mickey says. "I don't have what it takes."

Mutt stares into his son's eyes. "I tell you what, boy, I'd never throw away no opportunity like this if I had the chance. Would've killed anyone who came in my way. But all right. You ain't me. And if that's the way you feel, I might as well pack your bags for you. You can come on home and work in the mines like me. You coward." Mutt practically spits out the last word.

There was an awkward pause, as if Mutt is debating his next move.

"Time you stop acting like a little girl," he says. Mutt goes to the dresser, pulls out some of his clothing, and begins stuffing it into a cardboard suitcase.

"Time for my sissy son to come home, I guess," he says. He doesn't turn his head to look at Mickey.

Mickey begins to cry.

Mutt throws clothes into the suitcase hard. The clothes make a loud noise as they hit the lid and fall into the bottom. Mutt practically winds up and throws a shirt like a fastball, with extra effort, pushing all of Mickey's emotional buttons.

Lenny, I'm not . . . I can't watch this.

•   •   •

Mickey turns around in his seat, his head down. Lenny is transfixed by the scene and leans forward.

"Please, Pop, give me another chance. I want to stay here and play."

"Sorry, son, too late for that now. They don't allow crybabies in the big leagues."

Mickey fights to stop the flow of tears. He snuffles, then goes into the bathroom to blow his nose. He returns, trying to breathe deeply, his broad shoulders heaving. "I know I can make it, Pop. I don't want to go home. Please. I beg you."

Mutt stops flinging Mickey's clothes into the suitcase. He stares at Mickey critically, angrily. Finally, he sits down on the edge of the bed.

"Okay, boy," says Mutt, "but this is your last chance. One more bitch or moan, and you start in the mines the next morning."

The hotel room faded, and the noisy hustle of Toots Shor's returned.

He was a hard man.

He shamed me into continuing. How could that smug bastard say those things to me? When I thought about it sober, I loved him for it, for what he did, but also have never forgiven him for how he did it. Because baseball made my life. In a big way, it may have also ruined my life. That's the way baseball is: you can love the game, but it's very rare when baseball loves you back. That's the occupational hazard of making a living at the thing you love—you soon become a slave to it, and your source of joy can turn to hatred.

I felt the same way about writing. But let's get back to you. How'd you do after this scene with your father?

Since I was figuring I would be cut soon anyway, that how well I played didn't make a damn bit of difference, for the rest of my stay in Kansas City I relaxed at the plate, and when I did that I laid off the high pitches, and I hit everything those fuckers threw my way. By August I was back with the Yankees, and, wouldn't you know, that October I was actually playing in the World Series.

It was against the New York Giants, who had won the pennant on Bobby Thomson's home run against Ralph Branca. The "Shot Heard 'Round The World."

Dad came to see us play the Giants. He drove all the way from Oklahoma to New York City in his Ford pickup with two of his drinking buddies. Mom wanted to go, but he figured he'd have a hell of a lot more fun without her, and he ordered her to stay home to keep an eye on my younger brothers.

You learned how to treat women from your dad.

Sad to say. Once Dad and his pals arrived in New York, they hit the bars, and this one evening as they stood near the rail of the bar, one of Dad's friends started to feel sick. It was crowded, and he couldn't move, and so he did the only thing he could think of. He grabbed a fedora off a guy standing nearby and puked his guts into it. After that, you can believe that everyone moved out of their way.

A man goes to a local bar where he has drinks every night. One night he comes in and orders a club soda. The bartender asks him why. The man replies, "I don't drink anymore. Last night I blew chunks."

"So what?" said the bartender. "Everyone gets sick after drinking once in a while."

"You don't understand," said the man. "Chunks is my dog."

I didn't do shit in the first game against the Giants, and we lost. Casey had me leading off, and I was hoping someone else would play in my place in that second game, but no, he had my name on the lineup card again playing in right field. In the third inning I beat out a bunt for a single, then Scooter singled, and Gil McDougald hit a looper as I scored my first run in a World Series. I was proud because my father was in the stands watching. But I still had brown spots in my pants.

In the sixth inning Willie Mays hit a high pop between me in right and Joe in center. Casey had whispered to me to take anything I could because Joe's legs weren't any good anymore, and so I drifted over toward Joe, but when I heard him yell, "I got it," I stopped, my spikes caught, and when I tried to move, I heard a "pop" from my knee that could be heard all over the ballpark. The next thing I knew I was lying on the ground feeling as though someone had shot me. I later learned I had stepped on the rubber covering of a drainpipe. It was nobody's fault, just bad luck. But I would need surgery.

The next day Dad and I drove to the hospital in a cab. I didn't like hospitals then any more than I did later on. Dad got out of the cab first. I then hobbled out, holding my crutches in my left hand, and with my right arm I put all my weight across his left shoulder, and I couldn't believe it when Dad crumpled in a heap on the sidewalk as I fell on top of him. Dad had looked real skinny, but I had no idea how weak he had become. They put us next to each other in the same room in the hospital.

I had a knee operation, and afterward a doctor came in. He looked grim.

"Was the operation a success?" I asked. He nodded.

"Your father has cancer," he said.

"Is there a chance?" I asked.

"I'm sorry," he said.

Dad and I went home to Oklahoma. I took every penny of my World Series money and bought Dad and Mom a new house with it. Dad, who knew he was dying, wanted only one thing from me. When I got home, Merlyn had asked if I would marry her. I put her off because of Holly, who I was really beginning to like, but when I told my dad about her, he had said to me, "You marry your own kind. You marry that little ole gal back home. She's a good girl. I want you to promise me you'll marry her."

"But Dad . . ." I said.

How could I refuse my dad's last request? He was dying. He reminded me that I owed him so much. I couldn't say no to him, though every fiber in my body screamed for me to wait.

Why in the world did he want you to get married so badly?

He was afraid of the big city, afraid I was being attracted to city life, including the city women, and he was afraid his boy would leave Oklahoma and never come back.

So you did what he asked you?

So I did what I was expected to do: I got married. The ceremony took place on a Saturday around six at Merlyn's parents' home. She came out of the bedroom, and I came out of the bathroom. We spent our wedding night in a Hot Springs, Arkansas, hotel, where we were supposed to have been given a room for three days free of charge by Commerce's Chamber of Commerce, except that when I checked in, the hotel manager said he had never heard of me, and I could only afford to stay one night.

Speaking about weddings, did you hear the one about the guy getting ready to celebrate his twenty-fifth wedding anniversary? His wife says, "Why don't we go back to where we celebrated our honeymoon." He said, "Great," so they went to Hawaii, had a nice dinner, went back to their room, and she appeared in the doorway wearing a negligee.

She said, "Honey, this is the negligee that I was wearing twenty-five years ago. What were you thinking then?"

He said, "I was going to suck your tits dry and fuck your brains out."

And she said, "Honey, what are you thinking now?"

He thought a minute and said, "What a good fucking job I did."

Our honeymoon lasted one day. We drove home the next day. That afternoon I was out on the football field playing with the boys.

In a way that was the start and the end of our marriage. All these many years I was never faithful, had no interest in staying home, left her alone for months at a time, and despite all the women and the drinking and the humiliations, Merlyn never would leave me. I admire her tremendously. She was always faithful, and she helped raise our four boys, and she rarely complained about all the years I was away, all the time I spent with Billy or on the road escaping my demons. She has endured humiliations big and small, and I do regret treating her so shabbily. She didn't deserve it. I wish I could have helped myself. I wish I'd been strong enough to get professional help.

She always said she would be my wife on the day I die, and she was. Even after we no longer lived together, she remained loyal to me.

For her not to have left me after all I'd put her through says something about her, though I'm not sure what: either she deserves a medal or a padded room in a loony bin. 'Cause I got to tell you, I wasn't a worthy husband or father. Nor did I ever pretend to be. Like Billy, I believed I was never cut out for family life, which I thought of as boring and dull as going to the same restaurant and eating the same dish every meal, every day.

So you were never a good husband?

Only when it suited my purposes. Which wasn't very often. I made the big mistake of bringing Merlyn with me to St. Petersburg, Florida, for spring training in '52. Billy, meanwhile, had married his high school sweetheart, a girl named Lois, and we took adjoining rooms at the Soreno Hotel. One of the advantages of this arrangement was that it gave both of us the opportunity to sneak into the other's room at night to watch either of us make love to our wives. That was the challenge. We'd leave our doors unlocked on purpose so we could get into each other's rooms.

In fact, one time after spending a spring training afternoon at a bar, Billy thought it might be fun to go back to the Soreno, act like we got our rooms mixed up, and make love to each other's wives. Hey, Lois was a *real* good-looking girl. When she wore short shorts, she oozed sexiness, and I'd have given anything to get a poke at her. The thought of it really got me going. But Lois was not a person to pull pranks on, and at the last minute

Billy called it off. As much as he wanted a roll in the sack with Merlyn, he was afraid of what Lois would do after she discovered what we had done. Lois was drop-dead gorgeous, but serious as a heart attack. On some level, Billy knew that she would not only disapprove but might react real badly.

Like divorce him, which she did anyway. But I can tell you, I was sorely disappointed.

That spring Billy and I weren't surefire starters for the Yankees, but when we came to camp in St. Pete, we acted like we owned the town. Mastry's Bar was on Central Avenue not far from Miller Huggins Field, where we trained, and every afternoon Billy and me and some of the other guys would be in Mastry's drinking, while my wife and Billy's wife were left back at the hotel to lie by the pool or otherwise fend for themselves.

We'd have had more time for them, but from the first day when we sat down at that bar, distractions in female forms kept taking up much of our spare time.

During practice, high school girls, divorcees, secretaries—even married women looking for some excitement—would come up to us and bat their eyelashes or wiggle their shoulders and want to know what we were doing "later." Or if we were sitting at the bar at Mastry's, they'd ask us if we'd like to buy them a drink before driving them back to their place. A gal would look at me and smile that "Take me" smile, and my mind would be whirling a hundred miles an hour, and all I could hear was the stream of questions in my head that demanded to be answered: What color is her puss? How firm are her breasts? Is she a screamer or a moaner or a shouter or will she just lie there? Does she like to have her puss eaten? Would she like to put my dick down her throat? These were life's great questions, and I'll defy any man given the opportunity to walk away from finding out the answers if given the chance.

Weren't you taking a real risk dating married women?

Half the time I'd be wondering: Will this little ole gal's husband come home and fill me full of buckshot? Will I be the next Eddie Waitkus? But when you're twenty, every day means a new adventure, and add to that the fact we were in Florida, which is warm and steamy; well, I was in heaven all right. The one big downer of the whole experience was that Merlyn kept getting pissed when I didn't come home, and a couple times she burst out crying when she'd find stains on my pants, or lipstick on the collar of a shirt. Some years later Connie Francis sang a song, "Lipstick on Your Collar," and every time we were in the car together and they played that song on the radio, I'd change the station. If she found a stain, I'd have to make up a story that I had spilled coffee or beer or bourbon. One day I was feeling bad about it.

"She knows I fool around," I said to Billy. "I know she knows."

Billy didn't give a shit. He said, "Fuck her. If she fucking doesn't like it, she can go back to that fucking Dust Bowl where she came from. What's so special about her?" He felt that Merlyn's complaining was turning Lois against him, that she was more trouble than she was worth.

But Billy felt that way about all women. Loyalty to one woman was never part of Billy's vocabulary. For Billy, it was all about numbers. One time he started talking about this guy, Don Juan, who had such a reputation as a ladies' man that there was even a book written about him. Billy said to me, "Fuck Don Juan. The guy's an amateur compared to me." And that may have been the truth. Billy loved ground ball practice a whole lot, but he loved puss practice more.

Billy was such a renegade, so open about what he was doing that one day he learned he had gotten one of the St. Pete High School girls he was seeing pregnant. He walked around Mastry's passing out cigars. "I knocked her up," he told everyone. "She's having my kid."

"Is the girl going to have the baby?" I asked him.

"I don't give a shit what she does," he said. "She can do whatever the fuck she wants. It's not my problem. I'm married." And from what I was told, the girl went ahead and had the baby. I've often wondered how many of Billy's kids there are running around America. I guess I could wonder that about me as well. We never used protection.

When the regular season started in '52, things could not have gone better. DiMaggio had retired, and Casey wanted me in centerfield. The Yankees had traded away another Oakland phenom, Jackie Jensen, so I could play there. Then Case discovered I hadn't been doing my exercises to strengthen my bum leg during the winter, and I was still several weeks away from being able to play. In exchange for Jensen, Casey got Irv Noren, a veteran from Washington, a good guy and a pretty good player who got to play until my knee finally healed. But George Weiss and Casey were really pissed at me for being so lazy. It wouldn't be the last time.

In May of '52 Dad died. During the winter I had driven him on icy roads from Oklahoma to the Mayo Clinic in Minnesota. They opened him up, took a peek inside, and said there was no hope. I felt sad for my father, but at the same time he had made me tough. I wanted to cry, but if I had cried in front of him, he would have beaten me, even on his deathbed. You should be ashamed to cry, he would tell me.

When he died he was just thirty-nine years old. He had lived a hard life, was bitter and angry during most of the time I had known him, but when I heard he had died, a little bit of me died, too.

I beat myself up inside for being so callous, for never once telling him I loved him, even though while he was alive a lot of the time I felt like I hated him. I played in a ball game that night, and then, all by myself—I wouldn't take Merlyn—I flew to Dad's funeral and stood along with most of his miner friends, men like him who ended up dying too bitter and too young. Thirty-nine is too young to die. My uncle also died at age thirty-nine. You can't work in a mine breathing in that poison and live to a ripe old age.

As I told you at the beginning of this story, I figured dying young was in the family genes. I was born in '31. I figured I had until 1970 to live it up before I died.

But you lived until 1995.

Who knew? At Dad's funeral, I swore to myself that I would live life to the fullest, that I wouldn't get cheated like he had been, that I wouldn't end up a sad and bitter man, like he did. Of course, when I died at age sixty-three, I also died a sad and bitter man. Like father, like son. I look back and wonder what happened. That's part of why I'm talking to you now. I'm trying to figure out where I went wrong. As I look back on my life, I wonder to myself, *How could it have been any different? How could it have been better?*

What was it like to be so famous at such a young age?

When I arrived in St. Petersburg for spring training in '52, I discovered for the first time what it meant to be a professional baseball player. The press watched every move I made, and so many people asked me for autographs I hardly had a moment to myself. I could be standing at a urinal in the men's room of a restaurant, and before I could finish peeing, three guys would be in line, paper ready, pens in hand, wanting my autograph.

My picture was on the covers of a bunch of the big magazines, and I was feeling so overwhelmed by all the publicity that one time I even adopted an alias when I went out on a date. The name I chose was Melvin Oppenheimer. I was reading the St. Petersburg paper, the *Independent*, and I came across the name in a news story. Seems that Melvin Oppenheimer had come to St. Petersburg from somewhere in Ohio and opened a watch repair shop, and the paper did this little story on him. Andy Carey, who was a kid from California trying out for the Yankees, was dating this cute little number named Connie, and Connie had a girlfriend named Marguerite, and we went to the movies, and I told Marguerite my name was Melvin Oppenheimer, and she never did recognize me. When she asked me what I did for a living, I told her I was a miner, which wasn't a total lie, and I told her I liked to watch baseball games, which was true.

We didn't do a whole lot that night. Andy Carey wasn't anything like Billy. He was a choirboy, and after the movies we went to the Webb City malt shop and had sodas. Since I didn't have anything to drink, I reverted to being the shy country boy I always was, and when I brought Marguerite home, she must have thought I was the hickest boy she had ever dated. I often wonder whether she ever did find out who I really was or whether she still thinks she had a date with Melvin Oppenheimer, the miner from Oklahoma.

You and Billy didn't start playing regularly until the middle of the 1952 season.

During spring training Billy broke an ankle sliding while he was filming a pasta commercial. Joe DiMaggio was the star of the commercial, and he needed a teammate to make a slide into the base. Joe knew that Billy needed the money, so he was actually doing Billy a favor. Billy must have slid into that base fifteen times that day, and nothing had happened. The sun was going down, and the director asked for "one more take." This time Billy waited too long to slide, hit the bag hard, and busted his ankle. When Billy told Casey what happened, Casey didn't believe him. Billy had to go get Joe to back up his story.

I wasn't starting because after my winter operation, I had been more interested in drinking, chasing puss, and fooling around than working out and getting back into shape. For a few months it didn't look like either of us would get to play, but we were Casey's Boys, the light of the Old Man's life, and as soon as we healed, he put us in there and we started playing regularly. After that, nobody could get us out of there.

With Billy and me contributing, we held first place through the end of the summer.

Casey was the one who made me a centerfielder. The first time he saw me play, he knew I was a lousy shortstop. He told me he was putting me in the outfield where I couldn't kill nobody, and it was like I had played there all my life. I felt comfortable and I started to hit a lot of home runs.

I can remember in Cleveland one time Joe Collins, who was our first baseman, a good, good guy who could really drink, hit a home run. The ball must have gone 475 feet. I was on deck, and when he crossed the plate, he smiled at me and said, "Kid, go chase that."

On the next pitch I hit one even deeper into the bleachers. Joe walked over to the drinking fountain, and while he sipped the water, I said, "What did you say, Joe?"

"Go shit in your hat," he said. It was only my second full season in the majors, and I almost won the MVP award.

Billy's role, in addition to playing second base, was to be Casey's coach on the field. Casey hated mental mistakes, like throwing to the wrong base or missing the cutoff man. If you did that, he would get all over you, and when he was finished, Billy then would ream your ass out. Billy kept everyone on their toes. It was also his job to intimidate the other team. He had done that for Casey in the minors at Oakland, and they had won a pennant, and so Casey encouraged him to keep doing it in the big leagues. Casey loved it when Billy would challenge a rival player or call the other manager "a fucking bush league moron," and Casey especially ate it up when Billy would beat the shit out of someone. George Weiss would be mortified, but to Casey, Billy was an extremely important part of the Yankees' arsenal. Casey would wink and say to no one in particular about Billy, "That little bush leaguer, all he knows how to do is win."

The players all understood what a genius Casey really was. He platooned Bauer and Gene Woodling, and both hit over .300. Both of them wanted to play every day, and both of them hated the way Casey used them. But if you look at their numbers, you understand how smart Casey was in the way he played them.

It took years for the writers to figure him out. The writers were too fucking dumb to know.

Come on, Mick. We knew he was a great manager.

Most of those slobs either disliked Casey or they were his drinking buddies, and they'd write about his clowning and his funny language, but it took years for them to write about what a great manager he was. Casey believed if you could intimidate a team badly enough, you could win a game before it even started. So Billy's job was to swagger and brag and slide into base runners and spike them. He'd tag players on their heads. He'd even deliberately trip runners going around the bases. These same writers would talk about what a great player Ty Cobb had been, but they had a Ty Cobb in their own dugout and didn't even know it. I can't imagine that Cobb could have been any tougher than Billy, who was a sucker puncher with a right hand as powerful as Sugar Ray Robinson's. And Billy could go nuts, so if you were even half sane, you didn't want to mess with him.

Only the truly crazy guys were ever stupid enough to get into it with him. Billy once beat Red Sox centerfielder Jimmy Piersall to a pulp, and it was only a few months later that Piersall ended up in a loony bin. Billy beat up a catcher named Clint Courtney two separate times. Clint was a rockhead who was too stupid not to incite Billy. Clint would spike a player or tag him too hard, and Billy would pound him. They had gotten into it back in the minors, and Billy told me he relished pounding Clint's face every chance he got. "Besides," Billy said, "the guy can't fight a lick."

One time Billy and I were sitting with Ty Cobb himself at a banquet. Cobb was an old man by then. Billy knew he had this reputation for being a dirty player, for spiking guys. Billy turned to Cobb and told him, "The first time you spiked me, when I got through with you, your teeth would be down your throat." It was all we could do to keep the two apart. Boy, I'd have liked to have seen that one.

But like I say, you writers hated Billy cause Billy treated you like shit, and also because you were afraid of him. As you were of Casey at times. I can remember Billy was out of the lineup late in the season with a sprained ankle, and this sportswriter said to Casey, "Why isn't Billy in the lineup?" Casey growled to him, " 'Cause I don't want to win, you asshole. I only use him if I want to win."

No one knew it at the time but me, but during the summer of '52, Billy's wife Lois became pregnant, and right after that, she walked out on him, returning to her home in California. Lois decided that she hated being a ballplayer's wife, hated to have to sit at home while we were on the road, hated not knowing what Billy was up to while they were apart. More probably, she hated the knowing. 'Cause most of the time when we were playing at home, after the game Billy and I'd go out by ourselves and come home too exhausted and drunk to do anything but fall asleep. Lois noticed that when Billy was around me, we had fun, but when he was around her, he moped. She was no dummy. And she was not the type of person to let herself be humiliated. The writing was on the wall, and Lois could read. Lois told Billy she was going back to Berkeley to have the baby there.

Billy said, "Fine. If that's what you want. Go." He never suspected that she was leaving for good.

At that same time, Merlyn also became pregnant. She said she also wanted to go home, which was fine with me 'cause I knew she'd be happier at home with her parents in Oklahoma than sitting by herself in a hot, clammy Bronx apartment. It also made it easier on me. I didn't have to keep making up new excuses why I was coming home so late. But Merlyn was far more tolerant than Lois. She took my mistreatment and kept quiet. Later she said she was sure that one day I would change, but unfortunately for her, that never did happen.

Meanwhile, in the '52 World Series, Billy and I did what we could to help the Yankees beat the Dodgers—again. I homered in the final game, and I made a key play in the field when I threw out Jackie Robinson—after I faked throwing to first, he took off, and I threw him out at second. Casey had told me that Jackie liked to do that, and I was ready for him. Billy saved the game with one of the most famous catches ever made in any Series, when he ran all the way in from second base to catch a high pop-up Robinson hit between home plate and the pitcher's mound. No one else moved for it, not Joe Collins or Yogi behind the plate or the pitcher, cause the sun was in their eyes. If Billy hadn't caught it, we'd-a lost the game for sure, and probably the Series. That was Billy. As Casey often said about him, "That son of a bitch. He can't hit. He can't run. He can't field. All he knows how to do is win."

After the series I went back to Oklahoma only to get a call from Billy, saying Lois had given birth, but that she wanted a divorce. In his own way Billy really did love Lois, and Billy pleaded with her not to leave him.

Once Lois no longer wanted him, Billy wanted her worse than life itself. Billy had pride, and he couldn't stand the idea that Lois was walking out on him. Billy even got down on his knees and begged, but Lois was a girl with principles, one of the few I ever knew, and she refused to change her mind. If you want to know the truth, I think that deep down she didn't like the fact that Billy loved me more than he loved her. Can't say I blame her, either.

Just before spring training in '53, Billy pleaded with me to come to northern California to help him win Lois back. I moved in with Billy, his two sisters, and his mom and stepdad in their little house in Berkeley for a week while I tried to talk Lois into not divorcing Billy. Of course, asking me to talk for him was a joke. Lois hated my guts, and Billy was the one with the gift of gab. I was so shy I could barely get the words out. Still, I went to see Lois and the baby, Kelly Ann. When Lois opened the door, she was wearing a tight-fitting blouse and shorts. What a body she had! I had forgotten how sexy she was. My first thoughts, shameful as they might have been, were that I was sorry we didn't get to swap wives that one night in St. Petersburg.

"Why are you here, Mickey?" she asked me. She stood in the doorway, not even letting me in.

"Billy wants you back," I said. "He says he needs you."

Lois's face hardened. She told me, "I have no intention of getting back with Billy, ever. He doesn't know what it means to be faithful. He's no good. And the truth is, Mickey, you're no good either. You two are like two sixteen year olds. You can't keep it in your pants, and you don't care about who you hurt. I pity your wife. I tried to tell her what was going on, but she wouldn't hear of it. I asked her whether she intended to sit at home for the rest of her life waiting for a husband who was never there. All she did was shrug. I feel for her, 'cause she's gonna end up lonely and sad. Me, I want a life. And now that I have a baby, I don't need to take care of two babies. Tell Billy to leave me alone. I don't want to see him ever again, and tell the rest of the vultures in that perverted family of his to stay the hell away from me, especially his nut case of a mother. I don't want to have anything to do with any of them, either."

And then Lois slammed the door in my face.

God, what a great body she had. I never saw it again.

When I got back to Billy's, he asked me what Lois said. I didn't have the heart to tell him. I said, "Lois says she needs some time." I didn't tell him the time she needed was about a hundred years.

When he badgered me for details, I hemmed and hawed and fudged and lied. I never did have much guts.

It was during this trip that I met the woman who Lois had referred to as "that nut case," Billy's mom. Her name was Jennie Downey. She looked and acted like Ma Barker. She was about five foot one, weighed maybe a hundred pounds, but she was the toughest woman I ever met.

She and Billy fought every minute with a ferocity I had never seen before between mother and son. One time during dinner, Billy told me, she hit him with a frying pan. They cussed back and forth at each other— I never heard such language. But the funny thing about his Ma, if anyone dared say anything bad about Billy, she wanted to fight.

Billy told me one time that when he was a boy, the police from the neighboring town arrested him for slugging a cop. They called his Ma and told her to come and get him. She told them, "You took him. You bring him back or you're going to answer to me." They were afraid of her, wouldn't come in the house. They dropped Billy off a block away. His Ma always told him, "Never take shit from nobody." She never did. And neither did he.

During the week I was there, Billy and I got in the car and sneaked over to see his father, Alfred Martin, who lived a couple of towns over. Billy didn't want his mom to know, because she hated Alfred so much. When she was pregnant with Billy, she caught him in bed in a rooming house with a high school girl. She took all his clothes, threw them out into the front yard and stomped them into the mud. Al never came back.

Jennie, who had a way with words, told me, "When the bastard dies, I'm going to go to his grave, pull down my panties, and piss on him." She wasn't joking. I had no doubt she would.

Billy's dad turned out to be a sweet, sad guy who delivered booze to bars for a liquor company. We met him in a bar, and the three of us sat there for several hours drinking, not saying very much. And then we left. Billy said to me, "I was going to seek Dad's advice what to do about Lois, but when I thought about it, I decided he probably was not the right person to ask." We laughed. Billy said sadly, "Like father, like son, I guess."

So what's a seventy-year-old snatch smell like? Depends.

During my stay with Billy, we went to San Francisco to visit Joe D in the famous DiMaggio family restaurant at the wharf in San Francisco. When Joe walked in, he was with the most incredible-looking woman I had ever seen.

Let's see, 1953 . . . was Joe with Marilyn Monroe by then?

Hold your horses. I'm telling the story. I was twenty-one. She was twenty-five.

I don't believe in having sex with women against their will, but in this case I seriously considered it because I would have argued that she was an open invitation for sex, and no jury in their right mind would have sided against me. She had an absolutely angelic face, with pouty lips and silky blond hair, and she had a frilly little top that barely covered the most enticing breasts I had ever seen. She had a waist you could put one hand around and great legs. And when she talked, she sounded breathy, like a little girl, which drove me wild. I had never encountered a woman like this.

I asked Billy about her, and I was surprised to find out Joe's girl was a real honest-to-goodness movie actress. And she'd been in some big films—*The Asphalt Jungle*, *All About Eve*. He said her name was Marilyn, and Billy was real surprised I had never heard of her. Billy told me Joe and her had been going together for a few months. "I keep asking Joe for sloppy seconds," said Billy. He paused. "Then I start running as fast as I can."

"I guess I've been watching too many western movies," I said.

During lunch I whispered to Billy, "What would you give to fuck her?"

Billy whispered, "I'd be happy just to watch her soap herself in the shower." He wasn't kidding. I was happy just to sit opposite her fully clothed during lunch.

After we ate, Joe excused himself to go in the back to talk to his older brother, Tom, a short, squat Italian guy, who ran the restaurant. Billy got up, and I went over to him to ask him more about this girl. Billy said that Joe was head-over-heels gaga about her. He said that Marilyn had been the first girl Joe ever called a second time after fucking her on the first date. Billy said, "He also proposed to her after that first date."

"I guess Joe's not so crazy after all," I replied.

Billy walked off, and when I sat back down, Marilyn sat opposite me at the table. We were alone. I had had a couple of drinks, but not enough to loosen my lips sufficiently, and after sitting across from her without saying anything for what seemed like an eternity, Marilyn smiled and said,

"You have big muscles. I like to fuck men with bulging muscles." I stared into that angelic face not believing the smutty words coming out of that pouty mouth. My first thought was, *Are you shitting me?* And then I thought to myself, *You may just be the most beautiful woman in the world.* I mumbled something dopey, "I'd be happy to show them to you," and I gave her my best country-boy grin. Then I ordered a couple more doubles.

"How old are you?" she asked. I should have lied and told her I was older, but she had me hypnotized. I told her the truth. "I'm twenty-two," I said. She said she was twenty-five. "Am I too old for you?" she asked, adding, "I *love* younger men."

She took out a fountain pen from her handbag, and she purposefully walked around to where I was sitting. To my shock she unbuttoned my right sleeve, rolled it up a few inches, held my right forearm with delicate hands that had fingernails painted blood red, and wrote her telephone number on my arm in dark blue ink in big, perfectly formed numbers two inches high. She had a beautiful, flowery handwriting. She said in a whisper, "If you want, you can call me today at five, sharp." As she straightened up she gently brushed her left breast against my right cheek, and giggled.

Did she do that on purpose? I wondered. I couldn't think about anything but the electric charge of her body the rest of the day.

She left in mid-afternoon. I wondered whether I could go through with it. I worried what would happen if Joe found out that Marilyn had given me her telephone number. By now I knew how crazy the goomba sonofabitch was when it came to women. If Joe had recognized her handwriting on my arm, he'd have taken a baseball bat and bashed her brains out and then stood there and cried like a baby. Then he would have taken the bat to me. Billy told me a couple of times Joe came home and slapped the shit out of her after she had batted her eyes at some guy on the street. Billy said Marilyn was a born cock-tease, and that it made Joe crazy.

One time Joe suspected Marilyn of fooling around with some guy, and

Joe found out from a private detective he hired where she was going. Only the guy gave Joe the address of the house next door, and it was bedlam when Joe and Frank Sinatra and several of Frank's goons broke down the wrong door. It turned out Marilyn was practicing for a part or something innocent like that. But I hate to think what would have happened to that actor if they hadn't busted down the wrong door.

So Marilyn had to know she was asking for trouble by writing her phone number on my arm. But Marilyn was a little crazy herself. A bunch of years later she went to Madison Square Garden and sang "Happy Birthday" to President Kennedy in front of twenty thousand people. She did this even though she was having an affair with him. When the rumors started to spread, Kennedy broke it off, and she had an affair with his brother Bobby.

The story I heard was that Sam Giancana killed her as a message to the Kennedys to stop investigating him. I don't know if that's true or not. But her death was ruled a suicide—somebody was covering up something—so the Kennedys never got the message. Giancana then had John killed. Who knows—maybe he was behind Bobby getting killed five years later? Billy once met Giancana. He told me, "There's a guy you don't say no to."

The point of all this is that if Marilyn could seduce John Kennedy in front of twenty thousand people in Madison Square Garden, who was I to resist her charms? After all, she was an up-and-coming movie actress, on her way to stardom, who didn't take no for an answer. And she may just have been the most beautiful woman in the world. If Marilyn had her eye on something—or someone—who could refuse her? I kept the sleeves rolled down and made sure the buttons remained secure.

As I sat listening to Joe and Billy talk about the good old days when Billy wore zoot suits and beat up sailors and when Joe played baseball with the San Francisco Seals, the seven digits of her phone number remained hidden, etched on my arm under the shirtsleeve. All afternoon I worried that the ink had run and become illegible, a disaster which would have been worse than the sinking of the *Titanic*. A short time before five, I excused myself and went to find a phone. I pulled up my sleeve. The beautifully scripted numbers were clear and sharp.

As I looked at the numbers on my arm, the question I asked myself was *Should I or shouldn't I?*

Obviously, I called. Fuck Joe DiMaggio. It's not like they were married. And what had he ever done for me? He had retired and no longer was a teammate. And when he was a teammate, he had been an arrogant prick. And to be honest, I wouldn't have cared if he had been the nicest guy in the world or if she had been married to Al Capone or Joe Stalin. There was no way, I decided, I wasn't going to make that phone call.

I did get to fuck Marilyn. Or perhaps she got to fuck me. Did she like it? It was hard to tell. Working in the mines gave me muscles, and my muscles had muscles. Marilyn liked muscles. She couldn't help herself. She also liked exerting her considerable feminine powers over one of those muscles in particular. I saw from lunch that she liked rubbing her body against guys just to see the surprised looks on their faces. Hey, if you had the power to make every guy in the world walk around with a hard-on, wouldn't you do it just because you could?

She had told me to phone right at five, and that's what I did. For two hours I had stared at my watch until the hour hand was on five and the second hand started moving toward the twelve, and the moment it hit five on the dot, I dialed the final digit of her phone number.

Marilyn picked up on the first ring. She told me I could pay her a visit from six to seven, and promptly at seven I would have to go. She gave me the address. I told Billy I was on a secret mission and had to leave. Billy was no dummy. He knew exactly what I was up to. He had the same reaction I did: He said, "What if Joe finds out?" Then Billy paused. "Ahhh, fuck him." We both laughed.

I asked Billy if he wanted me to open the curtains a crack so he could watch, but Billy had already lined up a quickie with the wife of a guy he knew in town, and it was the only time she could see him. She had been a high school flame, and Billy figured he'd give her a poke for old times' sake.

So we went our separate ways. I took a cab, and—

Mick, I don't mean to sound like a pervert or anything, but would you take us there now?

It's gonna get a little creepy Lenny, but it might help you understand what happened that day.

They turn in their seats, but before the restaurant fades to black, Toots Shor comes waddling over.

"Wait, Mick, hold on."

"What's the matter, Toots? Is Joe coming in?"

"No, I ain't seem him for years. But I overheard you say something about going to see Marilyn. Mind if I join you?"

"Toots, this is kind of private . . ."

"Oh, it's all right, Lenny. I don't mind. Slide over."

Lenny scoots over on the bench seat at their booth to make room for Toots.

"You know, Joe used to bring Marilyn in here all the time when they was together. Nice girl. Very pretty. She once said to me—"

"Toots, shhhh."

"Oh, oh, sorry Mick."

Now the restaurant vanishes. The hallway and the interior of Marilyn's San Francisco apartment appears. Inside, the white walls are bare. All that's visible are a couple of teddy bears, a doll.

Mickey looks both ways down the hall to make sure no one can see him, then rings the bell. He nervously shifts his weight from one leg to the other, then back again. Finally, he hears footsteps, and the door opens. Marilyn Monroe appears. She's wearing a tight-fitting white satin blouse with the top two buttons open, no bra, yellow cotton short-shorts, and canary yellow high-heel shoes.

When she sees Mickey, a smile lights up her face. "Hi Mickey, you're right on time. Come in."

Mickey looks behind himself and walks into her apartment. She gives him a peck on the cheek, then she puts his arms around her and kisses him full on the lips. She rubs a bare leg against his crotch just to see if he has an erection.

I think she'd have been offended if I hadn't a-had one.

"Hold me, Mickey. Hold me tight," she says.

Looking back, Len, I think that's what she liked more than anything. And if that meant she had to fuck a guy to get him to hold her, hey, that's showbiz.

You're jumping ahead of yourself.

Yeah, I know. But I'll tell you, when she kissed me on the cheek, I almost fainted.

After Marilyn and Mickey break their clinch, Mickey inadvertently drops his gaze. He notices that the clasp above the zipper on Marilyn's shorts is open, allowing him a glimpse of the little swirls of dark blond hair below her belly button. He doesn't want to be rude and stare, but he can't help himself. As he forces his gaze upward, he sees the smooth, satiny outline of the two most attractive breasts he has ever seen in his life. Her nipples are tight against the fabric of her blouse.

Mickey gulps. His heart is pounding; he takes short, quick breaths. He feels like he's going to pass out.

She catches him staring and snuggles up to him again. Her body is radiating heat. Mickey is unable to speak, unable to move.

"Oh, Mickey, we're so naughty," she whispers in a warm breathy voice that would be imitated by every blonde film star for years to come. Every time she speaks his name he is aroused so strongly it is like a wave of hot lightning has gone through him.

She gives her upper body a little wiggle, whispers "Oooooh!," and she again puts her lips to his and sets his whole body on fire. Then she gently takes his hands, and places them right where she wants them so that each hand is cupping a breast.

"These are my privates, and pretend you are my general," she whispers.

Like any general worth his salt, Mickey attacks. He opens the remaining buttons on the blouse, and then he is fondling, licking, and kissing her breasts with an insane lust. He is like a man lost in the desert who stumbles upon the oasis and cannot drink enough to slake his thirst. He puts his face between them and holds his hands around them.

Marilyn squeals like a farm animal. After long, sensuous licks and dozens of kisses on every inch of them, she is breathing hard and whispering "Mickey . . . Mickey . . . talk dirty to me!"

Mickey stops cold. He obviously has no idea what to say. Does she want him to cuss? No woman has ever asked him to "talk dirty."

"Mickey, I want you to talk dirty to me," Marilyn repeats. She is petulant; angry almost.

Mickey squints, trying to think, to concentrate, to come up with the one thing he could say that would make her crazy. Finally, he blurts out, "I would really, really, really, really, really, *really* like to fuck you."

Marilyn can't contain herself. A giggle escapes her lips, and then she begins to laugh. "You really *are* a farm boy!"

Not wanting Marilyn to see him blush, he stands and walks around her, fondling those fabulous breasts from behind. As he does that, Marilyn grinds her perfect ass against his hard-on.

Let me tell you about them, Len. When I touched Marilyn's breasts, they responded as though they were living things.

Mickey's hands drop lower, and he slowly unzips her shorts. He pulls them down her shapely legs to the floor and then he s-l-o-w-l-y pulls down her satin undies. After Marilyn gives a little shake and then steps out of them, Mickey kneels down and plants his lips on the smoothest, classiest ass he has ever had the pleasure of kissing. Then he turns her around and kisses her on the other side. He buries his head in her bush. Her hands grab his head and she guides him to the right spot. When she's good and ready, Mickey stands up.

Marilyn reaches down and grabs his balls, but before he knows what's happening, he flows down her leg like Niagara Falls. He just couldn't help himself. Mickey doesn't know whether to apologize or say anything at all. Marilyn doesn't let go of him, and he stays silent.

She just stands there with her eyes closed, feeling the juices run out of Mickey and all over her.

She groans with pleasure. Something about this has really turned her on. And despite his embarrassment, Mickey's erection comes back. Sure she'd be pleased, Mickey guides her hand to his dick, but she just shrugs and walks over to the bed in the middle of the room. Then she lies down and passively spreads her legs.

Mickey enters her, going in nice and easy. The look on his face changes from excitement and pleasure to surprise and then disappointment. He waits for the yelling and the screaming, waits for her to tell him how good it was, waits for an ooh or an aah, any reaction at all, but no. Nothing. Mickey goes at it harder, and still nothing. While he works away at it, Marilyn just lies there staring at him with cold, accusing eyes.

She doesn't say a word, doesn't even sigh. Nothing. Orgasm? She doesn't even shudder.

There is a cold look on Marilyn's face—a look that says "I've done this a million times and I'm bored and disgusted."

When he's finished, he gets up, and she heads for the bathroom. She matter-of-factly tells him to let himself out, that it's time for him to go.

Mickey's last view of her is the delicate crack of her magnificent ass as she heads into the bathroom. The bathroom door closes. The apartment is silent except for the sound of faucets being turned and water rushing out of the showerhead. Mickey sits on the bed, stunned. He dresses, kicks the teddy bear, and leaves, shutting the door behind him.

What the heck was going on there? It looked like she was disgusted—bored and angry.

With me? With herself? I don't know. Later Billy told me that he'd heard she had been abused by her stepfather when she was a little girl and had once been a call girl, and that she had been so intent on becoming a movie star that she slept with anyone she thought could help her. Of course, when word got around, she started to get calls from all sorts of sleazy guys who promised her anything in exchange for getting into her pants.

Billy told me that when she signed her first movie contract, she told a friend, "I've sucked my last cock." But she was just kidding herself.

Later she told friends, "I've slept with producers. I've spent a great deal of time on my knees. It was no big deal. Nobody ever got cancer from a blow job."

Maybe not cancer, but all that bartered sex had hardened her.

Did you ever see her again?

I tried to call her again and again, maybe a dozen times. To say how wonderful it was? That would have been a lie. To apologize? For what?

But I never spoke to her again. The phone just kept ringing. Maybe she changed her number. Maybe she moved. And as it turned out, Marilyn and Joe got married, but it didn't last very long. They were married for nine months in 1954. As a wedding present she gave him an album of nude photos of herself. Joe didn't know whether to keep the photos under his pillow or burn them. He felt the same way about her as well.

When she sued him for divorce, she accused him of beating her, of treating her like shit. Big surprise. Joe was always pissed at her because when she was out making movies, Joe imagined she was out fucking some movie guy, an actor, a mogul, a flunky. Joe pleaded with her to quit the movie business and become a housewife because he couldn't figure out any way to keep her clothes on. Can you imagine it—Marilyn Monroe, a housewife? But knowing what I knew, who could blame him?

I think the biggest reason their marriage was a failure was that they weren't compatible in bed. Marilyn was a girl who loved the foreplay, the holding, the kissing, the fondling. She hated the fucking. Joe, meanwhile, was an old-time guinea who didn't go in for any of that foreplay stuff. He wasn't a fondler. He was a fucker. If Joe had asked me, I could have told him that if he would spend more time playing with her body and talking dirty to her, and less time fucking her, he'd have had a better shot at staying married. 'Course, I'd have never had the balls to tell Joe anything like that. If I'd said that to Joe, he and Sinatra would have come over to my house and butchered me with meat cleavers. And even if I run into Joe up here, I couldn't say it.

Here's the strange part. It was only after Marilyn died eight years later that Joe became the mythical hero he is today. She had supposedly done him wrong, and he had suffered as a result, and everyone loved him for that. Everyone, that is, except those of us who knew him. We still thought of him as a fucking lunatic.

After Marilyn left Joe, she switched to that guy who wrote plays, Arthur Miller, another guy she drove nuts. The poor guy didn't have a chance. Anyone who looks like her, who will flirt with the mailman or fuck any handsome guy who comes to the door, but who hates to fuck her husband as much as she did would drive any guy cuckoo.

All through Marilyn's marriage to the play guy, Miller, Joe never stopped pining for her. It was Billy and Lois all over again.

Joe even talked about how he intended to marry her again. It was wacky. She was married to someone else, for Christ's sake. Joe was just like Billy. Neither of them could stand it when a woman left them. Joe saw their divorce as some kind of personal failure, and so he was determined to undo the divorce by winning her back. For years after Marilyn divorced Joe, he never gave up the idea that he could get her to come back to him. Even when Marilyn got Peter Lawford to fix her up with President Kennedy, who Joe hated, Joe was sure he and Marilyn would get married again. That's what I mean about Joe being nuts. Marilyn was fucking her way up the ladder to the presidency and had passed Joe by years ago.

I still remember watching Marilyn sing "Happy Birthday" to Jack Kennedy not long before she died and he was shot. When she started singing there wasn't a pair of dry slacks in the house. The place reeked of male juices. I'd have loved to have been a fly on the wall to hear what Jack had to say before going to bed that evening. My guess is that he sounded like any ballplayer trying to explain a love letter found by his wife: "No dear. She doesn't mean a thing to me, really. She only *thinks* she's in love with me. It's all in her imagination. Who are you going to believe, your lyin' eyes or me?"

As I said before, when Jack Kennedy found out what a lousy lay Marilyn was, he gave her over to his brother Bobby, who had no problem sneaking off to Los Angeles to do the horizontal hokey pokey with Marilyn. As attorney general of the country he was supposed to be America's moral guardian and he had a wife and nine kids back home. It just goes to show you, the Law of the Land is certainly no match for the Law of the Puss. Never was.

Never will be.

Let me tell you, for anyone who came within ten feet of Marilyn, that woman was trouble with a capital T. She was a real wacko, like a lot of beauties I've met over the years. In fact, if there's one thing I learned, it's that the more beautiful a woman, the crazier she is, and the crazier she'll make you.

Either some relative has fucked her against her will when she was too young to keep him from doing it to her, or else after the first time he did it, she discovered she really liked it and kept letting him do it, or else when she was fifteen or sixteen she hooked up with some pervert and got into kinky shit a normal person wouldn't do, or else she'd been so spoiled rotten by her father that nothing you do for her is ever good enough.

I read somewhere that Marilyn had been in foster homes. And you know what they do to young girls in foster homes. Poor Joe. By the time he found out what I already knew, he was ruined as a man.

After Marilyn divorced him, he compared every woman he ever met to her, and none of them measured up, no matter how nice they were or how caring. Joe had become addicted to the idea of Marilyn's puss, and it was worse than if he had been taking heroin. Then when Marilyn died, she took her puss with her, and that made the poor bastard stark raving mad.

I once met one of Joe's later girlfriends. A real nice-looking girl, great body, really built, and she was a nice person, too. She told me that one time she came to the door naked to greet Joe with a rose in her mouth, and when Joe opened the door and saw her and that rose, he beat the living shit out of her. After he sat on her bed sobbing his apology, he explained that he thought she had been making fun of his devotion to Marilyn by holding the rose in her mouth. You see, since the day Marilyn died, Joe sent roses to her grave. Every day. So when he saw the rose in his girlfriend's teeth, he went nuts and slapped her around. Of course, while he was beating her around, she had no idea why he was doing it. After she was curled up in bed all bruised crying her eyes out and Joe saw what he had done, he sat on the edge of the bed and bawled. "I'm sorry, I'm sorry," he said. "I shouldn't have done that. I need help."

Boy, did he ever. Just like me. But he never got it. He had become a lifetime victim of Marilyn's puss. It made him plumb crazy, sort of the opposite of Alzheimer's. Those people can't remember anything, where Joe couldn't think about anything else but the golden puss that got away. He's been a wack job ever since.

When Billy and I returned to St. Petersburg for spring training in '53, Billy was living on the edge. I had never seen him so beside himself. Lois had carried through on her threat and served him with divorce papers. Billy was devastated. He would get drunk and punch walls. On the field he would taunt opponents and generally act obnoxious. All that year he seemed on the verge of a nervous breakdown. Still, that didn't stop Billy from being Billy.

In training camp Billy had met this real pretty young girl at a bar. She was from Miami, came from this wealthy family. Ordinarily, Billy didn't go out with rich girls. Not only didn't rich girls have sex on the first date, but Billy said their money made him uncomfortable, made him feel inferior. Billy had grown up poor, and he was always telling me how the rich kids in Berkeley had looked down on him and his roughneck friends. Billy bragged how he used to crash their parties, eat their food, make out with their dates, and dare anyone to throw him out. He told me how much he enjoyed punching them out when he got the chance.

Another reason he said he didn't date rich girls was that you were more likely to be dumped by rich bitches, and he always wanted to be the one doing the dumping. Also, Billy didn't like the buy-me-presents ritual that rich girls often demanded before they'd allow you to have sex with them. Billy's idea of a perfect relationship still was to meet a girl in a bar, get drunk with her, take her back to his room, then fuck her brains out for an hour or two. Then it was out the door and on to the next one.

No fuss, no entanglements.

But this girl was real pretty, had a great body, and treated him real nice, so Billy made an exception. I think he really took a fancy to her. He invited her to stay with him for the weekend, and to make a big impression, he went to Maas Brothers, a local St. Petersburg department store, bought a record player and a television, and he entertained her royally. Billy was a pro baseball player, this famous Yankee, but remember in '53 he was making maybe about $7,000 for the season, and a chunk of that was going back to Lois, so he really didn't have much to spend, so after she went back home, he took all the stuff back to the store, said the stuff didn't work, was no good, made up some kind of story, and got all his money back. Billy was a piece of work.

Their relationship didn't last long. The last time Billy ever saw her, we were playing an exhibition game in Miami, and this girl invited him to come over to her house for dinner to meet her folks. She lived in this big mansion on Key Biscayne. He said the family had a big yacht out in front. Billy said her house was three stories high, must have been fifteen rooms, marble columns, and he said the dining room was as long as a football field. Billy said he thought he was dining in the Taj Mahal.

He and this girl sat down at the dining room table with her folks, a full sit-down dinner, with real silver, plates with French castles painted on them, maids to serve them, very fancy.

Billy said that while he was eating, he thought how much he was enjoying this lifestyle, said he was pondering that maybe it made sense to marry this girl. He wasn't in love with her. He said she wouldn't give him head, but he told me he thought that she would learn. Plus, he thought he would enjoy living like a king.

And then in the middle of the meal Billy excused himself to go to the bathroom. He had to take a dump. As he was sitting on the can, he noticed that the bathroom sink had silver faucets and the floor was covered with fancy tile, but when he was done, to his horror he discovered there was no toilet paper on the spool, only the cardboard. Billy panicked. He looked everywhere for toilet paper, and when he couldn't find any, he took off his shirt and undershirt, and he used his undershirt to wipe himself.

Now Billy had to find some place to hide his soiled, shit-stained undershirt. Not knowing what else to do, he tried to flush it down the toilet. After he pulled the handle, he heard a gurgle, and then water began gushing onto the floor. Now Billy was in a serious panic. How could he explain the flood of water to the family of the girl?

What he did next was pure Billy. He opened the small bathroom window, crawled out, and disappeared. He hitchhiked back to the Miami hotel where the team was staying. He never saw the girl again. True story.

That was also the year Billy discovered that there was a school for secretaries and models across the street from the Soreno Hotel, where we were spending spring training in St. Pete. One day Billy told me, "Come with me," and we walked to Maas Brothers and bought a gigantic, expensive telescope on a weekly payment plan. For this telescope big enough to see Saturn's rings on a clear night, Billy agreed to pay something like twelve dollars a week over the next twenty years.

Was this the telescope you used on the roof of the Shoreham Hotel in Washington, the story I wrote about in Ball Four?

No, and if you hold your horses, I'll tell you why it wasn't.

After Billy brought the telescope back to the Soreno, we waited until dark, when Billy said, "Let's go." By this time I'd known him well enough to know that when he says, "Let's go," I go without asking any questions. We got in the hotel elevator and headed for the top floor. The elevator door opened, and with the telescope on his shoulders Billy headed for the stairs. I followed. We climbed those stairs to the roof.

Billy set up the telescope and pointed it toward the windows of the dormitory of the secretaries and models. We did this every night until we broke camp to go north. If a girl was careless enough to leave her curtains open, we could see everything she was doing inside very clearly.

For the first few nights we noticed that most of the time the girls would undress in the bathroom, where we couldn't see them naked, and when they came out they'd be dressed for bed. We couldn't believe that none of the girls slept naked, but then about eleven o'clock on about the fifth day of our secret surveillance our patience finally paid off. On the sixth floor of the dorm I was manning the scope when I noticed this one girl, who was real pretty, had dark hair, long legs—I imagined she was an actress, not a secretary. I said to Billy, "Showtime," and he said to me, "Give me a rating." I rated her a nine on a scale of ten, and then I began to get dry-mouthed when she began to dance suggestively in front of the window.

"Billy," I told him, "she's dancing." She was shaking her body all around. I paused. "Billy, she's taking off her shirt." Another pause. "Billy, she's stripping!" I gulped. "Billy, she's dancing topless." Billy thought I was making it up. He didn't believe me.

"You're full of shit," he said.

"Whatever you say," I said.

"Let me see," he said, but I wouldn't remove my eye from the viewfinder on the telescope. Billy stuck his head in front of the fat end of the device, blocking my view. "If I can't see, nobody sees," he said.

Billy got to watch for another ten minutes. When the girl finally quit dancing, we both went back to our hotel rooms. Merlyn wanted to know where I had gone so late at night. I told her the entire Yankee team had been on a visit to an old-age home. That sounded believable enough. St. Petersburg had more old people per square foot than any city in the world. They had green benches all over the downtown that the geezers sat on all day. A couple of times I had the urge to invite a couple of them to come up on the roof with us, because every night after that, that's where we'd be. Billy and I stopped going to the bars, didn't accept dates, didn't go out with the other guys. We had a date with our eye in the sky.

Billy made up a whole scenario as to who this girl was. According to Billy, she was the daughter of a professor and she was always shy in school but was finding out who she was in college. "She's a virgin," Billy said. "She's just a child learning to spread her wings."

Like clockwork every night around eleven this "child" would stand in front of her window, begin to sway to the music, pull her shirt over her head, unsnap her bra, and dance topless for about fifteen minutes. I suggested to Billy that we should wait for her outside her dorm, meet her, and ask her out. Billy was dead set against it. "That would ruin the fantasy!" Billy said. How do you argue with that?

Every night was like opening day. The excitement would build to a fever pitch. We couldn't wait to see whether or not she'd be there. Before we climbed the stairs to the roof, the air was electric with expectation. And rarely did she disappoint us.

And as the days passed, her dancing became more and more provocative. It was almost as though she was performing just for us.

When she danced, she raised her arms and shook her upper body so her breasts wiggled from side to side and then she'd move her hips in circles as though she was making love to us, and through the lens I could see she had a big smile on her face, and she would lick her lips, and sometimes she would grab her breasts and caress herself, all the while staring straight out the window at us.

One night Billy and I were watching her dance, and she was so into it she unbuttoned the fly of her shorts, pulled her pants down and started playing with herself. Billy had the telescope, and he began describing it to me. "Oh, you little doll," Billy kept saying. "You little doll."

"Let me see, Billy," I pleaded. But Billy was mesmerized.

"Please, podner," he said, "I think I'm in love. Don't break the spell." Billy was one with the girl in the telescope. It was one of his most powerful relationships. During the day he couldn't stop talking about her. He became so obsessed with her that I couldn't get her out of *my* head! Did she know we were there? Did she like it that we were watching?

There's a funny ending to the story. About three days before we broke camp to go north, Billy and I were invited by a couple of the veteran Yankee players to go to one of the strip clubs in Tampa, which was across the bay from St. Pete. It was after midnight, so we had to break curfew, but by now we knew it would be another couple of hours before Casey would come rolling in, so we knew we were safe. Besides, Casey didn't give a shit what we did, as long as we played well, and we were playing very well.

Billy drove us to this joint, and we paid five bucks for two drinks and all we could ogle, and sat at a table near the dance floor.

Get this. The very first girl to come out to dance was the girl Billy and I had been watching through the telescope! We couldn't believe it. She was no student. She was a stripper!

Billy was crushed.

"Big fucking deal," he said disgustedly. "I can see this for free any time I want. Let's get the fuck out of here." He threw back his drink and slammed his glass on the table. Then Billy and I got up and left. The other guys had to grab a cab back across the bay to our hotel.

The next day Billy returned the telescope to the department store. He said he didn't want it anymore. The store clerk gave him a hard time, but Billy told them he didn't care what the fuck he owed them, he wasn't going to pay them another dime. He said we were leaving town in a couple of days, and if they knew what was good for them, they should accept his offer to keep the money he had spent and keep the telescope as well. Reluctantly, they gave in.

So long as Billy thought he was watching a schoolgirl dancing topless, it was like he had died and gone to heaven. But once he discovered he was watching a topless dancer dancing topless, all the fun was lost for him. Billy was such a romantic.

Me, I'd have kept that telescope a couple more days.

10

Word is beginning to spread that Mickey Mantle is holding court at the far end of the joint. Several men, carrying their drinks and their chairs, drift over to where Mickey and Leonard Shecter are sitting, and they begin to gather around the booth just to listen.

Toots, certain that Mantle will want his privacy, starts to shoo the men away, but Lenny imperceptibly shakes his head "no," and puts his hand out as if to say, "It's okay, they can stay." Mickey hasn't really noticed the growing crowd around him.

Toots looks at Lenny and shrugs his shoulders.

How did you manage to avoid getting drafted for the Korean War?

Lenny, I didn't avoid it at all. During the winter after the 1952 season, I was called by my draft board to see if I was fit to serve. All through the '52 season, drunks in the stands on the road kept calling me "draft dodger" and "coward," but that wasn't really fair. I had suffered from osteomyelitis, a serious bone disease, playing football in high school, and when I went to sign up, I was turned down flat. Then the army made a new rule directed specifically at me saying that anyone suffering from osteomyelitis who had been treated successfully for the past two years now was eligible. A week after this new regulation was passed, I was called for a physical.

When one of the members of my draft board suffered a heart attack and died, the exam was put off until after the '52 season. When I showed up this time, I told them about the knee injury I had suffered against the Giants in the '51 series, and again I was given a medical deferment. The writers always talked about how much better I might have been if I hadn't hurt my legs, but you know, I might have spent a couple years in Korea getting shot at if I hadn't. I could've gotten killed. Instead of freezing my ass off in Asia, I went to sunny St. Pete in Florida.

We were playing an exhibition game in Brooklyn right before the start of the '53 season when the PA announcer told the crowd that I had become the father of an eight-pound, twelve-ounce boy. Merlyn was back in Oklahoma, and it was another month before I got to fly home to Oklahoma to see my son David. Meanwhile, for the season I had rented a nice house in Englewood, New Jersey, a short drive over the George Washington Bridge to Yankee Stadium, and as soon as the baby was old enough, Merlyn drove the fifteen hundred miles to join me. I was glad she came up, glad to be with her and my son, but their presence added to the tremendous amount of pressure I was feeling. With my dad gone, I had my own family to support in addition to my mom. I was just twenty-two.

I had hit some long home runs, but Casey was always telling me how far I was from becoming what he wanted me to be. He'd lecture me all the time. He'd tell me I had to play better in the outfield, had to study the game, had to become more serious about it. In other words, he wanted me to be more like Billy. He never had a good thing to say about me. There were times I really hated him for being so hard on me.

One day in Washington I went up to bat right-handed against a crafty left-hander by the name of Chuck Stobbs, who was famous for the expression, "Chuck her in there, Stobbs" that kids loved to yell at opposing pitchers. Stobbs threw me a high fastball that I uppercutted. I swore at myself because I didn't think I had hit it very well at first. But the ball went over the 370 sign on the left-field wall in Griffith Stadium, over a tall beer sign, then got into the wind and went completely out of the stadium into a nearby lumberyard. The next day the Yankee PR guy measured it at 565 feet. I wanted to say to Casey, "Let's see your fucking pet Billy do that."

That was also the year that Whitey Ford became a top pitcher. Whitey and Billy had played a short time together in the minors and had become friends, and so when he came up to the Yankees he began to join Billy and me playing golf and partying at night. Whitey could drink a little himself, and because he was a pitcher he only had to be ready to play every fourth day.

Whitey wasn't crazy or angry like Billy, and he wasn't excessive like I was. He liked to come up with fun-crazy things for us to do, and then he'd sit back and watch us do them. He could also play a practical joke or two. The three of us just liked to have fun. We loved being on the same team together.

I remember one game during the season when Whitey was pitching. Everyone was saying what a great pitch caller Yogi was, and I was always teasing him, ragging him by saying his pitch calling was horseshit. So this one day Yogi said to me, "If you're so smart, you call the pitches."

We didn't tell Whitey. For about six innings if I wanted a fastball I stood straight up in center field, and if I wanted a curve, I'd bend over. And Yogi would call whatever I wanted.

Whitey was pitching a shutout.

I said, "Shit, Yogi, it's easy to call a game."

We were just about unbeatable in '53. Casey was a real prick all season long, except for one week when we were losing, and then he was as nice as could be. During most of the summer I had a swollen right knee, but Casey kept putting me out there anyway. He wanted me in the lineup whether I was hurting or not.

In August my good leg gave way. Because of the injury in the '51 World Series my left leg always had water on it, was swollen and sore. We were playing the White Sox in August, and after a ball was hit to me in center, I planted my right foot to pivot and throw the ball back into second when my right knee buckled out from under me. I tore ligaments in the knee and had to wear a big, bulky brace. Despite the pain, I kept playing. I wanted to be in the lineup. I couldn't stand the thought of letting my teammates down.

We won the '53 pennant going away, and on the day we clinched it Billy drove in four runs against Early Wynn. People don't remember Billy's contributions. They've forgotten what an important player Billy was.

That night the Yankee brass threw us a victory party at the stadium, and afterward about eight of us went to the Latin Quarter. We all ordered steak dinners, maybe a shrimp cocktail or two, and we had a few drinks. Whitey thought the Yankees owed it to us, so he signed Dan Topping's name to the tab. The total bill was maybe $250, a lot of money in those days for us, but peanuts for Topping considering we had just won the son of a bitch the pennant.

Casey was always accusing Billy and me of causing all the trouble, but if you want to know the truth, Whitey was usually the guy who put us up to it. Whitey looked like a choirboy, but he sure could stir up the pot. And Whitey didn't give a shit about anything. If he wanted to do something, he did it.

"He's got plenty of dough," said Whitey, who rightly felt that Topping could have bought each of us fifty dinners, and he'd still be way ahead of the game.

We didn't know it, but Topping, a multimillionaire who himself was a pretty good skirt chaser, was also at the Latin Quarter that night. He didn't think it at all funny when the waiter brought him our bill. In fact, the next day the cheap bastard fined each of us five hundred bucks!

George Weiss accused Billy of being behind it, of course. God, Weiss hated Billy's guts, hated that he was on the team, even though Billy helped win him a pennant every single year he was on the team. Billy was a Yankee in 1951, 1952, 1953, 1955, and 1956. In '52 Billy won us the Series when he made a last-second catch of Jackie Robinson's pop-up.

Then in the '53 Series all Billy did was go 12 for 24, with two home runs and eight runs batted in. He was given the Babe Ruth Award as the Series MVP. Billy even got the winning hit to beat the Dodgers in the final game. We didn't win in '54 when Billy was in the army. Weiss should have worshipped the ground Billy walked on. Instead, he looked for every excuse to make Billy look bad.

A few days after it was announced we were being fined for signing Topping's name to the Latin Quarter bill, Topping's secretary called me and Billy to come over and get the five hundred bucks he was returning to us. The Latin Quarter fine was a mistake, Topping decided, after it was made public and he ended up looking like a sack of shit. He said he was sorry for the misunderstanding. My guess is that Weiss had really been the one who had fined us, but that Topping was the one who took the heat when the fines hit the papers. Topping told me to tell Whitey to come and get his money, but Whitey was so pissed he said, "Tell Topping to shove it up his ass." Whitey never did get his money back.

In that '53 series I only hit .208. My knees were killing me and that had a lot to do with it. Casey refused to give me an inch. We were expected to play hurt and keep doing well. Times sure have changed, huh? Can't imagine treating the players that way today. Like I said, Casey was a tough motherfucker, and he never let up on me. He told the reporters, "We keep telling him to cut down on his swing and hit down on the ball. The kid's got power to hit it in the seats just punching it like he did for the big one he hit. You tell him to stop trying to kill the ball, and he won't do it." I wanted to tell that stumpy-kneed, wrinkly faced bastard, If I'm supposed to stop killing the ball, why did everyone make such a big deal over the fact I hit that home run in Washington 565 feet? Why is it the traveling secretary carries around a tape measure to every game? And who is it who brings all the fans to the ballpark?

By '53 Casey had become as bad as my dad. Nothing I ever did was good enough for that big-eared son of a bitch dumb Dutchman bastard. At the same time Case would have kind words for Billy every single fucking day. While he was calling me a bum, he was calling him a great ballplayer. Great ballplayer, my ass, that scrawny little son of a bitch. For a long time I had to take shit from the two of them, Casey and Billy—I couldn't stand listening to their bullshit anymore.

Guys with a lot of talent often don't work very hard. Obviously, this was Casey's way of motivating you. He knew exactly who to stroke and who to dog. And Billy was a pretty effective motivator when he became a manager—sort of the linear descendant of John McGraw through Casey.

Now don't get me wrong, I really loved those two guys. I don't know where I would have ended up without them. For the first six years of my career, Billy and I did everything together, drank together, fooled around together, and helped each other out when things were looking dark. And Casey? Well, as much as I hated the way he talked about me in the papers, I really loved that guy. He made me the player that I became, taught me everything about the game, made me tough as nails, made me really care about being a New York Yankee. I guess that's what made the Old Man so special. A lot of guys play on teams, and for a lot of them it's a job. You go out there and hit and field and throw, and if you win, fine, and if you lose, fine. But it wasn't that way with Casey when he was managing the Yankees. He demanded that you play the game right, that you throw to the right base, that you hit the cutoff man, that you pay attention to the signs, that you move up the runner.

We always knew that Casey wouldn't screw up the game, that he'd have the right guy pitching or the right guy pinch-hitting or the right guy playing defense in the late innings, and in the ten years I played for him, he never once made a mistake. He looked like a funny old man, but he was the best manager who ever was. To me, he was what made the Yankees special. Against our will he made us learn the game right and play it the way he wanted us to, and at the same time the players developed a special camaraderie with each other that few other teams had. We were the Yankees. We were special.

Not just because we won, but because Casey made us feel that way.

Even after he was fired at the end of the 1960 season, every time I put on those pinstripes to get ready for a game, I thought of Casey. I remember how my legs would be killing me, and I wouldn't want to play and that gnarled son of a buck would come up to me and say, "I guess you're hurting too much to play today, huh Mick? Too bad, because we sure could use you." And he'd say it in a way that would make me just furious, and I'd say, "Who said I'm not playing, Case? You better put my name in that lineup," and he'd say with great sarcasm, "You sure?" and that would make me madder, and I'd play, and on those days usually I hit one out just to show him.

To me, those pinstripes symbolized his leadership and strength. I only wish I had been able to open up to him a little bit more so I could have told him how much I loved him. When I was a ballplayer I never believed in God, but even though we fought like dogs, from the day I became a Yankee, I always believed in Casey Stengel, the son of a bitch.

We played the Dodgers in the 1953 World Series just like we did the year before. Everybody talked about what a great team the Dodgers were, but they were only great when they played in Ebbets Field. They had an almost entire right-hand hitting lineup, guys like Campanella, Hodges, Furillo, Reese, and Robinson.

The only left-hander was Duke Snider, so whenever they came to Yankee Stadium, we'd just let them hit long fly balls and stand out in the outfield and catch them. Don't forget, this was before the renovations in the seventies. The outfield was huge, real deep in left and something like 457 feet in center. It was nicknamed "Death Valley" back then 'cause that's where fly balls would go to die. It was so deep the three monuments to Ruth, Gehrig, and some old manager were in the playing field.

We didn't think the Dodgers were all that good. Billy was always talking trash about the Dodgers, saying he was just as good as that loudmouth Jackie Robinson, complaining that Jackie got all the publicity and he got nothing but grief from everybody, including the Yankee owners. His whole life Billy felt cheated about something. It was the way he was.

But I think it also made him a better ballplayer. He felt he always had to try harder, or else somebody was going to come and take his job.

A guy comes home from work, walks into his bedroom, and finds a stranger fucking his wife. He says, "What the hell are you two doing?"

His wife turns to the stranger and says, "See, I told you he was stupid."

After the '53 season ended, Billy came to Oklahoma to visit. Billy wasn't the sort of person who could sit still, never mind sit at home. He needed companionship, and he begged me to let him come visit me in Oklahoma. Merlyn didn't want him to come, really didn't want him coming to visit, because she knew what was going to happen as soon as he arrived.

Sounds like you enjoyed spending time with Billy more than you did with her, no?

I guess I must have, because I told him to come on down, even though she didn't want him around.

Looking back, I wonder if my life would have turned out any different if he hadn't come. Cause we had so much fuckin' fun. I didn't think a guy could have that much fun. And it was all because of Billy. He loved the action, and the crazier it was, the more he liked it. So we'd tell my wife we were going hunting or fishing, and we'd drive to Missouri to drink and chase puss.

Billy knew just what to do. We'd walk into a bar, check out the two best-lookin' broads in the place, and we'd buy them a drink. Billy would tell the bartender to tell them, "Tell the ladies these drinks are compliments of the two biggest stars on the world champion New York Yankees," and almost every time when those girls'd see who it was, they'd be taking their clothes off even before we got out the door. We'd rent two motel rooms, go at it, and then if Billy was in the mood sometimes he'd get on the phone and ask if my girl wanted to switch rooms. And more often than not, she would! God, we had fun. One time we picked up two sisters. Good-looking girls, too.

Billy was fascinated that a girl from the same family would have sex in the presence of her sister. That really turned him on. We took them to our hotel room, and while I sat on the couch, I watched in amazement as Billy asked the two girls if they would take off all their clothes so he could check to see the family resemblance. I thought to myself, *This is pretty kinky. They're not going to fall for that.*

But they did. Willingly.

"Would you undress each other?" Billy wanted to know. I thought to myself, They're going to get pissed off at Billy and walk out of the room.

But they didn't.

Rather, they started taking off all their clothes until the two girls were standing in front of us buck naked. Billy then asked them to stand back to back so he could compare them. And they did it. I couldn't believe it, but they were happy to do it!

They stood there giggling while Billy measured the diameter of their breasts with his fingers, holding one breast of each of them, and then he stood them side by side so he could compare the size of their asses, which he rubbed all over with his hands as he pretended to compare them. And then he turned them all the way around and put his face about three inches from their pubic hair to see if there was any difference there, and when he got done examining, he declared that the only way he could know for sure who was sexier was if he could have sex with both of them, after which he would make a judgment.

The girls looked at each other, giggled, and said okay.

Billy even made a little ceremony of it. He flipped a coin to see which sister would go first.

So Billy had sex with one of them, while the other sister and I watched, and then Billy had the other girl play with him until he was ready to do it again, and then he had sex with the other one! And when he got done, he declared that it was a tie, that they were in fact both as beautiful as the other! Which tickled the girls to no end.

Billy asked the girls if they would have sex with me too, and they were willing, but I had had enough just watching them, and I took a raincheck. The girls got dressed and left, and we went back to the bar for some serious drinking.

"Nice upbringing," I said to Billy.

How can you tell when two lesbians are twins? They lick alike.

What's it mean when two lesbians make love? It doesn't mean dick.

Billy sure loved to drink. He would order three or four vodkas at a time, and he'd down them one after another, and sometimes he'd feel like talking, and he'd go on about his ex-wife, and how much he missed her and how badly she had hurt him, and how he wouldn't be around to watch his daughter grow up, and once in a while he'd start to cry, but sometimes all it did was make him mad, and heaven help the guy who sat down near us and said the wrong thing to Billy when he was in that mood. Boy, Billy could pop a guy so fast, you didn't even see the punch. And I'd have to run Billy out of there before the police came.

My problem was that I would get drunk a lot faster than Billy did. I had serious trouble holding my booze, but I enjoyed the feeling it gave me, so I did it anyway. Billy was only in town a month, but I guarantee you I came home wobbling every one of those days. Merlyn sure didn't appreciate it, but at that point I didn't care. Billy had shown me there was a world out there, and I was determined to take advantage of it.

After Billy went back to California, I found myself more and more attracted to the company in the bars, and at night I'd go to one of my favorite bars, drink boilermakers, and then stumble home. One time, instead of going home, I went fishing with my neighbors—fishing, honest—without telling Merlyn. I came home two days later. She thought I had been kidnapped and had called the police with a missing person's report.

I have to admit I treated her pretty shabbily. I don't know why I was the way I was. Maybe I hated feeling tied down. Maybe I couldn't help myself. I had watched my dad treat my mom the same way; it was all I knew. Still, that's no excuse. But all through the winter of '53–'54, I drank a lot and treated Merlyn terribly. I was never abusive. I just stayed away a lot. One time she ran off—down the street to her parents—but she came back after I sobered up. No matter how drunk I got, she would come back. I put her through a lot. I really did. To this day I can't figure out why she insisted on staying with me, though I'm glad she did.

Women. Go figure.

You want to know the perfect breakfast? Your son is on the cover of *Sports Illustrated,* your mistress is on the cover of *Playboy,* and your wife is on the back of a milk carton.

Billy was drafted into the army for the '54 season.

He never should have had to go. But Billy was a dumb fuck when it came to anything outside of baseball. He was a wiseguy, tried to play the angles, but more often than not he'd screw things up worse than if he had just left the situation alone.

Billy had first been drafted in '50, but he didn't want to have to interrupt his baseball career. Casey had promised to bring him to the Yankees in '51, and he was afraid he'd never get another chance if he spent two years in the army, so he cooked up one of his harebrained schemes. He got his stepfather to quit his job so that Billy could tell the draft board he needed a hardship discharge because he had to support not only his wife, but also his mother, two sisters, and his poor ailing stepfather.

It wasn't a bad plan, even though it made his stepfather furious. When his stepfather quit his job, Billy paid him instead. And remember, Billy wasn't making more than $5,000 a year with the Yankees!

The army, impressed that Billy was supporting all these people, discharged him after five and a half months. Billy was sure his plan had worked. But Billy didn't bother to study the regulations. As usual, he was flying by the seat of his pants.

If he had been in six months, the army wouldn't have been able to take him in again. Billy should have waited two weeks more before going to his hearing. Then he'd have been in the clear.

But after Billy got the winning hit in the 1953 World Series, his draft board looked back at his records and discovered he was eligible to be drafted again. Bye-bye Billy.

So we didn't have Billy in '54, and that was one of the two times under Casey when the Yankees didn't win the pennant. The Cleveland Indians just wouldn't lose that year. We won 103 games that year; they won 111. If you'd heard George Weiss, you'd have thought we had been terrible. My knees got well, and I almost won the Triple Crown that year, hit .300, drove in more than a hundred runs, but that cocksucker Weiss still tried to cut everybody's salary, including mine.

Maybe if we'd had Billy, we'd a-won it. I say this because in '55 Billy was still in the army, and as late as early September it didn't look like there was any way we were going to beat out the White Sox and the Indians 'cause Andy Carey was killing us at third, and our offense was horseshit. It was the second of September, and I walked into the club-house, and I could hear Casey chattering away telling a group of reporters, "That little bastard is back, and them guys better watch out." I knew immediately Casey was talking about Billy, and I looked around for him, and sure enough, Billy was there in the trainer's room.

"All right, podner," I said, "what's on the menu tonight?"

"Something special," he said beaming. "We have a date with the Heavenly Twins." I had no idea who the Heavenly Twins were, but I knew I'd be in for a treat. Billy had been in the army for a year and a half, but he had maintained a sexual network in cities where we played—and in cities where we didn't—that was simply amazing. If I had said to Billy, "I'm going to be in Boise, Idaho. Do you know a girl I can look up?" he'd have one. Or he'd have a friend who had one. And it didn't matter which city. Elko, Nevada? Augusta, Georgia? Bumfuck, Iowa? Didn't matter.

In this case when Billy was in the army he had met an Italian guy from New York who was part of the Gambino family, and after Billy and he became friends, he told Billy when he got back to New York, he had to get in touch with these incredible twin twenty-year-old girls. Since Billy had this thing for twins, there was no way he was going to pass this up. Their name was Minelli or Scarpelli or something like that, and they were identical, incredibly beautiful, dark-haired, really stunning, he said, and what made them so special, Billy's friend said, he had called the girls and told them that no matter what Billy asked them to do, they should do it.

"We have love slaves for the evening," Billy told me. Whoever heard of such a thing? I don't remember any love slaves in Oklahoma. We didn't even have love in Oklahoma, and the only slaves back home were the miners like my uncle and my dad.

After the game Billy and I went back to Billy's room at the Hotel Edison, and waiting for us were these two doe-eyed girls—identical twins with large bouncy breasts like water balloons. This time I wasn't going to be a spectator. I drank a few vodka-and-tonics to get myself into the mood.

"I've always had this fantasy about being the cream in an Oreo cookie," I said, making what I thought was a lewd, vague request, but those doll babies knew exactly what I was talking about, and garment by garment they began taking off their clothes, and when they were totally nude, they posed for us provocatively for a few seconds to show us they were twins in every way. After I undressed, one of them wiggled over to me and snuggled her breasts against my chest and the other held me from behind and rubbed her breasts against my back.

"Like this?" one of the innocent looking twins asked. I nodded, speechless. I was too excited to say a word, because I was being held in a vice of four firm and meaty breasts.

While they squeezed me from both sides, one of them rubbed her puss against my right leg while the other rubbed her puss against my left leg. I was a prisoner of puss. I grabbed two cute asses at once and held on for dear life.

It was better than going to an all-you-can-eat ribfest. My wish was their command.

Just seeing the twins naked, with their flat stomachs and those inviting breasts, that was the most memorable part of the evening. Though the rest of it was pretty terrific, too.

Billy told me they'd do whatever I wanted them to do, but being a very traditional guy, all I wanted to do really was to be able to stare at their naked bodies, to touch their breasts, to grab their pusses. I don't need to do much more than that. To me, getting a strange woman to take her clothes off is really enough. It's the moment of truth. After that, it almost doesn't even matter whether you have sex with her or not. The mystery is what's under those clothes. I even feel that way about fat girls. I see a girl who weighs 240 pounds. I wonder, *Is she wearing a bra to hold up her breasts? If I rub her nipples, will she feel it? Will I be able to find her puss under all that flab?* Since I was a boy I always wanted to know the answer to those questions, and if the girl would let me, I was intent on finding out.

Billy always thought I was crazy 'cause I would pick up girls of all shapes and sizes, colors, and types. I was a Nixon Republican when it came to politics, but a Kennedy liberal when it came to puss. If she had one, I wanted it. Billy was like the Republicans, a lot more choosy: he only liked them young and white, and he only wanted them built. And as he got older, his girls got even younger and even more built. I would tell him, "Making love to a fat girl is just as much fun as making love to a skinny one. You just have to be sure you're always on top, that's all." Billy would make a face.

Two deaf people get married. During the first week of marriage they find they cannot communicate in the bedroom with the lights out. The wife signs, "Honey, we need to agree on some simple signals. If you want sex, squeeze my left breast. If you don't, squeeze my right breast." The husband signs, "Great idea. If you want to have sex with me, reach over and pull on my dick one time. And if you don't want to have sex, pull on my dick . . . fifty times."

Sometimes I'd go to a party, and if I saw a pretty girl I'd stare at her for an hour, trying to imagine what she looked like with her clothes off. Of course, if I stared at her long enough and if she knew who I was, chances were she'd eventually come over and give me a phone number or hotel room key, and later that evening I would get the chance to find out. When Joe D or Yogi, or whoever it was, said "I'm lucky to be young and a Yankee," that's what he meant. If she took off her clothes for me, that meant she wanted me to look at what she ordinarily wouldn't let some run-of-the-mill guy see, and I always felt that was a wonderful compliment. Now, if the girl lying there naked also was pretty, then emotions came into play. Once I got an erection, it would kinda make me mad if she didn't let you get rid of the pressure in one way or another. But over the years the thing I've observed about women is that once they go to the trouble to take their clothes off for you, usually their intention is not to just lie there. They want as much fun as you do.

As long as you didn't slap them around or humiliate them or point out their disfiguring features, chances were she'd let you fuck her, or at the least she'd give you a blow job.

That was another thing I noticed: girls who dug sex loved to give blow jobs. It was like a game to them, to see how much semen they could produce by rubbing your dick with their tongue and mouth. And the ones who really loved sex wanted to swallow it. None of this "I promise I won't come in your mouth" bullshit. Oh no. In fact, it was just the opposite. They would ask me NOT to tell them when. They wanted it to be a surprise, because the challenge for them was that once it started coming, they wanted to swallow as much of it as they could without choking on it. It was amazing to me that so many women loved to do this. And when they'd get done, almost every time they'd have a big smile on their face.

Almost as big as mine.

Back to the Heavenly Twins. They were professionals of the finest kind. They were private property of New York mob boss Joseph Gambino himself, and apparently the guy Billy knew in the service was Gambino's cousin or brother or some close relative who let us enjoy their services free of charge for the night because Mr. G was a big Yankee fan and he was showing respect to Billy and me.

Billy said I could go first, and I had the twins lie next to each other with their legs spread apart. Since they looked alike, I picked one at random, laid on top of her and had sex with her while I rubbed the crotch of the one lying next to me.

It was so great. To me, this was the best part of being a professional baseball player. I made good money, but the money never meant anything. I didn't care about the money, except for the puss it could get me. I had grown up poor, and I was perfectly happy when I didn't have anything. Besides, usually there was nothing I really wanted to do except get drunk and fuck. Most of the other guys on the team were exactly the same way.

Yogi was different. He had a nice wife and a bunch of kids, and he had the first nickel he ever made. In fact, when we were on the road and we ran out of money, we knew we could always borrow a few bucks from Yogi. By the time he retired, he had a mansion in Montclair, New Jersey, and never had to go to autograph shows to keep himself afloat. That Yogi didn't need the money was also one reason George Weiss had such trouble bargaining with him. Yogi would say to him, "If you don't want to pay me, then trade me." But Weiss never hated Yogi, even though he gave Weiss a hard time. No one hated Yogi.

As for the rest of us, there were times when George Weiss forced us to hold out, knowing we couldn't stay away for very long. We always caved during negotiations, and the reason was that the more days we missed in training camp, the more puss was going to the other guys.

Billy had missed the first five months of the '55 season. The Heavenly Twins were a stark reminder of what he had missed.

Part of the fun of being with a girl is seeing how much bodily fluids you can produce from her. Podner, these two girls made rivers. By the end of the night, the bed was a sticky, smelly mess. I loved it. God, I loved it so.

What Billy loved was the idea that there were two of them the same.

He had a mathematical mind, and so he began to try to figure out all the different sexual combinations to which he could subject the two girls. His biggest problem was that they had two vaginas, and he had only one dick. He tried to position them so he could alternate thrusts into a different girl, but they were all giggling so much he didn't get past the second thrust.

Billy decided that more than anything else he wanted to experience a blow job from one girl while he was administering oral sex to the other one. He must have spent fifteen minutes moving the girls around, trying to put them in the perfect position to attain his pleasure. After having them lie back to back, then front to back, then crossways, then on top of each other, this was his solution: he laid on his back, and he had one twin sit with her puss on his face and gyrate while he held her breasts, while the other one lay on her stomach, took his dick in her mouth, gave him a blow job, and rubbed his stomach. I never heard so much moaning and groaning. Billy kept screaming, "Don't stop. Don't stop," while he was licking one girl and the other one was licking him. Lenny, if anyone who starts to read this book is a prude they'll probably put it down long before they get to this part, but if they make it this far, I can assure them, it was fascinating to watch. Billy was delirious about that combination, and after Billy had an orgasm—which he announced proudly at the top of his lungs to all of New York City—he declared that as soon as he could get erect again, the girls should switch positions.

Billy was like a sexual Dr. Salk. He declared this to be an important medical experiment to see which twin had the better blow job technique. Me, I couldn't tell them apart. That's the thing with identical twins. If you've fucked one of them, you've fucked the other one, too. 'Cause they're exactly the same. Same puss. Same tits. That is, after all, what it means to be identical.

To this day I don't know if I had sex with both of them or fucked one of them twice. And you know what, I don't give a rat's ass either. They were beautiful and a lot of fun to be with.

All I know is that it was some welcome home party. By the time we fell asleep, it was about four in the morning, and none of us had any juice left in our bodies. Billy and I were exhausted. The next morning we got up and went to the ballpark.

When I told Casey about the twins, the old goat was genuinely pissed that we hadn't invited him, too.

Where did your wife fit into all of these sexual shenanigans? After all, you did have a wife.

I did have a wife, and I had a baby son, too. What you have to understand is that in baseball you spend a lot of time by yourself, and you are in constant need of some companionship. You also have to understand that when you're a ballplayer, there's a lot of fun out there, and often you just get caught up in the moment. Hey, ninety percent of the guys are married, but no one holds it against each other that they do it. When you're out doing these things, it's not out of disrespect to your wife, you don't love her any less, it's just that you're out with the guys, and they're doing things, and you are, too. It's part of the life. During the game you're out in the field. After the game you're still out in the field. The real Field of Dreams.

Sounds like pretty lame excuses for guys cheating on their wives, Mick.

Sorry, Len. They're the best reasons I can come up with. How about, My dick made me do it. That any better?

Did you ever fall in love with any of these girls?

I rarely got attached to them. But having sex with them was normal. It was taken for granted you did these things. Home was one part of your life. Away from home was a separate, entirely different deal.

Did any of these girls become attached to you?

You did have to watch out when you went out with a girl. You had to be aware of her emotional state. All because of Eddie Waitkus.

But that was the exception. If the girl was a groupie, which was the lowest rung on the puss ladder, she had probably been out with other ballplayers as well. If she was a hooker or a topless dancer, that was much better, because all she wanted was to show off her equipment and get laid by fame. She wasn't trying to corral some guy. Some of the groupies were hoping that maybe they'd strike lightning and make it with a player who would fall in love with her. It didn't happen very often, though it has happened. Would *you* marry a girl who has opened her legs for fifteen or twenty other ballplayers? Like I say, it happened.

The guy who marries her is too blind or stupid to know.

I can remember one time I was dating this really beautiful girl when the team played in Detroit. She was a model. In the middle of the season one of the Baltimore Orioles pitchers got traded to the Yankees, and when we arrived in Detroit, I had a date with her, and when I came into the bar she was sitting with this guy traded over from Baltimore. I looked up at him and asked, "What are you doing here?"

He said, "What are you doing here?"

The girl said, "Oh, my God."

We sat and talked and I found out both of us were dating her. When the Orioles came to town, she went out with him. But that happens.

Whatever team you play on, most guys end up at the same bars. In Detroit it was the Lindell Athletic Club. In Cleveland you went down to The Flats. In Boston, we used to go to King's Row. In New York the visiting players went to Maxwell's Plum or Tittle Tattle. Everyone knew where to go. It was a secret shared among the baseball people. The clubby knew. It was kept secret from the guys of the outside world—though the girls somehow all knew.

She may have been dating a guy from the Red Sox and another guy from the Indians for all I knew or cared. Obviously, she liked ballplayers. But if she was a great-looking girl, and I enjoyed being seen with her, and she liked spending the night with me, I didn't care who she was with after I left town. She made the days spent in Detroit a little bit nicer. Without her, I might not have hit all those long home runs in Tiger Stadium.

What's the difference between a dentist and a gynecologist? The teeth.

Why did the gynecologist go to the eye doctor? Everything was looking fuzzy to him.

Very funny. So what happened when Billy came back?

Because of Billy, we ended up winning the '55 pennant, and again we faced the Dodgers in the World Series. I had torn a thigh muscle and sat on the bench the last two weeks of the season. Hank Bauer tore a thigh muscle in the second game of the Series, and so Casey had to use two rookies, Ellie Howard and Bob Cerv, while we could only sit and watch.

The Dodgers won three of the first five games, but Whitey pitched a beautiful game to tie the Series at three each. If Hank and I could have played in the seventh game, we would have won it for sure. Johnny Podres started for the Dodgers. I had batted against Podres in Game Three and hit a home run that cleared the center field wall in Ebbets Field. Podres had a good fastball and a good change, but he was nothing special. I don't think he won ten games all season. All afternoon I sat on the bench wishing I could play. In the sixth inning we were losing 2–0 when Billy led off and worked Podres for a walk. Gil McDougald singled him to second. Yogi was the batter. We all felt Yogi would hit one out, and we'd be champs again.

We had beaten the Dodgers in '41, '47, '49, '52, and '53. The Dodgers were a mediocre ball club compared to us. Their pitching was fair. Roy Campanella was a great player, and Duke Snider had good power, but the rest of the team was only fair. Jackie Robinson was over the hill, and Pee Wee Reese was okay, and Carl Furillo had a real good throwing arm in right. Gil Hodges couldn't hit, and I can't even remember who was playing second and third and left. If Hank and I had been healthy, the '55 Series would have been over in five games.

Yogi was looking for the change, and Podres threw him an outside fastball. Swinging late, he sliced the ball down the left-field line. The ball was headed for the seats. As I watched from the dugout, the only question was whether the ball would bounce into the seats or go straight in for a home run.

Playing in left was a journeyman outfielder by the name of Sandy Amoros, who I had never heard of before. Why the Dodgers manager, Walter Alston, put him out there I never did know, because Yogi usually pulled the ball to right field, and what did he need a lefty outfielder in there for? Didn't make any sense. It's fifty-some-odd years later, and it still doesn't make any sense. But Amoros raced after the ball, and just before he reached the seats, he caught Yogi's ball. Being left-handed, Amoros was just able to stick out his right hand and catch it. The runners were sure it would be a hit, so they were on their horses, and after Amoros threw the ball back in, Gil was almost to third when he had to turn around and head back to first. The throw beat him to the bag, a double play. When the next batter grounded out to end the inning, our big chance had gone.

For the rest of the game we sat on the bench mumbling how that motherfucker Alston, who couldn't manage a meat market, had gotten lucky when he put Amoros in the game. "No way anyone else catches that ball," we kept saying over and over, and we were still saying it after the game ended with us losing 2–0.

After the game Billy and I both sobbed. I couldn't believe we had lost the World Series to the pathetic Dodgers. How would we live it down? Billy was bawling, and when he entered the locker room he began punching the lockers with his fists, making them bloody. I just felt so bad. I felt I had let my teammates down, let Casey down, let the city of New York down. Losing to the Dodgers was an absolute disgrace. They may have been National League champs, but as a team they couldn't hold our jocks.

Even now, here in heaven, when I think about losing to the Dodgers in '55, my stomach turns.

But think of all the Dodgers fans you made happy that day. Poor bastards, little did they know that Walter O'Malley was going to take their team away from them two years later. Don't you think they were entitled to a little joy and happiness, Mick?

(Several of the men standing around them are nodding in agreement.)

I hated to lose, Lenny. I especially hated to lose to teams that had no business beating us, like the '55 Dodgers and the fucking lucky Pirates in '60. Podres had no business throwing a shutout, and Amoros had no business even being out there. We never should have lost to Brooklyn. Never. Never. Never. Campy wasn't as good as Yogi. Pee Wee wasn't as good as Scooter. Podres wasn't as good as Whitey. And Alston wasn't in Casey's league, which in this case was the major league.

And I suppose you were better than Snider in center?

As Casey used to say, Len, you can look it up. Look how long it took for Snider to make it into the goddamn Hall of Fame. That's not me saying it—that was you guys—the writers.

Okay, fair enough. Now was 1955 the year you went to Japan?

Unfortunately. We had played 154 games in the regular season and seven games in the Series, but we still weren't allowed to go home. Weiss had scheduled twenty-four games for us to play in Japan. None of us wanted to go, but the Yankees said we could all take our wives. Since Merlyn was pregnant again, she stayed home.

Once we arrived in Japan, Billy and Whitey and I drank hard and played hard the whole time—my thigh had healed up pretty good. We went to the geisha houses, which we thought were bordellos, but they weren't. The ceremony of getting your back rubbed was very nice but too tame for us.

Billy and I headed for the fancy whorehouses for some prime Japanese puss. A girl cost about ten bucks back then. They'd stand in a row wearing those pretty, colored robes that were open down the middle, and you'd walk along, and if you saw a girl you liked, you bowed in front of her. Billy asked the madam the age of her youngest girl. Billy was told she was sixteen. "I want her," Billy said. The girl came forward, and when she opened her robe so Billy could see what he was buying, I could see that she barely had breasts. Billy went off with her anyway.

I picked the most exquisite little Japanese girl you can imagine. I love girls who are short but who have big breasts, and this one little girl was about five-one and she was shapely and beautiful, and she was about the sweetest girl I ever met. She told me she would take off my clothes, and when she did, she made a big show of how impressed she was with the size of my dick. She took my hand and led me to a pool of hot water, and I got in, and she got in beside me and rubbed soap all over me, washed my armpits and my crotch. She then led me to a small room with a bamboo mat and she invited me to lie down on it. She began to sweetly sing to me in Japanese, and then she rubbed an aphrodisiac that smelled of rose petals over my entire body. She served me sake, which didn't hit me until the third glass. I asked if she would do Mickey-san the honor of taking off her robe. She did, and I was staring at perfection. And if you're wondering whether the pubic hairs of Japanese girls are straight, they aren't. They are as wonderfully curly and enticing as those of American girls.

But unlike a lot of American hookers, who were only interested in getting it over and getting out of there, this girl made me feel as though I was the king of the universe, as though everything she was doing she was doing just for me, that everything she was doing she was doing because it made her so happy to please me, and not because I was a baseball star. Unlike most American girls I slept with, this girl made it seem that she was actually enjoying the experience, that she really wanted to be doing this.

Now maybe this was an act, but if it was, she was sure convincing. She asked if I had ever tried the lotus position for lovemaking, and I shook my head, and then she had me sit up, and she did the same, and she showed me how we could make love facing each other in such a way that I would penetrate deep inside her, and I must say in that position, I felt we were joined in a very spiritual way. While I was moving back and forth inside her she gasped often and praised my manhood. When I began to have an orgasm, she squeezed my balls with her delicate fingers in a way that produced the most exquisite sensation I have ever experienced. I literally shrieked with ecstasy. When we were done, I was wishing I never had to leave that little room with the bamboo mat.

"Can I see you again?" I asked her.

"You have to see mama-san," she said demurely, reminding me that this hadn't been a date but rather an encounter I had paid money for. Over the next seven days I paid for her six or seven more times. And each time I felt the exact same way, that I was the most incredible lover she had ever had. I certainly felt that way about her.

She was so fabulous that I seriously considered quitting the Yankees, signing with the Tokyo Giants, and moving in with this girl. Billy was the one who talked me out of it. He told me I was nuts. "You're gonna move to Japan to live with a hooker?" he asked. "You've got a wife, a kid, a kid on the way, and a contract. What do you think George Weiss would do? You want to start World War III?"

Billy was so concerned I was serious, he concocted a fake telegram, informing me I better go home cause my wife was having the baby. (David wasn't born for another two months.) I fell for it and flew home. I was really furious at the time, but looking back, I can see that Billy saved my career and my marriage. If I had stayed another couple of days, I'd have bought that little Japanese girl outright and lived with her forever in Japan.

When I went back to the States, it was back to the good old Protestant missionary position, back to the girls who wanted to fuck me just because it was an opportunity to tell their girlfriends they had had sex with The Mick. Not that I'm complaining, mind you. When you're all alone on the road and you've had a few drinks, and a really cute girl gives you the eye in the bar, and you're wondering to yourself, I wonder if she'll let me pull her skirt up and fuck her from the back? Then she comes up and says hi, and you ask her if she'd like to go back to your room with you, and she says yes. And when you get there, you ask her if she would do you a favor, and she says, "Anything." And you say to her, "You are incredibly beautiful, and I am turned on more than you can know. Would you do me the great pleasure of taking off all your clothes?" And she goes for that first garment, and your heart races.

And I watch intently, because not all girls take their clothes off the same way. Some girls take off their skirt first, and others start by taking off their blouse. Some girls leave their shoes on, and others take them off. Some girls like to pretend they are doing a striptease, twirling each garment and throwing it around the room. Some take off their own undies, and others will insist that you do it. Some aren't wearing any.

Any way she does it is fine with me. I'm not picky. Some turn around so I can see their attributes, modest or impressive, and others ask if there is anything special I'd like them to do.

Always, they smile. Several ask if I want to spank them first. I am happy to oblige.

"Be gentle," some say. "Be rough," say others. Some of the other shouts prior to intercourse that I can remember were "Ride 'em tiger," "Hop on, Hopalong," "Ramming speed," "Fill 'er up," and there was even one chubby girl from Washington who said to me, "Chuck her in there, Stobbs." And in I'd go, the cavalry to the rescue. I never went unsatisfied.

When you're twenty-four, life is an endless parade of passing puss.

And every single one of them was special and memorable. I never once ever regretted putting my dick in that special spot. Even after I had puss after puss after puss after puss after puss.

I always looked forward to the next one. Every morning of my life after I became a genuine American hero, I would wake up wondering, What new puss is in store for me today?

What a life!

You had the season of your career in 1956. Did it change your life very much?

Whatever fame I had achieved before 1956, you could have multiplied that by a hundred after the season I had. I was twenty-five years old, still a shy, scared hayseed wet behind my ears, and all of a sudden I couldn't go past a newsstand without seeing my picture on the cover of a magazine, couldn't go anywhere without a crowd rushing up to me. It became impossible to go anywhere—to eat in a restaurant, to go to the movies, to do much of anything, without people coming up and asking for my autograph or wanting to talk baseball, which ordinarily I do not like to do because most of the time talking baseball is just so much hot air.

Some players crave the attention. I hated it. Always did. I never learned how to handle the attention. That year I became a prisoner of my fame. I had to stay in my hotel room, killing the day until it was time to go to the ballpark, wishing I could be left alone, like everyone else.

There was nothing you could do?

Over the years I thought a lot about it, but I never could figure out a way to keep the public away. Everybody recognized me, even the few times I tried going out wearing a disguise.

You wore a disguise?

Once I tried wearing fake glasses and a beard, but people seemed to know me just by the way I walked, and I got mobbed for autographs anyway. They told me they dug the disguise, then asked for autographs. I really wish I could have been more like Muhammad Ali, who treated every fan who came up to him like a long-lost friend. One time I was with Ali at a banquet, and I watched as a steady stream of people came up and shook his hand or asked for an autograph, and Ali smiled and joked with them and acted like he was happy to see them the whole night. As I watched him, I wondered why I couldn't be that way. But as much as I wanted to be like that, I just couldn't.

Why not? Just be nice. How hard could it have been?

It wasn't that easy. Being in a crowd made me very nervous. Male strangers frightened me. Kids made me uncomfortable because I never knew what to say to them. It goes back to what I was saying: why would people want to be in my company just because I could hit a baseball? I couldn't make myself understand.

You were their hero.

I never asked to be their hero. I didn't want to be their hero. To me, I was just another guy trying to make a living. I was paranoid about what people wanted from me, and I just didn't know how to handle the situation. Plus, a lot of people can be a pain in the ass. Once they corner you, they don't ever want to leave you alone. We called the pests "green flies," like what buzzed around the piles of cow shit in the fields back in Oklahoma. Like you guys hanging around and listening now—no offense, fellas.

The men surrounding their table look at their feet and shift in their seats, but no one leaves.

• • •

So you reacted by acting surly? That's no way to be.

I was trying to scare them away, to get rid of them the only way I knew how. How would you like it if I cornered you while you were eating lunch and started asking you a bunch of questions?

I'd probably have answered a couple of their questions.

I tried that, but then after I'd say, "Excuse me, I'd like to finish my lunch," the guy would get all huffy and unload on me for being so rude. This way I just skipped the middle part. That's why so many people who met me back then remember me as being a prick. I feel bad about it, but at the same time if I had to do it over again, I don't know that I could have done any different. I wanted people to respect my privacy, and this was the only way I knew to do that.

Didn't you want people to like you? Everyone wants people to like them.

I really didn't give a shit. I just wanted them to leave me alone. Fortunately, baseball and my nightlife kept me sane.

You were baseball's biggest star in 1956.

It was one of my two greatest seasons. Whenever I look back at my life and want to relive some of my happiest memories on the ball field, I think about that year a lot. Despite my leg injuries, I could still run to first base in just over three seconds, ran like the wind in the outfield, could hit a baseball farther than anyone else, and after the games were over—party time. I also had an MVP year.

Do you remember your statistics that year?

Of course I do, but you need to understand that statistics never meant jack shit to me like they did to some other players, like Pete Rose, who probably remembers every hit he ever got, or Joe D, who could talk in great detail about every hit he got off which pitcher during his fifty-six-game hitting streak. Maybe Joe didn't need friends because he always had his statistics to keep him company. It was Joe's fate to live in the past. He had his hallowed streak, and he had his memories of Marilyn, and he worked very hard to keep them both alive. Like me, Joe went from card show to card show signing autographs and taking home piles of cash from a generation of people who never saw him play but who saw him more as an investment than as a hero. I did that, too, but the difference was that that was Joe's whole life. He needed to do it in order to remind himself how important he still was. I did it because it paid my bills.

Mick, let me list your '56 statistics for you. You led the American League in just about everything. That year you batted .352, nine points higher than Ted Williams. You hit fifty-two home runs, twenty more than Vic Wertz, drove in 130 runs, two more than Al Kaline, and scored 132 runs, twenty-three more than Nellie Fox. In addition to your winning the Triple Crown, you were the Most Valuable Player and you won the Hickok award, given to the top professional athlete in America. Say what you want, but that's pretty damn good.

Everyone made such a big fuss about that year, but if you want to know the truth, I could have done a whole lot better than that if I hadn't hurt my leg in September. I probably would have broken Babe Ruth's record of sixty home runs in a season, because by mid-July I had thirty-five home runs, including my most famous home run of all off Pedro Ramos of the Washington Senators. It was during a Memorial Day doubleheader, and I hit one left-handed, which I really thought was going to be the first fair ball ever hit out of Yankee Stadium.

I was there that day. I remember the ball hit the façade in right field above the third deck.

I bet it didn't miss going out by two feet. Ramos had a great curve ball, but I was figuring he would throw me a fastball to get ahead in the count, and he threw it right where I expected it, and I swung from my heels.

That baby would have gone six hundred feet if it had cleared the top of the stadium.

I know it. I couldn't believe it myself. I really hit the shit out of that ball. Understand, when you do something like that, it's like you're a spectator along with everyone else. I watched the ball rise up just like the rest of the people sitting in the stands. The only difference between them and me was that when the ball finally hit the filigree of the roof, I still had to run around the bases.

You guys ran away with it in '56. Not much of a pennant race.

We took the lead in early May and never lost it. We were so good that when we went out there onto the field none of us ever expected to lose a single game. Whitey won almost every game he pitched, it seemed, and whoever else went out there was usually better than the guy we were facing. Yogi was the best catcher in baseball, and he drove in over a hundred runs. Billy kept everyone on his toes, and Casey was the best manager in baseball. We were a well-oiled machine.

Of course, despite all our success, that cocksucker George Weiss made sure to let us know that no matter how good we were, we always could be replaced. On Old Timers' Day, in late August, the Yankees invited Lefty Gomez, Red Ruffing, Red Rolfe, and all the living guys who played for manager Joe McCarthy in the 1930s and early 1940s. Phil Rizzuto, whose first manager was McCarthy, was still on the Yankees. He had played with a lot of the Old Timers. Rizzuto was a great shortstop and a great little guy. He was probably the best shortstop the Yankees ever had, until Derek Jeter came along.

Phil was very superstitious. He was afraid of spiders and snakes and bugs, and we loved to go to the novelty stores on Broadway and buy rubber snakes and fake bugs, and we'd put them in his glove between innings and wait and watch to see what would happen. Phil would grab his glove and run out to shortstop, and he'd put his hand in the glove, and the next thing you knew, he'd throw that thing fifty feet into the air, screaming and hollering in front of all those fans and holding up the game. We'd be laughing like a son of a bitch.

One time Tom Sturdivant put a live lobster in Phil's uniform pants. Fortunately for Phil, Sturdy didn't remove the rubber bands around the claws.

Phil put on the lobsterless pant leg first. We were watching. Nothing happened. Then he pushed his other leg into the other pant leg, and that's when he discovered something spiny and cold and wet wriggling around in his trousers. Phil led out a loud yell, and when he found he couldn't get his leg out, he began to panic. We rolled on the floor laughing while Phil ripped those pants to shreds getting them off.

Back to Old Timers' Day. Before the game, Weiss called Phil into Casey's office in the clubhouse. Weiss began by telling Phil that he had been an important part of a lot of Yankee pennants. "But," he said, "a couple of left-handed bats are hurting, and I acquired Enos Slaughter from Kansas City to fill in until they can get healthy. Someone has to go. Any suggestions?"

Phil named about seven guys, bench guys, relief guys, players who he thought the Yankees could afford to let go, and each time Weiss shook his head no and gave him a reason why. Finished with the list, Phil suddenly realized there was only one other player left who hadn't been mentioned: Phil himself. Here it was Old Timers' Day, and now Phil was one of them.

We never imagined the Yankees would be so coldhearted as to let him go in the middle of the season. And certainly not on Old Timers' Day. The timing seemed cruel.

Phil cleaned out his locker in tears and disappeared, ending a long, illustrious career. He was smart enough to know to keep his mouth shut, and the next year the Yankees brought him back as our announcer, and he broadcast Yankees games for the next thirty-five years. "Holy Cow!" Along with Mel Allen, Phil was the Voice of the Yankees.

Weiss was tough. He ran the team like a business, not a hobby like Tom Yawkey and his Red Sox or Phil Wrigley and his Cubs. Weiss made money, and he won pennants.

Weiss always wanted us to be aware of what a heartless prick he was, wanted us to play scared, to realize we were only a phone call away from being traded or released, and I'd have to say his tactics were very effective. Even though I was the highest-paid player, I know I was *way* underpaid. For all the fannies I put in the seats, the Yankees could have paid me triple and still would have gotten me cheap. But this was long before the coming of player agents or free agency, and I was making plenty to live on, so I was happy. Plus, I never felt I was anything special, so when Weiss sent me a contract, usually I'd just sign it and send it back. I never got too upset because I was just happy to be playing baseball.

Billy, on the other hand, hated the way Weiss treated us, and he carried with him a deep resentment of Weiss and his power. Of course, Billy didn't make near the money I made. Billy and I would talk about Weiss all the time. His very first year Billy had been sent down to the minors by Weiss. Billy, in tears, went to see Casey, who wanted him to remain on the team. Billy asked Casey what to do, and Casey told Billy to go to Weiss's office and talk to him. Casey should have known better. When Weiss refused to budge, Billy got mad and reamed him a new asshole. Weiss never forgot or forgave. For all his toughness, Billy more than anything just wanted to be loved, and Weiss always made it a point to let him know how little he thought of him.

Billy would say to me, "What more does the son of a bitch want from me? I won two World Series for him. I helped him win a bunch of pennants. Why does he hate me so much?"

How can you wonder why anyone hated Billy? I know he was your friend, but you weren't blind, Mick. He was a despicable little bastard. Every sportswriter in New York hated him. Me included.

Billy never thought sportswriters should have that much power. Billy thought sportswriters should be cheerleaders, like Arthur Daley or Milton Shapiro.

Or Drebby.

Or Drebby. Yeah, you've got a point. Billy wasn't going to put up with you, or Jimmy Cannon, or Stan Isaac. But Billy never understood the downside of making enemies. He was the worst politician I ever knew. He only knew one way to approach a problem: if someone was standing in his way, he would go right through him. With Weiss, Billy figured he was safe because he was Casey's boy, and Casey would always protect him. But Weiss was Casey's *boss*, and Casey didn't tell Weiss what to do. Weiss told Casey what to do, and Billy should have realized that. Not knowing who was boss was a problem Billy had his whole life, especially after he started managing. He would always find a way to piss off the guy who signed his paycheck or decided his fate. Billy hated authority, and he seemed to go out of his way to offend that person. Then he'd get fired, and he'd wonder why. You'd see him on TV crying.

Part of that was because Billy was always afraid he was going to get fired, and his fears would make him a little crazy. Once he thought he was going to get fired, he then figured as long as he was going to get fired, he might as well take his best shot before getting canned. Half the time his best shot was the thing that ended up getting him fired.

I thought you were an Oklahoma hayseed. You're not as dumb as you look.

Thanks, Lenny. I think. But you're right. I know what I saw. Billy avoided George Weiss whenever possible. Except for that one time his rookie year, Billy rarely said a word to Weiss, who was one of the few people Billy genuinely was afraid of. All through 1955 and 1956 Billy would say to me, "Weiss is going to trade me to Kansas City, you watch." I'd say, "What are you talking about? You're our regular second baseman. You're the guy who makes us go. Casey loves you. Don't talk crazy."

"Weiss hates me," Billy would say. "He's always hated me. As soon as he can find someone who plays as good as me, I'm gone." And there would be tears in his eyes, especially if he had been drinking. I'd listen to this crazy talk and shake my head. But that's the funny thing about paranoid people. It's not paranoia if people really are out to get you.

In the end Billy knew what he was talking about.

Billy didn't have much of an education, but he was a lot smarter than anyone ever gave him credit for.

You said you got hurt in '56. How did that happen?

I lost my chance to catch the Babe in early September when I pulled a groin muscle running the bases. I played hurt, because I wanted the record and because I never wanted to let my teammates down by not playing, but the rest of the year I hit like shit and I started swinging at bad pitches like I used to, and I'd kick that metal water cooler so hard it was a wonder I didn't break my toes.

Despite my playing lousy, we clinched the pennant in mid-September, Casey's seventh pennant in eight years with the Yankees. When we won, we barely shook each other's hands. We were so used to winning pennants that we took it for granted. So did our fans, which was why the Dodgers and Giants fans hated Yankees fans so much. Our fans knew we were going to win. Their fans could only hope and pray.

You still had a really great season.

Yeah, but Casey still found a way to sour it for me. After the season, a reporter asked Casey who he thought was the better player, Joe DiMaggio or me. After the year I had, I was sure Casey would say me, but the son of a bitch said DiMaggio was better. He said something dumb like, "DiMaggio didn't need a manager. My guy does." Now what the fuck did he mean by that? And how could he have picked DiMaggio over me knowing that Joe had always hated his guts? It was like I was back home hitting baseballs against my dad. "Can't you do any better than that, son?"

Your father figures had mean streaks.

What was it about me that caused them to treat me like that?

I doubt if it had anything to do with you, Mick. Sounds to me like you just had bad luck. There's a lot of meanness in the world. Could it be Casey was just trying to use psychology to make you play better by goading you?

He was. It was his way of telling me not to get a swelled head, but I didn't need a slap in the face to make me play better. A pat on the back would have worked just as well. I was really disgusted when I read what Casey had said. Casey let outsiders think he was this funny old story-telling clown, but as far as how he treated me, he could be a real prick. Nothing I ever did for that bastard was good enough for him. I thought to myself, *Fuck Joe DiMaggio and fuck you too, Case.* I would have daydreams of playing for the White Sox or the Indians or even the Senators, so I could get up against the Yankees and beat him with a long home run just so I could run around the bases and have the last laugh. For a long time after reading what Casey said, I would daydream that after hitting a home run I'd be shouting, "Ha! Ha! Ha! Let your fucking Joe DiMaggio catch that one!"

You took out your anger on the Dodgers in the World Series.

It was our chance to avenge '55. Two of the stars of that series were Tom Sturdivant and Don Larsen, guys I loved to hang with because, like me, they were drinkers and knew how to live life to the fullest.

We called Sturdivant Flakey. He was a pitcher who was at his best when he was angry, so Casey and Billy did everything they could to keep him pissed off out there on the mound. Billy would yell at him from second base that he couldn't have broken a pane of glass with the shit he was throwing, and Casey would go out to the mound and call him a "Dumb Dutchman." Casey would say to him, "To what do you attribute your record?" And Tom would say, "My fastball. It's my best pitch." And Casey would say, "Son, when are you going to throw it?" And Tom would seethe, and he would throw smoke.

Tommy loved to laugh, have a good time, party, play practical jokes. When we went on the road, he enjoyed dropping water balloons on the guests from his hotel window. One time in Kansas City he called me up on the phone and told me to fill my wastepaper basket with water and bring it up to his room. I did as I was told.

We were staying at the Muehlebach, a very fancy hotel. When I walked into Flakey's room, I found seven of my Yankee teammates there along with Tommy, all with their wastepaper baskets filled with water. The room was on the fourth floor, above the main entrance door, and as the guests walked out of the building, Tommy would dump the water out, duck back inside laughing like a hyena, and then peek out the window to view the outrage of the fancy-pants guests below. We never did get caught, though one time Casey looked at Sturdy and asked him if he knew why so many guests were getting rained on. Sturdy looked Case right in the eye and said no. The rest of us were laughing like hell.

But Casey never said anything because Sturdy had a great year in '56. For two seasons, '56 and '57, he was as good as any pitcher in the league.

He had a good riding fastball that he threw up and in, and a dinky little slider that he threw outside, and he told me that what he tried to do was get the batters to hit fly balls to me in center. I swear I ran so many miles chasing balls hit off Sturdy that I could have played another five years if he hadn't been pitching for us.

But after those two great seasons, he hurt his arm, which was a shame, because he was a great guy and deserved better.

Sturdy won Game 4 of the '56 series. Don Larsen pitched the next day. What do you remember about that fifth game?

After Whitey and Larsen lost the first two games of the Series, Whitey came back and won Game 3, and then Sturdy beat Carl Erskine in Game 4. Billy drove in the winning run, and I hit a long home run to put it away. It was one of the best games Sturdivant ever pitched, but we started calling him "Queen for a Day," because the next afternoon Don Larsen, who we called "Gooney Bird," and who called everyone "Baby Doll," pitched the only perfect game in World Series history. "Gooney" should have been the last person to have done that.

Two years before he lost twenty-one games pitching for the Baltimore Orioles.

That was a really bad ball club. He was good when we got him, but he was never great. He was like me, never took the game seriously. But without my talent. His first spring training with us he crashed his car into a pole at five in the morning. He told everyone he had gotten up early to begin his workout. We really chuckled when he said that. Gooney hadn't gone to bed yet, and he was driving back to the motel. Casey never fined him a red cent. Casey understood. As long as he pitched well, which he did, Casey didn't give a shit what Don was doing during his free time. But no one would have bet ten cents that he could have or would have done what he did, even with two outs in the ninth. I don't think anyone in his right mind would have. But Don had developed the no-windup delivery, and he had started pitching really well in September, so . . .

Talk about the game and the day.

Ask any Yankee fan who remembers October 8, 1956, and he'll tell you what a great day it was. It was a vivid memory for all of us because that might well have been the greatest game in Yankee, if not baseball, history. That day the Yankees were perfect in every way, especially our pitching and fielding, which was what Casey stressed most.

How close did the Dodgers come to getting a hit?

There was a play in the second inning where Jackie Robinson hit a ground ball wide of third that Andy Carey nicked with his glove. The ball bounced over to Gil McDougald at short, and Gil threw Robinson out by a step. It was a great play, but of course we had no idea how important it was at the time he made it.

Don kept getting them out, but so did Sal Maglie, who was mean and smart. In the fourth inning he threw me a fastball up a little too much, and I hit the ball into the stands for a home run. It was all Don needed.

The next inning I made the most famous catch of my career. People remember it because it saved Don's perfect game. Gil Hodges pulled a ball to deep left center. I went back for it, and as I did I swore to myself I would crash into the wall to get it if I had to, not because of the perfect game, but because we were only ahead 1–0, and we needed to win the game. I caught the ball with my gloved hand raised high just as I reached the warning track. I never thought it was any big deal. You see, baseball really is a very simple game. You run after the ball. You catch the ball. That's all I did, really.

Are you serious?

Very. We went back into the dugout, and I bumped into Larsen, who was smoking a cigarette in the runway leading back to our clubhouse.

"Do you think I'll make it," that crazy Gooney Bird asked me. I refused to talk to him and walked away.

So you believe in that silly superstition that you don't mention your pitcher is throwing a no-hitter in the middle of the game?

He made it, didn't he? What I remember most about that game was the deafening silence in jam-packed Yankee Stadium as Don went out to the mound to start the ninth inning. It was so quiet you could hear the wind blowing. Out in center field, my only concern was the smoke billowing from the stands. When you look back, it seemed that everyone smoked cigarettes then, and the accumulation of smoke gave the Stadium a shimmering haze that made it hard to see the ball sometimes.

Quickly, somebody flew out to Hank Bauer in right, and then Campy grounded out to Billy for the second out. A lot of people forget that Billy was the second baseman that day. One of the most famous photos in baseball history is the one of the field and the right-field scoreboard just before Don threw the last pitch. Standing at second behind Don was Billy.

After two were out, the tension became unbearable. I wanted very badly for Don to get the final out because it was our chance not only to beat the Dodgers, but to humiliate them for all time. There was no love lost between the Dodgers and the Yankees. The writers always made the Dodgers out to be the good guys, the underdogs, the people's team—I guess because of Robinson, and they portrayed us as corporate bullies, the emotionless robots who kicked ass. Weiss was certainly like that, but the players weren't. As far as Billy, Whitey, and I were concerned, we were the good guys, and of course Billy saw himself as the lovable underdog. Plus, Billy was always comparing himself to Jackie Robinson, and he hated it that the writers and the fans always gave Jackie the edge.

"How many fucking World Series did he win?" Billy would say to me. Billy had won four and was about to win his fifth. Robinson had won exactly one, and he had been lucky to have won that one. But what did you fucking writers know? You never played the game.

You can't tell me with a straight face that Billy was a better player than Jackie. Jackie was a Hall of Fame ballplayer. He was the quickest base runner who ever lived. Billy was a mediocre player on a great team.

Like hell he was. Billy was as important to the Yankees as Robinson was to the Dodgers.

Hey, Mick, Jackie Robinson was perhaps the most exciting baseball player in the history of this game. You can't tell me with a straight face Billy was as good.

Hey, Lenny, we won World Series rings with Billy in 1951, 1952, 1953, and 1956. How many rings does Robinson have? One. And he shouldn't have gotten that one. Goddamn Sandy Amoros. A career minor leaguer. Son of a bitch.

Calm down, Mick. We can argue this from now until the end of time. Tell me about the final out of the Larsen game.

Dale Mitchell, a veteran who had played for Cleveland for many years until coming over to the Dodgers to give them a left-handed bat in the Series, came up as a pinch hitter. The year before, Walter Alston had put Sandy Amoros in as a substitute left fielder, and Amoros had won the game and the Series. This time Alston, who may have been the most boring push-button manager who ever put on a uniform, was hoping Mitchell would make him look smart again.

The first pitch was a ball. Then Don threw a called strike, and then Mitchell swung and missed. I remember a large airplane flew overhead, drowning out the crowd noise. Larsen then threw a pitch which looked a little outside from out in center field, but the home plate umpire, Babe Pinelli, called it a strike, and the game was over. It was the last pitch Pinelli ever called. And it was the last pitch Mitchell ever saw. They both retired after the Series.

Gooney had done it! He had pitched a perfect game! And anyone who saw it will remember Yogi jumping into his arms, and Yogi had to jump pretty high because Don was a big guy. Don carried him from the mound to the foul line until the rest of us could get to them and dump them to the ground as we made a big pile of bodies. We were cheering as loud as the fans. We were stunned. It isn't often that you know immediately that you've gone down in history.

That put you up three games to two, right?

Yes. We had to win one more game. The next day Bob Turley pitched another great game, but the Dodgers won 1–0 in ten innings when Enos

Slaughter in left allowed a line drive hit by Robinson to go over his head. Slaughter said he lost it in the sun when it left the bat. The shadows in left made playing there awfully tough, but Billy was furious that Stengel had even played Slaughter, who he called "that National League bobo," and told him so.

"Who would you play?" Casey asked Billy.

"You better play Ellie in left and get Moose back in there at first," said Billy. Even then, Casey knew Billy had what it took to be a great manager. "I taught the bastard everything I knowed," Casey would say.

And that's what Casey did, and we beat the snot out of the Dodgers in that final seventh game, 9–0. Moose hit a grand slam and Yogi hit two homers, and Johnny Kucks, who pitched the best game of his short career, shut them out.

After that final game, I felt happy, because we had won. Billy and I celebrated by going out and getting very drunk. The season was over. I couldn't wait for spring training to roll around again.

Did you spend the off-season with your family?

I was home for Christmas. I always made it a point to be home for Christmas. But after the Series I was invited to so many banquets and awards dinners and I was signed up to do so many commercials and appearances that I wasn't home very much. I felt I owed it to myself to earn as much extra dough as I could. So I wasn't home very much.

You had another excellent year in '57.

For me, it was one of the worst. Not that I hit badly—I hit .365, but after I hurt my leg in a golfing accident, I only hit 34 home runs and failed to drive in a hundred runs, so I felt I had let the team down, and, of course, 1957 was the year the Yankees traded Billy away, and I lost the best friend I ever had. Baseball was never as much fun again.

How in the world did you hurt yourself playing golf?

To be honest with you, I guess I shouldn't call it a golfing accident. Rather, it was a golfing cart accident.

Billy and I were playing a round of golf in St. Pete during spring training. We each rented a golf cart, and at first we were happy just to race the carts to our next shots, but Billy started to get pissed because my golf cart was faster—they never should have allowed Billy to drive anything—by the seventh hole, he decided it would be more fun to play bumper cars than play golf. At full speed he faked right like he was going to drive away from me, but then he turned left and rammed right into the side of my cart, tipping it over. I fell onto the ground, and the cart fell on top of my leg. I suffered sprained ligaments in my left foot and never was right all season long.

Did you ever think that this was one reason Weiss thought Billy was a bad influence on you?

It was an accident. I should have been paying attention. He didn't injure me on purpose.

What did you tell the Yankees?

I had to make up a story. I told Casey I had stepped in a hole during fielding practice. I didn't think he believed me, but Billy and I were the only ones who knew, and we weren't telling anyone.

I didn't play much during spring training, and when I finally took the field in April, I was limping badly. Billy, meanwhile, was approaching thirty, and during a wrestling match we were having one night in his room at the Soreno Hotel, Billy sprained his neck. He also suffered from tonsillitis, and then he missed a few games after getting beaned, and all the while Casey was playing this young kid by the name of Bobby Richardson at second, and Billy would point to Bobby and say to me, "That's the guy who's going to replace me. That's him." I told Billy he was being ridiculous. What did I know?

Despite my injury, Billy, Whitey, and I continued to play golf all through spring training. That was the year I discovered how great golf was. I could spend three or four hours competing in almost complete privacy. I could sit in the golf cart until the golfers ahead of us teed off, and I could relax with my friends without having to worry about gawkers and green flies. And I could hit a driver 300 yards. I held the club down at the end and let her rip. Of course, the ball almost never went straight. I could go through twenty balls in a round and never think twice about it. But there was something about golf that Whitey, Billy, and I all loved, and that spring we went out and played whenever we could.

One time I even skipped practice to play. Whitey had the day off because pitchers and catchers were excused, but I needed an excuse, so I told Casey I had a stomachache, and he gave me the whole day off.

Whitey and I headed for the golf course, and on the eighteenth hole, I noticed a short, balding man in a three-piece suit holding the flag. I said to Whitey, "Isn't that George Weiss?"

"It sure looks like George Weiss," Whitey said. Who else but Weiss, who dressed formally every day, would have been standing out on a golf course in a suit?

I didn't say a word as I holed out, while Weiss held the flag stick. Weiss asked, "How is your stomachache, Mickey?" I admit the man made me nervous, but by then I was a veteran. I didn't flinch.

"Eighteen holes is the best thing in the world for a stomachache, Mr. Weiss," I said, and Whitey and I left him standing there as we headed for the clubhouse. It's a wonder Weiss didn't trade me to Kansas City right then and there. But he didn't. He traded Billy instead.

Weiss had always complained to Casey about how bad an influence Billy was on me, and this was the year Weiss took the opportunity to split us up after an eventful evening at the Copacabana nightclub in New York.

What really happened that night? Didn't Billy punch out somebody that night?

The story of the fight at the Copa has become legend, but it never was reported right. If it had happened today, we'd have been viewed as heroes. The NAACP would have thrown a benefit for us, because we were defending the honor of Sammy Davis, Jr., one of the great entertainers of all time. But he was black, and this was 1957, during a time when blacks couldn't even stay in a hotel in New York. During the performance these two drunk Italian guys from a bowling party sitting near us started yelling racist shit at him in the middle of his performance. Back then, that happened all the time, and usually no one said boo about it. But we had heard all the racist junk from racist fans aimed at Elston Howard, our friend and our catcher, and it infuriated all of us. We didn't think Ellie had to put up with hearing it, and the same went for Sammy. So we decided to defend Sammy's honor, and that's when all hell broke loose.

Wasn't this an evening to celebrate Billy's birthday?

Yeah, timing is everything, and Billy had the worst timing. A group of us got together to celebrate Billy's twenty-ninth birthday. We picked May 15 to go out because originally we had an off-day the next day and we figured a late night wouldn't hurt anyone. But after we made the arrangements, we had a rainout, and the league scheduled us to play, which, looking back, made the whole thing seem worse than it was.

We really painted the town that night. Me, Whitey, Hank, Yogi, and John Kucks, a young pitcher, went with our wives, and Billy came by himself. We went to three nightclubs. We started with dinner at Danny's Hideaway; moved on to the Waldorf-Astoria, where we watched Johnny Ray sing "Rain"; and from there we went to the Copa.

We were treated royally. We were given a large table, and we were having a wonderful time as we toasted Billy and let him know how much we loved him.

Sammy really put on a terrific show. He sang and danced, talked to the audience, and told jokes. Right in the middle of a number, some drunk at the next table stood up and called Sammy a "jungle bunny." It made us all furious. "Shut the hell up," Hank Bauer told the guy.

"Make me shut up," the drunk yelled back. One of his buddies, a fat guy who was also drunk, chimed in, "Don't test your luck tonight, Yankee."

Billy, of course, jumped out of his chair and was more than ready to test his luck. He told the fat guy if he wanted to settle it, they could take it outside.

"Let's go," said the drunk.

Billy got up and headed out with the drunk right beside him. I trailed them, because I knew the poor slob was in for a bad beating. When the fat guy also got up, Hank Bauer went with him. Hank's wife tried to stop him, but Hank was beyond listening to anyone. Whitey and Yogi went after Hank. Too late.

Before Billy got his chance, Hank and the fat guy had gone into the men's room, and by the time Whitey and Yogi arrived, the guy had been beaten up real bad. Hank always swore that two Copa bouncers beat up the fat guy, but we really didn't believe that. Hank had been a Marine and had been wounded on Iwo Jima. If anyone could have pounded that guy to a pulp, it would have been Hank. And we were glad he did.

So before Billy could get into it with the other guy, we all decided it would be best to get the hell out of there, but our bad luck continued. Right after we headed out the back door of the kitchen to the street, who should walk into the Copa but Leonard Lyons, a gossip columnist for the *New York Post*. Lyons interviewed the fat guy who had been beat up. The guy told Lyons that Bauer had punched him without provocation. Fucking liar. But since we had already split, Lyons didn't get our side of the story.

We knew we were in deep shit the next morning when a crime reporter from the *Daily News* called Hank and said the fat guy was charging him with assault and battery. He wanted a comment. Hank hung up on him.

The newspaper had the words YANKEES and BRAWL in the headlines. George Weiss was beside himself with anger. He had spent most of his adult life building the Yankees into a respected institution, and here we were involved in a brawl in a nightclub after curfew on a night before a ball game.

Weiss called us all in and informed us that no matter what the papers said, he knew that Billy had hit the guy. Weiss wanted us to tell him why Billy did it.

That's a natural conclusion. Billy had the reputation for being a brawler. Why would Weiss think it was anyone else? And you had told Casey you were sick when you went and played golf. Why should Weiss believe any of you?

He didn't even believe Yogi! Weiss took him in a corner and asked him, "Please tell me what happened."

Yogi told him, "Nobody did nothing to nobody."

We had to go to court, but it didn't even take the DA an hour to drop all charges.

That should have been the end of it, but it wasn't. The bad publicity gave Weiss the opening to get rid of Billy, and he took full advantage. And there wasn't anything Casey could do about it this time. If Casey had threatened to quit, I suspect Weiss just might have let him go.

Weiss was the boss, whether Casey liked it or not, and besides, Casey—unlike Billy—was too smart and savvy to lock horns with the guy who was signing his paycheck. Casey loved Billy, but he wasn't about to cut his own throat to keep him after what had happened, not when he had a young player as talented as Bobby Richardson to replace him. After the Copa incident the season resumed, and we all waited and wondered whether any of us would survive the trade deadline of June 15.

Billy made matters worse in early June in a game against the White Sox. Larry Doby, the Chicago center fielder, had to eat dirt after an inside pitch by Art Ditmar, and Doby told Art if he ever did that again, he'd stick him with a knife. When Ditmar told Billy what Doby had said, Billy ran from the dugout onto the field and started swinging at Doby until they could be pulled apart.

Two days later, Billy was traded. In the middle of the game Casey started asking around to find out where Billy was. No one knew, because he was hiding out in the bullpen under the tarp. The trade deadline was midnight, and Billy figured if he could avoid being told about a trade until then, he'd be safe.

Midnight, unfortunately, came too late for Billy.

Billy was found, and he was told to see Casey in the dugout. After a long run down the right-field line, Billy went up to Casey, who told him, "Well, you're gone." Casey said a lot of nice things to him, but Billy was in such a state of shock he didn't hear a word of it.

In the dugout after the game Billy, Whitey, and I cried like babies. We couldn't believe the Yankees could do this to us. Casey hadn't wanted to lose Billy, but it wasn't his call, though Casey took it out on the guy we got from Kansas City for him, Suitcase Simpson. In protest, Casey refused to play him much, and he was traded back to Kansas City a year later.

"I'll play who I want," he said.

That night Billy, Whitey, and I went out and got very, very drunk. We talked about the good times, vented our anger at Weiss, and Billy vowed to get revenge. Whitey and I both knew that was bullshit. The only team Billy would ever care about was the Yankees, and when Weiss got rid of him, his career was as good as over. He played a few more years, as teams like Kansas City, Detroit, Cleveland, Cincinnati, and Minnesota got him in hopes his winning ways would rub off on their players, but away from the Yankees Billy was only a shell of himself. His motivation for playing his best was pleasing Casey and honoring the Yankee pinstripes. He played hard because he wanted Casey to be proud of him. After leaving Casey, he just went through the motions to earn a paycheck. Not only that, but players on bad teams aren't interested in hustling and playing hard the way Billy did, and a lot of those veterans just ignored Billy's rah-rah approach. It wasn't until he became a manager that Billy could make the other players follow his lead.

Billy blamed Casey for not doing everything in his power to keep him on the team. "He should have threatened to quit," said Billy, "but he didn't." And Billy didn't talk to Casey again for a long, long time—almost ten years.

And when we learned who Weiss had gotten from Kansas City in exchange for Billy, we thought he was out of his mind. Weiss, of course, knew exactly what he was doing, fleecing Kansas City for all they were worth. Rarely did anyone get the better of a deal with Weiss, who traded

Billy and three decent prospects for Simpson, and a pitcher by the name of Ryne Duren. I had faced this guy during spring training. He was so fast and wild I told Casey it wasn't worth it for me to bat against him, because I didn't want to get killed.

Duren turned out to be one of the finest relief pitchers I ever saw, but his career was very short. He was a drinker who turned nasty when he had too much, but I'll tell you, when he took the mound wearing his coke-bottle glasses and started throwing those BBs every which way, for a few years no one could hit him.

Was Duren the biggest flake on the team?

Oh no. That honor went to another pitcher we acquired from Kansas City. I'll call him Mike, but don't bother looking it up. There weren't any Mikes on the Yankees at that time. I don't want to name him because his reputation was that of a conservative, family man. But there was nothing conservative whatsoever about this guy.

I remember the first road trip he went on with the Yankees. We were in Chicago. Mike was carrying what looked like a briefcase, and he was standing near the check-in desk of the hotel where we were staying. I saw him and asked him what he was up to.

"This is the hotel where all the stewardesses going in and out of O'Hare stay," he said, something, of course, I knew very well. "Let's go sit down and wait and see who shows up."

We had played an afternoon game against the White Sox, and it was coming on seven in the evening, and I had nothing else planned. I was intending to hit the bars around eleven, so I had time to kill. Mike seemed to know what he was doing, and he said to wait, so I waited, and watched.

The stews started to roll in, and whenever one stood at the counter to fill out her check-in card, Mike would say to me, "What do you think?"

I would say, "I think she's great," every time, because for me it was enough a girl was wearing that stewardess outfit to look great. It's like girls who have the hots for cops and firemen because of the uniform. I love all girls in uniforms, whether they're stews or nurses. For me, there's something very exciting about that uniform. Like trying to take it off, for instance.

Every time I approved, Mike would say, "We can do better. Patience."

After about forty-five minutes a stewardess came to the desk wearing a dark blue Pan Am uniform. This gal was drop-dead gorgeous. She was a knockout, and she wore those high-heel pumps stews loved to wear, which made them seem even sexier.

"She's the one," Mike said.

"She sure is," I replied. I still had no idea what he was up to.

He stood up, and I followed, and we walked over to the bank of elevators. When Miss Pan Am got into one of the cars, we followed and went to the back behind her. I could smell her perfume and imagine the taste of her lips.

After she exited the car at the ninth floor, Mike held the door a few seconds, letting her get ahead of us, and when she turned left to go down the hall, we went around the first available corner and peeked out to see what room she was staying in without her knowing we were on her trail. When she closed the door behind her, Mike ran up to it and made sure he wrote down the room number.

We went back to our hiding spot down the hall.

"Now we wait," he said, looking at his watch. "It's dinnertime. She won't be long." And sure enough, about twenty minutes later, Miss Pan Am opened the door, walked to the elevator dressed in a beautiful blouse and skirt, and headed down.

"Keep a lookout," said my teammate, as he laid his case on the hotel hallway floor and opened it. Inside I could see an arsenal of drill bits and a couple of small hand drills.

"Most hotel rooms have the same plan," said Mike. "The bed is in the same place in every room, and so is the bathroom. In this hotel you get a great view of both."

I admit I still had no idea what this guy was talking about.

Then he began drilling, turning the drill handle with speed and dexterity. He was a master. As a pitcher he was famed for his control, and at door drilling he was just as masterful. Very quickly, he drilled a series of small holes all the way through the thick wooden hotel door.

"Take a look through this one," he said. I looked. I could see the bed. "Look here," he said. I could see into the bathroom.

"Now all we have to do is wait for our gal to come back home," he said. He continued drilling more holes.

"There are holes for you, me, and one other guy. Pick someone, but pick someone you trust." I called Sturdy from a house phone in the hall, and he came up as fast as he could. Then we went back to our room.

We called room 366 every fifteen minutes. At eleven thirty, she picked up the phone.

"Is Mary in?" Mike asked.

"You must have the wrong room," she said.

Quickly Mike, Sturdy, and I left our room, got on the elevator, and went up to the ninth floor. We quietly walked over to her door, and we manned our peepholes. We could see she was lying in bed in her bra and panties watching television.

You'd have thought it would've been hard for three guys to watch her through the door at the same time, but Mike had drilled the holes a couple feet apart, so we all could watch without getting in each other's way. Every time the elevator bell rang, we had to pretend we were going somewhere or doing something so no one called security on us. Fortunately, it was late, so we didn't have to scatter often.

After midnight Miss Pan Am got up to take a shower. We switched to the other set of holes and watched her undress and shower in all her glory. She toweled herself off, got into her PJs, and went to bed. My only regret was that Billy wasn't there with us. When she turned the lights out, we left. The next night Mike picked a different stew, and we followed the same routine.

For quite a few years Mike and I hung around hotel check-in counters waiting for the right girl or girls. We got to see a lot of very beautiful girls naked, and even today, you can go to these old hotels, and if they haven't replaced the doors and you know where to look, you will find the holes still there. We never did get caught. Mike was too much of a pro. He belongs in the Peeping Tom Hall of Fame.

How did you react to Billy's getting traded away?

Believe it or not, it made my drinking worse. I was a lot lonelier after he was traded. Boozing had become an important part of my daily routine by 1957. Billy had shown me how much fun it was to go to a bar and sit in the corner so you could see what was going on without being bothered—you could drink for a few hours and either leave or try to pick up the sexiest girl in the place, even if she came with a date. I was amazed at how often it worked.

If the date went to the bathroom or left her unattended while she was sitting at a table, he'd hand her his room key with a note: "I'm having a party in my pants, and you're invited." Invariably she'd show up, even if it was two in the morning.

Anyway, I really loved the ritual of sitting with my teammates and drinking. Didn't matter what kind of booze it was. I could drink scotch, bourbon, gin, rye, rum, vodka, anything.

One time I was visiting Tom Sturdivant at his home in Jersey during the season. I started out drinking Cutty Sark and water, and I was saying to Sturdy, "There isn't any kind of drink I can't taste." And all the time I was saying this, his wife had a bottle of vodka, and when I emptied my glass, she started pouring me vodka, straight, and I'd finish the drink, and she'd fill it up again. Don Larsen was in on it, and so was Yogi and Johnny Kucks, and a couple of other guys, and they kept talking to me, agitating me, and I kept drinking what was in my glass, and she kept refilling it, and I kept insisting I could taste any kind of drink. Sturdy's wife said, "Are you sure you can taste vodka?" I said, "You're darn right I can." And right about then I tried to get up from the couch to go to the bathroom, and I fell back, and I literally couldn't get up. That's when I found out you can't taste vodka, no matter how hard you try.

Sturdy and I loved to play golf together. We didn't play for money, because Tommy wasn't making none, but we'd bet something like $5,000 in make-believe money to make it interesting. This one day I had him down by one going into the ninth hole. I hit a beautiful drive just to the right of the hole, and he dribbled his first shot, and I started agitating him all the way down the fairway. He hit his next shot onto the green, and I chipped up onto the green. He had a thirty-five-foot putt, and I had a three-foot putt. Tommy sank his, and I missed. So Tommy tied me, and he started laughing like a hyena. As he was coming off the green I was standing under a tree, and I tried to chop down one of the lower branches with my putter. I swung with all my might, and I missed the branch and sliced that putter right through my shin down to the bone. I began bleeding like a stuck pig.

Tommy wanted me to quit right there and go see a doctor, but I was so mad he had tied me I insisted we finish the match. I was so angry. I tied a handkerchief around the wound, and you could hear the blood squishing in my golf shoes as we walked.

Again I had to make up some cock-and-bull story about how I hurt myself. The rest of '57 I limped because of my "shin splints."

Mick, pardon me for saying so, but that's pretty fucking stupid. How many games did you end up missing?

I know. I missed fifteen games.

And yet you still hit .365, drove in 121 runs, and hit 34 homers.

I'd-a hit a lot more if it hadn't been for the pain, which made it hard for me to plant my front leg. Casey, of course, was disappointed I hadn't done better. I was furious with myself. Even though my stats were pretty good after Billy got traded, I always felt it was a bad year.

You were still named the American League MVP for the second year in a row.

Yeah, but the golf club injury cost me the Triple Crown again, and I cost us the World Series. We were playing the Milwaukee Braves, who should have been no match for us. They weren't even as good as the Dodgers.

Come on. The Braves had some great players. They had Warren Spahn, maybe the best left-hander who ever pitched, Eddie Mathews, and Hank Aaron.

For my money, Whitey was the best left-hander who ever pitched, Len. I don't care what the records show. Whitey was better than any of them. But the guy who really beat us was a spitball pitcher—Lew Burdette—who had been a Yankee farmhand when I first came up.

Whitey won the first game easy, and Burdette and Bobby Shantz were tied 0–0 in the second inning when Hank Aaron hit a fly to center field that I misjudged. The ball bounced behind me and rolled a million miles before I could get it and throw it in. Aaron was given a triple, and a single scored him. We ultimately lost on an error by Tony Kubek, the young kid who took Phil Rizzuto's place at shortstop.

We flew to Milwaukee for three games. Kubek made up for his error when he homered early in Game 3 off Bob Buhl, who then walked me and Yogi. Buhl, rattled, spun to try to pick me off at second, but he threw the ball to the wrong side of the bag. Red Schoendienst leaped to catch the ball and missed, but I couldn't go to third because he landed right on top of me full out. When I tried to push him off, I tore ligaments in my right shoulder. I told Casey I couldn't throw, but he said the team needed my bat, so he left me out there. He instructed Bobby Richardson to come way out to take the cutoff throw. But because of this injury for the rest of my career I had trouble batting left-handed.

I eventually scored, and we won the game easy. Kubek hit another home run, and I hit one off Gene Conley, who also played basketball with the Boston Celtics—talk about a guy who loved to drink! One time when Gene was playing with the Red Sox against us in Yankee Stadium, he jumped off the team bus while it was stuck in traffic near the Lincoln Tunnel. He then ducked into a bar, got royally smashed, and then decided he was going to fly to Jerusalem to find Jesus. He even bought his ticket at the airport, but he didn't get to go because he didn't have his passport. I don't know why Conley never became a Yankee. He would have fit right in with Sturdy and Gooney Bird and Billy and Ryno and the rest of us.

The next day we read in the papers that Braves fans had thrown garbage on the front lawn of Tony Kubek's parents' home, who were living in Milwaukee. How bush league is that? Milwaukee is one bush league city still. The only thing it has going for it is its beer.

We lost Game 4 because of a shoe polish smudge. Tommy Byrne, who was a wild lefty and who later ended up mayor of the town of Wake Forest in North Carolina, threw a curveball into the dirt. The umpire called it a ball. The batter, Nippy Jones, a guy nobody ever heard of, argued the ball had hit his shoe. Yogi was right there. He told me no way the ball hit his shoe. But the Braves' third base coach, who we were sure had scuffed up the ball himself on his shoe, showed the home plate umpire a black smudge on the ball, saying it was proof the ball had hit Jones's shoe, and Jones was given first base. Casey was really furious, but we got nowhere.

Jones ended up scoring, and that was the run that beat us. The guy who ran for Jones was bunted to second, and at that point Casey, who knew how bad my shoulder was, took me out of the game because he knew we'd lose if the next batter hit a ball my way. I wouldn't have been able to throw out the runner at home. I didn't play the rest of the way.

After blowing a game we should have won, Whitey, the best money pitcher in all of baseball, allowed six singles and one run in Game 5. Burdette allowed seven singles and no runs. I couldn't play, and neither could Moose Skowron, our brittle first baseman.

One more loss, and the Series would be over.

Hank Bauer homered to win Game 6, but we were no match for Burdette in Game 7, as he shut us out and won 5–0. It was his third complete game of the Series. I'm convinced if I hadn't gotten hurt, I'd have been able to do something to keep us from losing to the Braves. They weren't all that good. But like '55 when we lost to the Dodgers, it was another World Series where I was hurt and didn't do much.

Even though we lost, our fans didn't suffer nearly as much as the Dodgers and Giants fans. They lost their teams forever.

I have never forgiven that prick O'Malley. I had rooted for the Giants as a kid. If O'Malley hadn't left, the Giants wouldn't have left. You know how O'Malley made his money?

I have no idea.

He was a lawyer who foreclosed on properties from people who lost all their money and went bankrupt during the Depression. The man was evil. He packed up in the middle of the night and took the team away, and suckered Horace Stoneham into joining him in California with the Giants. O'Malley left because he saw blacks were moving into Brooklyn, and he got Stoneham to leave because of all the blacks living in Harlem, where the Polo Grounds sat. When O'Malley built his park in L.A., he made sure all the customers would have to drive to the game. That way, there'd be no blacks or poor people in the stands. Meanwhile, the fans left behind mourned for the rest of their lives. Did it make any different to you that the Dodgers and Giants had left?

Nah. We had the whole city to ourselves, at least for a few years.

Mickey Mouse goes to court to get a divorce. The judge says, "I can't give it to you. I find no evidence to support your claim that Minnie is crazy."

Mickey says, "Your honor, I didn't say she was crazy. I said she was fucking Goofy."

When we began spring training in 1958, the whole pitching staff was hurt, and we couldn't win a game. Casey worried, but none of us did. We were used to winning, and Denver, our top farm system, was sending the

Yankees so many great young players that Casey didn't know who to start, and once the season began we almost never lost.

We were 25–6 by the end of May, and our pitching was better than it had ever been. Whitey finished the season with only fourteen wins, but his ERA was 2.01. He was unhittable all year long, and what made his record all the more remarkable was that Casey only pitched him against contending teams. Bob Turley won twenty-one games that year. He was one of those guys Casey didn't trust because he didn't drink and instead of reading the *Sporting News*, he read books. But I loved Bob because he was the best reader of pitchers and pitches I ever saw. He could study a pitcher and know from his delivery whether he was going to throw a fastball, a curve, or a change-up. Before I went up to the plate, Bob would tell me what to look for, and I could see for myself what the pitcher was doing. Other times I couldn't pick out the difference even when Bob told me about it, and so from the dugout he would whistle to let me know what was coming, and I can't tell you how many home runs I hit because I knew exactly what was coming.

The funny thing was the pitchers knew what Bob was doing, but we had worked out a simple system to confuse them. The first whistle would be a fastball, and the second whistle would be a curve, and the third whistle would go back to the fastball again. The pitchers all thought they had us fooled, but we weren't fooled at all. Sometimes Bob would want to go to the bullpen to get some work in, but he was so valuable to me that I would go to Casey and tell him to get him back on the bench. One time after Bob was injured he was placed on the disabled list. We arranged for him to sit in the stands close by the batter's box, where he could whistle what was coming.

As straight-arrow as Turley was, that's how drunk and crazy Ryne Duren was. Ryno, we called him. He was a big, burly relief pitcher who loved to drink like we did, except that after a couple of pops he would get nasty and try to fight everyone in the joint. Ryne was what you'd call a mean drunk. When he was playing in the minors his team was in

Louisville. He and a few of the other players were in a bar when Ryno picked a fight with five men, who proceeded to beat the shit out of him. He ended up in jail for the night. After he retired Ryno got drunk, drove onto the railroad tracks, sitting in his car and waiting to die. Only he parked on tracks that hadn't been used in years. That's when he turned himself in to the psycho ward.

I can't remember a pitcher who was as much fun to watch as Ryno. He'd come in from the bullpen and take the ball from Casey. He'd then wipe off his glasses—big, thick glasses like manhole covers—and he'd put them back on his face. He'd then go into the stretch, and he'd throw the ball so wildly that the guy standing in the on-deck circle wasn't safe. In fact, when he was pitching in the minors, one time he did hit the guy in the on-deck circle! Most of the time that first pitch would hit the top of the screen or bounce three feet in front of the catcher. We'd be laughing like hell, because we knew Ryno was doing it on purpose, just trying to intimidate the shit out of the other team. They didn't know that, and they just hated the idea of getting hit in the head with a 95-mile-an-hour fastball. In 1958 Ryno saved twenty games and had an ERA of 2.02.

I remember. Whitey and he were an unbeatable combination.

By the summer of '58 everyone was crying, "Break up the Yankees," and for good reason. All of a sudden we were a very young team: Ellie Howard was twenty-nine. Moose twenty-seven, I was twenty-six, and all those guys from Denver—Richardson, Kubek, Jerry Lumpe, Norm Siebern, and a kid named Marv Throneberry, who was very highly touted—were all younger than me. Wherever we went, we won, and the opposing fans booed us. When Casey complained, they just booed louder.

And as we kept winning, Casey became grumpier and grumpier. There were times when the Old Man was insufferable. We had a ten-game lead, but he became fixated on the idea we would somehow blow it and make him look bad. It was ridiculous.

But it wasn't that ridiculous. In 1914 Casey was playing for the Dodgers. He remembered that the Giants had had a huge lead, but the

Boston Braves came roaring back to overtake them. Casey had experienced it firsthand. He knew what he was talking about.

Nineteen fourteen? That's a long time ago.

You know what—there was less time between 1914 and 1958 than between 1958 and now. To Casey, it was like the 1914 Braves were something that happened yesterday. So he rode us hard, chewed us out in the field and in the clubhouse meetings, and drove us without mercy. He didn't say much to me, but the ones I really felt sorry for were the kids, Kubek, Richardson, Jerry Lumpe, Clete Boyer, Ralph Terry, guys who got second-guessed all the time. When Casey first became manager of the Yankees, he loved working with the young kids. I was one of them. But now he was nearing seventy, had won eight pennants, and he had absolutely no tolerance for rookies and their mistakes.

I remember one time Tony booted a ball that cost us a run, and Stengel screamed at him, "Goddamn it, Kubek. How the hell can you miss a goddamn ball like that? What the hell is the matter with you?" Young pitchers got second-guessed every time they gave up a hit. If the pitch was a curve and the batter got a hit, he would say, "How the hell can you throw that guy a curve?" It seemed like Casey was hazing them. It made the ones who survived tough as nails. The ones who became nervous and jumpy didn't last.

Richardson and Kubek survived Casey. Guys like Norm Siebern and Jerry Lumpe didn't and were traded to Kansas City. Neither player ever did become the star he was supposed to be. Clete Boyer was another player Casey tortured. Clete was an all-world fielder, but he didn't have a lot of success hitting, and so Casey would pinch hit for him in the middle of the game, once in the second inning. Clete ended up getting traded to Kansas City, but the Yankees got him back, and he became a star after Casey left.

You had a seventeen-game lead in August.

Yeah, but then our pitchers started going down with sore arms. After Whitey pitched his seventh shutout, he didn't get another win all year. Sturdy was fooling around in the outfield before a game, got spiked, and suffered a gash in his heel and had to go on the DL. Two guys who Weiss got from Kansas City, Virgil Trucks and Duke Maas, saved us. Even though we played under .500 ball the last two months of the season, we still finished the year with ninety-two wins and won in a walk. We beat out the White Sox by ten full games.

You had a strong finish that year. You hit .331 the last two months, and you finished the year with 97 RBIs and 42 homers.

It was an okay season, not a great one. We held our pennant-clinching party in Kansas City at the Muehlebach Hotel. We started drinking champagne and never stopped. After the party we boarded a train for Detroit. We continued drinking way past midnight. Ryno, inebriated and wobbly, got it in his head that he could win a fistfight against Ralph Houk, our first base coach and a Marine veteran. Houk had been Ryno's manager in Denver the year before. He was a big, burly guy just like Ryno.

Ryno said to Ralph, "You know what I think I'll do? I think I'll push that cigar you're smoking right down your throat." Ralph, who knew how Ryno could be when he drank, tried to calm him down, but Ryno was far too gone. He began pushing the lit cigar down Ralph's throat. Ralph then swatted him away with the back of his hand, scratching Rhino above the right eye with his World Series ring.

Ryno began to blubber something like, "After all I've done for this team." He was so drunk he didn't remember what happened the next morning. The other players tried to subdue him, and they were finally able to put him to bed, but not before Ryno kicked Don Larsen in the face, cutting the inside of his mouth. Nothing much came of any of this, but I suspect it was one of the reasons George Weiss put private detectives on us when we arrived in Detroit.

How did you know they were private detectives?

Whitey noticed a couple of suspicious guys watching us. One had on a Panama hat and red shoes, and the other one was wearing a London Fog raincoat. They were looking over the tops of newspapers like cops in the movies.

"This should be funny," Whitey said to me and Darrell Johnson, one of our young players. "Let's go." We walked out the front door of the hotel and got into a cab. We watched as the two men jumped into another cab. Our cab raced off. They followed.

"Go around the block and stop back in front of the hotel," Whitey ordered the cabbie. When he stopped and opened the doors to get out, we could hear the squeal of the brakes behind us. We waved to the detectives and walked back into the hotel.

Whitey wanted to give them something to tell Weiss, so he decided we should play hopscotch on the sidewalk. We hopped on one leg up the sidewalk, turned around, and hopped back. Then Whitey led us into a nearby Catholic church. We snuck out the back door and lost them.

A couple of other guys were following the milkshake drinkers, Kubek, Richardson, Bobby Shantz, and Johnny Kucks. They were followed into the YMCA, where they played Ping-Pong, and then they went into a movie theater. Kubek, who was very smart, had made them as detectives sent to spy on us, and so the four went into the theater. But they didn't buy tickets. They only bought popcorn.

When Tony saw the detectives buying their tickets, he and the other guys walked out of the theater, leaving the assholes with wasted stubs. After I told a couple of the reporters all about it, mysteriously the next day the story appeared in the newspapers.

You *gave a reporter a story?*

Hey, compared to George Weiss you guys were princes. But after it came out in the papers, Weiss looked so stupid he never did that again. Kubek, for one, was furious. We had won the fucking pennant, for crying out loud. What did the SOB want from us?

When Casey read about the detectives the next day, he called us together and told us about the time he was playing for John McGraw on the Giants. On one road trip, Casey said, McGraw had a detective follow him and another Giant outfielder, Irish Meusel. Casey said he told McGraw, "I don't deserve that kind of treatment, you putting detectives on me and Irish."

"How should you be treated?" McGraw wanted to know.

"I got a right to have a whole detective to myself," he said. "I don't believe in no sharing."

I guess Casey was always a character.

He was wonderful. While we were playing for him, none of us fully appreciated how lucky we were to have him as our manager.

You beat the Braves in the 1958 World Series. You should have lost.

Says you. The Yankees should never lose. Never. Ryno pitched great in relief in the first game, but we lost. He was great when he pitched one inning, good when he pitched two, but after two, he became human. Billy Bruton beat us in the tenth.

In the second game Milwaukee creamed us, even though I hit two home runs. Lew Burdette pitched his fourth straight complete Series game against us.

We were down 2–0 in games. I was sitting in the dugout before Game 3 when Howard Cosell came to interview Casey. He asked Casey whether the Yankees had "choked up." Cosell and Casey were two of a kind—smart and mouthy. Cosell was the sort of guy who would ask if he could talk to you. You'd say to him, "Sure, Howard, as long as you don't ask me about the pimple on my ass." Howard would say, "No problem, Mick." And we'd sit down, and the camera would start to roll, and Howard would say, "Mickey, the first thing I want to ask you, how is the pimple on your ass?" He did that a lot, but I knew just how to deal with him. Either I'd stare straight into the camera for five minutes without saying a word, or I'd say the word *fuck* every other word, as in "The fucking pimple on my fucking ass is fucking fine." Because I knew there was no way the television station was going to run any answer with the word *fuck* in it.

Anyway, when Howard asked Casey whether the Yankees had choked, I thought Casey was going to wrap Cosell's microphone cord around his neck and pull it tight. Casey told him, "I haven't choked up and none of my players have choked up. Ballplayers don't choke up. But if anybody's gonna be choked up it's the guy holding the microphone." I doubt if Howard aired that one either.

That day, Gooney Bird pitched a shutout, the second-best game he ever pitched. In Game 4 Whitey lost 3–0 to Warren Spahn. We got exactly two hits. Spahn kept us guessing all day.

Now we were down three games to one. We had to win the last three games in a row to win the Series.

If I remember right, everyone was down in the dumps.

I got to tell you, before the start of Game 5, you'd have thought we were holding a funeral. The Braves were tooting their horns, telling everyone how they had this one locked up, and we were really seething about it. After the fourth-game loss, fucking classless Burdette told reporters he wished the Yankees were in the National League. He said we'd be lucky to finish fifth. Johnny Logan, their shortstop, said he thought we were "over the hill." Spahn had the balls to predict that they'd win it all the next day, that the last two games wouldn't be necessary. Their team had no class, and neither did their fans, who we hadn't forgiven for throwing garbage on Tony Kubek's parents' lawn the year before.

I went to a novelty shop on Broadway, and I bought one of those arrows that fit over your head with a wire to make it look like the arrow goes in one side and comes out the other. Before the game I walked into the middle of the locker room and said to everyone, "Now I know how Custer felt." The guys started laughing, and so did the reporters, and I think I even saw Casey smile. After that, the atmosphere seemed to lighten, and we went out there and kicked their asses. Bob Turley was overpowering. He allowed five hits and no runs. And so the Braves were forced to go back to County Stadium, despite Spahnie's prediction.

It was at this point that Braves manager Fred Haney made a very stupid decision. He decided to start Spahn in Game 6 on two days' rest, rather than save him for a seventh game. It was stupid, because if we won Game 6, he'd then have to pitch Burdette on two days' rest. Which is exactly what happened.

We won Game 6 by the skin of our teeth. After they tied us in the ninth, we scored two runs in the top of the tenth, and Casey brought in Ryno to finish them off. With one out, Ryno ran the count to 3 and 2 on Johnny Logan, then threw him a perfect strike. Yogi went to throw the ball down to third. Duren pumped his fist. And then the home plate umpire called it a ball for ball four. I couldn't believe it. Before the next pitch, Duren put his hand to his neck to show the ump up, but the ump didn't see it or he let it go. Ryno ended up getting fined $250 because commissioner Ford Frick saw him do it on national TV. When reporters asked Ryno about it, he denied giving the choke sign. Instead he told them, "I was fixing my tie." Ryno was a beauty.

Duren struck out Eddie Mathews, and then Ryno had a brain fart. With a runner on first, he went into his windup, letting Logan go to second without a throw. Rattled, Duren allowed a single by Hank Aaron to score the run. Joe Adcock then singled Aaron to third. The tying run was ninety feet away.

I was praying for Casey to get Ryno the hell out of there, and Casey did do that, but Case, who could be very unorthodox, surprised everyone when he brought Bob Turley into the game. Bob had pitched a complete game the day before, and you'd have figured his arm was sore, if not shot. But all Bob had to get was one out. The Braves manager sent up a left-handed hitter, Frank Torre, to pinch-hit. You know, Joe's older brother.

Turley threw one pitch, a rising fastball that Torre hit toward second base. The fans thought it might loop over Gil McDougald's head, but the soft line drive died in midair, and Mac caught the ball easily on the outfield grass. The Series was tied at three games each.

An hour before the final game Casey told Don Larsen he was starting. Burdette, as planned, pitched for the Braves on two days' rest. Milwaukee scored a run in the first, and we scored twice in the second. When Gooney Bird gave up a couple of hits in the third, Casey went to his pen. For the third day in the row he brought in Bob Turley!

I thought Casey was nuts. I didn't think there was any way Turley could get them out, but he did. He pitched the rest of the way. That would never happen today. The guy's agent would object, fearing an injury. The pitch counters would go crazy. But Bob was a gamer, and it was one of the great performances in Series history, though no one remembers it anymore. That's because Turley was a quiet family guy who never said boo to anyone. But while Bob cut through that Braves' lineup, we kicked the shit out of big-mouth Burdette. We scored four runs with two out in the eighth. Moose Skowron's home run into the bleachers clinched it.

Once again, we were World Champions, like we were supposed to be. Casey could smile for the first time all season. In the clubhouse, Turley reminded everyone that he, Larsen, and Ryno, the winners of the four games, had all been members of the St. Louis Browns before the Browns moved to Baltimore. Bob said all we were missing was Satchel Paige.

On the plane ride home we all got drunk and said nasty things about the Braves. Whitey took champagne corks, burned them, and painted designs on everyone's faces. When he got to Casey, he painted big dollar signs. When Casey walked off the airplane, with dollar signs etched on that lined face of his, he told everybody, "I guess we can play in the National League after all."

He didn't say it smiling.

14

If I remember right, things started off badly in 1959 right from the start. What was going on?

When we arrived for spring training in 1959, Casey was extremely agitated. So was I. The owners, Topping and Webb, had taken over the team in the mid-1940s and had won eight pennants in nine years, making millions of dollars in the process. As our reward, they went on a cost-cutting campaign. They got rid of our instructional school, which had allowed Casey to train our best prospects, and they tried to cut everybody's salary, including mine. I was so angry I told Topping to his face he could go fuck himself, that he should trade me if he was so unhappy with the way I was playing. I was making $80,000, and he wanted me to take a $10,000 cut. Why? Because Topping was one of those guys who had inherited all kinds of money, never had to work a day in his life, had nine wives, screwed around on the side with actresses and models and showgirls, even married one of his brother's ex-wives, and tried to fuck with people's lives because it gave him pleasure.

No one knew it, but Topping and Weiss were actually preparing to sell the team. Although that wouldn't happen for another five years.

We had no idea. Casey was so angry, I thought he was going to quit for a while. But he had played for John McGraw, who had won a record ten pennants, and Casey had nine, and Casey wanted to leave the game tied with McGraw, so he came back for '59. But we could see during spring training that Casey was drinking more than usual, and for Casey that was saying something. Weiss had to get Casey's wife Edna to come to St. Petersburg from California to keep an eye on him.

We started the season with another epidemic of injuries. Don Larsen and Tom Sturdivant had sore arms all year. They were never the same again. I hurt my throwing shoulder making an off-balance throw, and then in batting practice I was hit on the right index finger by Duke Maas. Tony Kubek played center in my place. Bill Skowron tore a back muscle running out a ball. The whole team was hit by the Asian flu.

We sank into the cellar for the first time since before World War II. We were in dead last, eight full games behind the leading White Sox, and all the Yankee haters were having a field day. What bugged me was that our fans booed us loudest of all, and me in particular. I was playing in great pain—my right index finger and right shoulder were killing me—and at Yankee Stadium I was getting booed for my efforts. The day we fell into the cellar, I hit two home runs, and I got booed as I ran around the bases! You ask me why I had contempt for the fans when I was a player? You don't have to look much beyond that.

In addition to the booing, the other thing that really upset me was that Casey was getting too old to manage. Not that he wasn't as sharp as always. But his drinking and staying up all night was taking its toll, and he began to fall asleep during the middle of games, especially when we were playing doubleheaders.

Even that had its funny side. Casey had been feuding with our third baseman, Andy Carey, who was one of those hitters who tried to pull every pitch, and it drove Casey nuts because Carey struck out a lot on outside pitches. Casey wanted him to go to the opposite field on the outside pitch, but Carey stubbornly refused to do it. Casey would give him shit all the time.

To get back at him, Andy would wait for Case to fall asleep on the bench during the game, and when a Yankee batter got a base hit, he'd creep up on him and scream right in his ear. Startled, Casey would jump up, pace the dugout for a minute or two, sit down again, and fall back to sleep.

In the end, of course, Casey got the last laugh. George Weiss traded for another third baseman, Hector Lopez.

What a Pair of Hands Hector. What was it like for you when the Yankees fell into the cellar? How bad was it?

I felt it was all my fault. I was embarrassed, and I was determined to do everything I could to get us back on top where we belonged. I began bunting and stealing bases whenever I got on, and when I started doing that, I noticed that the fans stopped booing and began cheering every time I got on base. I wanted everyone out there to understand that I was a guy who played the game hard every game. I didn't take care of myself as good as I should have, and I didn't go to bed as early as I should have, but whenever I walked out between those white lines, I played the game as hard as anyone. I ended up second in the league in steals that year with twenty-one, and that was one statistic I was very proud of.

The Yankees weren't in the cellar for very long.

We had Ryno to thank for that. In '59 he was almost unhittable. The SOB would walk out onto the mound, throw that first pitch up against the screen at a hundred miles an hour, then wipe off his thick glasses. His drinking and fighting had become known around the league, and that made him even more fearsome. No one wanted to hit against him. During one stretch he pitched thirty-six straight innings of scoreless baseball. During one span he struck out fifteen of nineteen batters.

I remember one game in late June we were playing against the White Sox. Ryno came into the game in the seventh and struck out three batters. He struck out two more in the eighth and three more in the ninth. I don't think I ever saw a better performance for a relief pitcher.

We started going great, closing in on the Sox when I hurt my ankle badly the last day of June sliding into a base. It hurt the team as much as

it hurt me. In July I came to bat with fifty-seven runners in scoring position. I drove in exactly four of them. In August I drove in exactly two
more runs. I felt like jumping off a cliff.

*For a guy who says he hates stats, you sure can remember the negative ones
in great detail.*

I was horrible, and I could barely live with myself, I was hurting my
team so bad. I drank more heavily than ever. I couldn't face my teammates, refused to talk with reporters, and I scowled every time a fan came
near me. I'd say to anyone who tried to come close, "Get the fuck away
from me." I could see the pain in the guy's face, but I didn't care. When
you're going as bad as I was, you don't give a shit about anyone or anything. I had enough pain of my own to deal with, and I pretty much had
to do it alone. With Billy gone, I really didn't have anyone to hang out
with like I had with Billy.

Even Casey turned on me. He rode me hard, but I never gave him the
satisfaction of letting him know he was getting to me. Casey was second-
guessing worse than ever. Casey had told me that was why anyone who
played for John McGraw hated him so much, and here Case was turning
into McGraw before our eyes. But part of the reason Case was turning up
the heat was that Dan Topping, who thought Casey had gotten too old,
was second-guessing him. Years later Casey told me Topping wanted to
fire him after '58, but he didn't do it because he had two more years to go
on his contract, and Topping didn't want to pay him for not managing.
Topping went so far as to tell reporters that the Yankees would win the
pennant if Casey would just quit so he could name Ralph Houk manager.
But Casey, who had as much pride as anyone, believed he was the best
manager in baseball and deeply resented Topping's backstabbing after all
he had done for him. When George Weiss sided with Casey against
Topping, I thought for sure both Weiss and Casey would be gone after '59.
Only Topping's cheapness kept them on.

The '59 season was a disaster.

We had injury after injury. Moose bent over to field a ground ball and felt a sharp pain in his lower back. He went on the DL. Hector got hit by a pitched ball and was out a while. Kubek suffered a concussion when he ran into Gil McDougald chasing a pop fly. Tony was knocked out, and Gil suffered from dizzy spells. Then in late July Moose broke his arm in two places when a guy on Detroit ran into him at first base. When the pitching went south, we were dead. We finished third that year, fifteen games behind the punchless White Sox.

So you didn't know Topping was intending to fire Casey after '59?

I didn't.

Topping decided to hire Al Lopez, who had led the White Sox to the '59 pennant. He even offered him the job, but Casey and Lopez were close friends, and Lopez wanted no part of backstabbing his friend. He turned Topping down flat. When Lopez said no, Topping decided to let Casey finish out his contract and manage in 1960. He didn't fire Weiss, either.

And it's a good thing he didn't, because Weiss, who knew his job was coming to an end, made what was perhaps the greatest deal in his career when he sent a bunch of guys he didn't want anymore to Kansas City for Roger Maris, who became my good friend and who would make baseball history.

To me Roger was a prick.

That's okay, Len. He thought you were a prick.

He was even more of a red-ass than you were.

Let me tell you about Roger. You may have found him surly and nasty and hard to talk to, but to his friends, Roger was the nicest person you'd ever want to meet. He loved his family and loved to play ball, but he just wanted to be left alone, like me. Roger would have been better off not leaving Kansas City, where there wouldn't have been a media circus. New York was the *wrong* place for Roger. I told you, just because you're a star athlete, that doesn't mean you're prepared for the publicity and the fame. I hated it. Roger hated it more. But bringing Roger to New York was the greatest thing that ever happened to me. Before he came, whenever anyone wanted a story, they came to me. Once Roger came to New York and started hitting home runs, they went to Roger and took a lot of that off me. And with Roger added to our lineup, I didn't feel I had to carry the offense on my back anymore. If I made out, Roger would come through. For a few years, as far as I was concerned, Roger Maris was the best ballplayer in the major leagues. The very best.

Were the Yankees upbeat in spring training after the trade?

The Yankees were pissed in spring training because after finishing third the year before, now Topping really wanted salary cuts. Weiss wanted to cut me by $17,000, too much to stomach. I had shown up on time for practice, figuring Topping would be fair, but when I arrived, I found him defiant and ornery. He told me I had had a mediocre season, that I didn't deserve the money he was paying me, and that he didn't care if I played or not. Okay, I told him, I won't play until you offer me a fair contract.

We were still training in St. Petersburg, and that afternoon I was invited by a wealthy fan who owned a powerboat to take a ride out into the Gulf of Mexico with a couple of teammates and a group of party girls he knew. We got out there, and all of us started drinking, and one of the girls asked if it was all right if she sunbathed topless, and we said we didn't see anything wrong with that. In fact, we suggested she might get a more even tan if she took the bottom of her bathing suit off too, and she thought that was a great idea. Then we took our clothes off, and some of us jumped into the water, and while we were swimming around, grabbing the girls, flames began rising up from the back of the boat. I'm not exactly sure how that happened, but the fire burned all our clothes, and the boat sank.

You're lucky no one got killed. It could have been a bigger scandal than the Copa.

Oh yeah. Fortunately, we had been able to call the Coast Guard before the boat sank, and when they came to pick us up, they found the boat owner, me, a couple of teammates, and four young gals all buck-naked holding onto floats for dear life. I was standing on that Coast Guard boat, ass to the wind, when this one guy came over and asked me for an autograph.

"Dickhead, can't you bring me a towel first?" I said.

Good thing Topping didn't find out.

As it was, he made me hold out for two weeks. During that time I didn't practice, and it drove me crazy. As the first week of inactivity went by, I started getting antsier and antsier. I couldn't stand being away from the game, and though I'm sure I could have avoided a pay cut if I had held out all spring, after two weeks I let him cut me $7,000, from $72,000 down to $65,000.

So your salary went from $80,000 to $72,000 to $65,000. He was cutting salary more than even we knew.

The worst part was the layoff ended up hurting me. When I went out to play, I tried to do too much too soon, and I hurt both my right shoulder and right knee. I was so angry, I told Casey to tell his buddy Weiss to trade me the hell away. Casey was sympathetic. He told me what they did was wrong. He said he had spoken to Weiss, who told him Topping was trying to cut everyone's salary, that it was out of his hands. He said he and Weiss were powerless to do anything. But after I got hurt, Casey and Weiss stopped speaking to each other. Nobody thought we had a prayer to win the pennant after spring training in 1960.

But that year you ended up winning the first of five pennants in a row!

Which we couldn't have done without Roger, who carried us on his back the early part of the season. He was leading the league in everything, including homers, when one of the reporters asked him whether he thought he could break Babe Ruth's record of 60 home runs in a season. Roger hit the roof.

I was the reporter who asked him that. I felt I was paying him the highest compliment. I was comparing him to Babe Ruth. He didn't have to be such a grouch about it. How fucking hard would it have been to answer my question?

A question which he would be asked only about a million times.

It was a legitimate question, Mickey. He should have answered the fucking question. At least he should have answered it the first time it was asked.

Roger felt it was tough enough to play the game without the added pressure put on him by the press. I remember what he said to you, that the question was silly because he felt he hadn't even made the ball club, and here you were talking about Babe Ruth.

How could he have felt he hadn't made the ball club? He was leading the league, leading the team. He made me look stupid for asking a perfectly reasonable question.

All you had to do was write about what he was doing, and you had a great story right there. Who cared how he felt about what he was doing anyway? What difference did it make how he felt about it? And who gave a shit whether you felt stupid? You didn't have to take it out on Roger. Roger was doing something special, something important, and you guys were ruining it for him. You had no idea how much strain everyone was under.

The strain of being a baseball player? Give me a break. What strain?

The pressure coming from Topping and Weiss after the horrible year in '59. Everyone's jobs were at stake.

What about the strain I was under to get a better story than the reporters from the other papers? You guys didn't care about the strain I was under. My job was at stake, too, and I made a hell of a lot less money than you did.

The strain of being a sportswriter? Give me a break! What strain? Whatever pressure you felt was nothing compared to what Casey was feeling, and it took its toll. In late May he got real sick and had to leave the team and go to the hospital for a couple of weeks. Ralph Houk, who was a coach, took over for him, and we played .500 ball under Ralph, nothing special. I liked playing for Houk, who didn't ride us the way Casey did, but still I was happy to see Case return in early June. I really did love that old cocksucker. I loved him like I loved my dad. And it was only after he was gone that I realized it. Looking back, all he wanted was for me to be the best player I could be, and it saddens me to think how much I must have let him down sometimes.

The day Case came back, someone asked him how he was feeling, and he said, "I'll tell ya something. They examined all my organs. Some of them are remarkable, and others are not so good. A lot of museums are bidding for them." Casey was hysterical. That just cracked us up. Even Roger laughed.

We won that day, and the next, and the next. Our pitching staff recovered, and during the next two weeks we won every game but one, fourteen in all, and we climbed into first place after beating the White Sox four games in a row at the Stadium.

One of the pitchers who couldn't seem to lose was a lanky rookie by the name of Jim Coates, who we called The Mummy, because he slept with his eyes open. One time Coates fell asleep on the bus a couple of rows behind Edna Stengel, and she turned to Casey and whispered, "Dear, I think one of your players is dead."

Coates, who was from the South, was a nasty guy who pitched sidearm and hated blacks, and loved to throw at them. He was an SOB, and Casey loved him for it. He said Coates reminded him of Carl Mays.

Mays was the only pitcher ever to kill a batter in major league history. Ray Chapman of the Cleveland Indians, back in 1920. I heard that Mays was a mean, ornery drunk.

Casey's kind of guy! Coates wasn't that good a pitcher, but that year we scored a bushel of runs for him every time he pitched, and he won twelve games, and we'd tease him that he was the luckiest SOB in all of baseball.

By June I started hitting better, and with Roger, Yogi, and Moose all hitting, we returned to being the Yankees of old. It was like we had been caught in a nightmare for a year, but then it was over, and everything could go back to being like it once was.

Moose Skowron was one of our unsung players. He was quiet, and modest, and he didn't say very much, but what a nice guy. What I found most amazing about Moose was that during a big chunk of his career with the Yankees, he was having marital problems. I was one of the guys he would talk to about it. The way Moose told it, his wife never had enough—enough clothes, enough jewelry, a big enough house, a fancy enough car. Moose felt he was spending every penny he earned on her, but it was never enough. And when Moose went on the road with the team, his wife would be calling him up all the time, accusing him of fooling around on her, which was a joke, because unlike a lot of us, Moose didn't dare fool around, because he was afraid she'd find out. When Moose told me this, he'd be near tears.

So Moose took a lot of grief, without getting any of the benefits. I told him, "Come on, Moose. I'll get you some puss. You deserve some pleasure."

"Oh no, Mick, I couldn't do that. My wife would kill me."

She was killing him anyway.

Through the summer of '60 we held a slim lead over the Baltimore Orioles. I was playing in constant pain. In mid-August we were playing a doubleheader against Washington. Roger was on first, and I grounded a ball to the infield, and in my frustration I didn't run to first. I stood at the plate, disgusted with myself, while Roger was sliding hard into the second baseman, hurting his ribs and putting him on the DL for two weeks. I thought Casey was going to kill me. I'd never seen him so angry. I was the third out of the inning, and as I waited for my glove, Casey sent Bob Cerv out to play center field in my place. As Cerv trotted out to center, the fans booed and booed me.

After the game Casey came over and said, "You have a bad habit. When you make an easy out, you quit hustling. For your own good, you have to stop acting like a spoiled brat."

I felt awful. I told him I'd try harder.

You were almost a ten-year veteran by then.

He didn't care. I was his protégé when I came up, and I had never stopped being his protégé. And he was right. The Orioles came to town for a four-game series. When my name was announced the boos were so loud they scared me. I could hear people screaming I was a bum and I stunk from as far away as the bleachers. It was real ugly. Casey told me he never saw fans boo anyone as badly as they were booing me. He told me to ignore them, that as soon as I hit a home run, they'd start cheering again.

The next time up I decided to show everyone, and I hit a long home run over the right center field fence into the bullpen to tie the game. When I crossed home plate, I decided to tip my cap to the fans. I wanted them to see I wasn't a robot, but a flesh-and-blood human being.

Late in the game the Orioles were up by a run, and when I batted there was a runner on first, and I could still hear the boos ringing in my ears. Hoyt Wilhelm was pitching in relief, and that guy gave me fits because he threw a knuckleball that darted this way and that, and it was a wonder anyone ever hit him. Wilhelm threw me a knuckler, and I swung, and I popped it up behind the plate. Clint Courtney, the catcher Billy got into those fights with several years earlier, dropped the ball. Billy always said Courtney was a horseshit player. I was given another life.

Wilhelm threw me another knuckler, but this one only rotated a little, enough so I could track the flight of the ball, and I hit that son of a bitch nine miles on a line into the right-field seats, and I'll tell you, I don't think I ever received a louder ovation in my entire life. The fans just stood there and cheered and cheered, and after the terrible game I had the day before, I was grateful. And for the rest of the season, Casey never had a bad word to say to me. I had redeemed myself in his eyes, and really, that was all that mattered to me.

You really showed us something that day. A person had to be awfully cynical not to be impressed.

The next day, for the first time, the reporters wrote about the fact I was hurting and talked about my courage and commitment to the game, and really, after ten years of playing with the Yankees, that was the first time I really felt wanted. Wanted by Casey, wanted by the Yankee fans. Even when I was winning two MVPs and all those World Series, I always had a nagging doubt in the back of my mind, a concern that Casey wouldn't want me anymore or Weiss would trade me away. For years those insecurities ate at me, but after that game against the Orioles, I began to feel I really belonged. I really began to feel at home.

We never told you this, but you were our hero, too. That's why we reacted so negatively when you treated us like shit. We wanted so badly to be your friend, but you made it clear you thought we were garbage.

I guess I never stopped to think that you guys had feelings. Most of you were so arrogant, so sure of yourself. You were educated, got paid to write things. And you were a bunch of unathletic, scrawny guys who never played the game, and so we avoided you like the plague.

You never considered how that would make us feel?

The only thing we felt was that our jobs would have been so much easier without you guys around all the time.

Didn't you realize that without us, no one would have read about your heroics, Roger's heroics, the Yankees' heroics? Without the publicity from the newspapers you'd have played in front of empty houses?

I didn't read the newspapers. For me, I never saw the need. If I wanted to find out the news, I'd watch it on TV. All I knew was that you guys were always wanting to know what we were thinking before doing something. It always seemed like you were second-guessing, and we had enough of that from Casey.

I wasn't second-guessing. I was trying to find out what was going on in your thick skull. You were a smart ballplayer, and I wanted my readers to understand your thinking.

Why didn't you say so? That never occurred to me.

What we had, Mickey, was a lack of communication. We couldn't have been that much of a distraction, because you ended up winning the 1960 pennant in a cakewalk.

With fifteen games to go, we had a small lead, a game and a half. We won our last fifteen games, ran the table. We left the Orioles in the dust.

You must have felt a great sense of accomplishment.

We won it to show Weiss, and we won it to show that prick Topping. But the guy we won it for most of all was Casey. We all knew it was going to be his last year. Before the end of the season Del Webb, the other owner, a builder of casinos in Las Vegas, had called Casey and told him he wanted to discuss his retirement plan. When Casey said he didn't want to retire, Webb told him he had no choice. Casey told him he didn't want to be around if he wasn't wanted. Casey told me of the conversation a few minutes later. He was bitter and resigned. He said that a lot of times he had managed without ever signing a contract. He said he had been a good soldier all along, going along even when Weiss or the owners did something he didn't approve of. Casey told me he told Weiss not to trade Billy, but Weiss did it anyway. Casey said Topping and Webb were a couple of bastards and predicted Weiss would be fired as well. Casey was right, as usual.

We all knew how much Casey had wanted to win that tenth pennant to tie McGraw. And we were able to get it for him. The day we clinched, Casey came over to me and gave me a bear hug. We both had tears in our eyes.

And when Casey went in front of the microphones, the player he praised was me. He told them, "I believe the most powerful factor has been Mickey, who hit forty home runs and drove in ninety runs and played fifty hours through three doubleheaders on a bad knee without asking for relief or flinching. He has worked hard and hustled and in my mind he was my most valuable player."

I never felt so proud.

That day I loved the Old Man. I thought how hard he had tried to make me a better player, no matter how hard I fought him, and how proud he was to see me play well. I also knew when he left, I would have to play the rest of my career on my own, that I wouldn't have Casey there behind me anymore. I was twenty-eight years old, and my childhood was over. I broke down and cried.

15

If winning the 1960 pennant was our greatest triumph, losing the 1960 World Series to a bunch of crumb bums like the Pittsburgh Pirates was a low point. In the three games we won, we kicked the shit out of them by the scores of 16–3, 10–0, and 12–0. The Pirates had one decent pitcher, Vern Law, and he beat us twice, and we lost a third one when we didn't hit their best reliever, Roy Face, who threw a forkball that dropped off the table when it came up to the plate.

Game 7 should have been a piece of cake, because we were playing at Forbes Field, a bandbox, a great place for us in that any fly ball was a potential home run, unless you hit it to straightaway center field. But after Bob Turley gave up two runs in the first inning, Casey yanked him for a rookie, Bill Stafford, who loaded the bases with no outs, then got two outs before giving up a dinky seeing-eye hit and two more runs.

Bobby Shantz then came in and pitched brilliantly. He held the Pirates through the eighth while we crept back into it. Moose hit a home run, and we scored another run off Law, and then the Pirates brought in Face, and I hit a ball up the middle to score the second run, and then Yogi, who may have been the greatest clutch-hitter in the history of the game, hit a three-run home run into the upper deck to give us a 5–4 lead. I was sure that was the game, right there. We even added two in the eighth on hits by Clete Boyer and John Blanchard, two young players who quickly became close drinking buddies of mine.

We took the field for the bottom of the eighth. Shantz was still out there. It was his fifth inning, and he hadn't pitched that long all season.

The first batter singled. Bill Virdon then hit a three-hopper right to Tony Kubek at shortstop, an easy double play. Tony moved over, about to catch the ball when the ball hit a rock or a clod of dirt, took a high hop, and hit Tony right in the neck. The runners were safe as Tony lay on the ground trying to breathe. He had been hit in the Adam's apple, and our trainer saw that if we didn't get Tony to the hospital, his larynx might swell up and choke off his oxygen. He signaled for an ambulance. Kubek, just a kid but a smart cookie, whispered to Casey that he should leave Shantz in the game because it was a bunt situation, and Shantz was one of the best-fielding pitchers in the game. Casey later expressed wonder at Tony's cool head.

But Dick Groat didn't bunt. He swung, and he singled to make the score 7–5. Case took Shantz out and brought in The Mummy, Jim Coates. This time the Pirates did bunt, moving the runners to second and third. The next batter flew out to Roger in right. The runner stayed put, not wanting to challenge his great arm. We needed one more out to get out of it.

Roberto Clemente was the next batter. He had a big mouth, but he was a great hitter, and we should have walked him. To this day I don't know why Casey pitched to him. We had an open base, and Clemente was impossible to get out. As it turned out, all Clemente did was ground wide to Moose at first. It should have been the third out.

They say that the team that allows extra outs in an inning loses, and that's what happened to us. Moose caught the ball and made a run for the bag, and when he did that, Coates, running halfway to first, stopped. But Clemente was lightning fast, and when Moose saw he couldn't beat him, he went to throw to Coates, but Coates was nowhere to be seen. Clemente was safe, another run scored. It was now 7–6.

Hal Smith, their catcher, was up next. He wasn't much of a batter, but anyone with a bat in his hand is a threat in tiny Forbes Field, and Coates was so upset about not covering first that he lost whatever composure he had. On a 3–2 pitch he threw Smith a letter-high meatball that Smith hit up over the left-field wall for a three-run home run. In disgust Coates threw his glove ten feet in the air. Before it came down, Coates was out of there.

Ralph Terry had been warming up throughout the game, and he finally got his chance to pitch. He ended the inning, but not before the Pirates had taken a 9–7 lead.

We were really up against it. It was the top of the ninth, and we needed to score two to keep it going. Bob Friend, who we had beaten mercilessly, was pitching for the Pirates.

Bobby Richardson singled, and then Dale Long singled. Friend got the hook, and Harvey Haddix, a left-hander, came in to pitch to the left-handed Maris. Roger popped out. I was next, batting righty. Haddix threw me an outside fastball, and I lined a single to right center, scored Bobby, and moved Long to third. We still needed one more run, with Yogi up. Gil McDougald ran for Long.

Yogi hit a scorcher, a one-hopper inside the first base line. Their first baseman, Rocky Nelson, was protecting the line, and he caught the ball and stepped on first for the second out. I was stranded five feet off the bag, and if I didn't get back, the game and the Series would be over.

I dove back as hard and fast as I could. Nelson, who wasn't the most agile fielder, hit me with his glove, too late. My hand was under him, and the umpire yelled "safe." More important, Gil scored with the tying run.

I was sure we were going to win it when we took the field for the bottom of the ninth. Ralph Terry, who was just a kid but who had great stuff, went back to work. Bill Mazeroski, the Pirate second baseman, was the lead-off hitter. Yogi, our veteran catcher, was in left. John Blanchard, Yogi's backup, was behind the plate. I will always wonder whether things might have been different if Yogi had been back there.

The first pitch was high. John told me he told Ralph to get the ball down. On the next pitch he got it down all right, about waist high, and Mazeroski hit it high and deep, far over the left-field wall of Forbes Field. Yogi didn't even move. All he could do was watch it crush us. Meanwhile, Mazeroski ran around the bases, holding his cap in the air, a famous moment that has always made me sick to my stomach every time I see it. End of game. End of Series.

I tucked my glove under my arm and trotted in from center field to the dugout, as the Pirates and their fans celebrated. It was a madhouse of cheering, stomping, crazy fans, but all I could feel was a total emptiness, a feeling of abject failure, of having lost something I'd never get back again. I had felt bad after losing the Series to the Dodgers in '55 and to the Braves in '57, but this was something far worse. I was struck with a sense of hopelessness and desolation.

I descended the ramp leading to the clubhouse, headed for the trainer's room, where the reporters couldn't get to me, and I sobbed for what seemed like hours. Real men aren't supposed to cry, but I never felt a loss as deeply as this one. One reason I cried was I was sure George Weiss was going to trade me away. I had been Casey's boy all those years, and it was clear Casey would be fired, and I was sure Topping and Webb were going to ship me off, too. And even if I stayed, I was overwhelmed by the thought of having to play without Casey there behind me, and it was as though he had died, which in a baseball sense, he had. Some of the guys came over trying to console me, but I couldn't stop crying, no matter how hard I tried.

We had kicked the shit out of the Pirates in every way imaginable and lost the Series. None of us could believe it. We all walked around saying, "I can't believe this shit." We were all shaking our heads.

The only one who didn't seem to be upset was Casey, who had seen it all. "That's baseball," was his comment. "Tra la la."

Casey was fired right after the Series.

Topping and Webb held a press conference in New York and tried to tell everyone that Casey had retired. We knew Casey too well to fall for a bunch of bull like that. The first question he was asked was, "Were you fired?"

"You're goddamn right I was fired," he said. "I'll never make the mistake of being seventy again," Casey told everyone.

Topping and Webb had thought they had seen the last of Old Case. Boy, were they in for a surprise.

What was it like for you without Casey?

When we arrived in St. Pete to start the '61 season, everything was different. Ralph Houk, the guy Topping and Webb wanted so badly, was the new manager. I thought I was going to hate it, but the funny thing about baseball is you never know what's going to happen. When Ralph took over, baseball became a lot more fun. Ralph treated us real nice. He didn't second-guess us like Casey. He didn't dump on the players in the newspapers the way Casey did.

It was as though a weight had been lifted off my shoulders, and I know the younger guys, Richardson, Kubek, Boyer, and the kid pitchers could feel it too, because we'd talk about it. Ralph had coached all those guys at Denver, and they trusted and believed in him. Richardson, in particular, thrived under Ralph.

Casey had picked on Richardson and Kubek more than anyone, because they were young and made rookie mistakes. At one point Bobby came to me and told me he was going to quit baseball and become a minister. Bobby was a great defensive player. I didn't know how well he'd hit, but I always hated it when the game made a player unhappy, especially when he's talented, and besides, I liked Bobby. He was funny and sincere, and he always tried real hard, so I did what I could to make him feel better. I told him not to take what the Old Man had to say so hard. I told him Case had told me he was special. I advised him to keep playing and that things would work out.

I'm sure he appreciated that.

I have no idea whether what I said had anything to do with his not quitting, but he stayed, and when Ralph took over, Bobby just blossomed. He became the best second baseman in the American League. His buddy, Tony, was a lot tougher. He would swear at Casey under his breath whenever Casey was too rough on him. Under Ralph, he took over at short, and he also became an All-Star. Ralph gave Clete Boyer the third base job, and in '61 Clete led the league in assists. Casey had always batted Clete at the bottom of the order and often pinch-hit for him in crucial situations. Houk told him he was the best third baseman in baseball, left him alone, and Clete made him look like a genius. The three anchored one of the best infields in baseball. You can have Tinker, Evers, and Chance. I'll take Boyer, Kubek, and Richardson any time.

Houk made some other changes as well. He made Ellie Howard our first-string catcher and played Yogi, who was getting on, in left. And he announced he was going to have a four-man rotation and that Whitey would pitch every fourth day no matter who we were facing.

Another thing Ralph did—which meant so much to me—was tell me every day how much I meant to the team. I had played for Casey for ten years, and I can count on one hand the number of compliments he paid me. All I ever heard was, "When is Mickey going to fulfill his potential?"

From the very first day of spring training Ralph told me I was the best player in baseball, that he appreciated me, and that he would do all he could to make sure I was happy. He said he wanted me to be the team leader. He said, "Mickey, the other guys look up to you. They like you. You have to go out there and show them the way." I promised him I would.

I started the '61 season hitting a whole bunch of home runs. The only other player in the league who did as well was Roger.

In spring training that year I asked Casey whether he thought Roger could break Ruth's record. Casey said he thought he could.

So did I. I thought I could, too. The league had added two expansion teams, Washington and Los Angeles, and there were a lot of young and not-so-talented pitchers in the league. By June we had hit so many home runs that fans were taking bets on which of us would break the record. Roger hit fourteen home runs in June, and was leading the league with twenty-seven.

On July 1, I hit two home runs, my twenty-sixth and twenty-seventh, and that day Roger hit number twenty-eight. The next day I hit number twenty-eight, and Roger hit twenty-nine and thirty. Moose, Ellie, and Blanchard were also homering, and by the time summer came we were hitting so many home runs that everyone was comparing us to the 1927 Yankees of Ruth and Gehrig. Baseball had become fun again. We went out there every day convinced we were going to homer and win.

That may have been the best baseball team I ever saw. You won twenty games in July.

By the end of the month, I had thirty-eight home runs, and Roger had forty. Ellie was hitting around .350 and Yogi was homering in bunches. John Blanchard hit four home runs in consecutive at-bats in three games.

Roger and I chased the Babe through the month of August. On August 2, I hit home run number forty. On August 4, Roger hit number forty-one. Two days later I hit three home runs.

Whitey Ford, meanwhile, was having the finest season of his career. By the end of August, his record was 22–3.

Johnny Sain, our pitching coach, had taught him a slider, a fast curve that became his out pitch. In '61 Whitey was the best pitcher in baseball.

We flew to Washington, and in three games against the expansion Senators, I hit home runs forty-four and forty-five. Roger hit forty-three, forty-four, and forty-five.

You were sixteen games ahead of Babe's pace. You and Roger roomed together. Tell me about your relationship with Roger.

We shared an apartment together in northern New Jersey with Bob Cerv. The funny thing was, I don't think we ever talked about the home run race even once. Records didn't mean much to me, and they certainly didn't mean anything to Roger. All we cared about was winning games. All I wanted to do was make Ralph happy with the way I was playing. But once we left our apartment and went out into the public, the whole world was only interested in one thing: who was going to break Babe Ruth's record? Roger's answer was always the same: "How the fuck do I know?"

Which is why we called him "Red Ass Roger."

Roger had a great sense of humor. When he was asked why he was crabby, he told a reporter, "Anyone can be nice when they're going good." And he meant it, too.

Because of Roger, you became the fan's favorite to break the record. Roger became the bad guy who was between you and breaking it.

Yeah, that year I became the Yankee fans' hero that I was for the rest of my life. Before that, the fans had taken me for granted, or else they felt about me the same way Casey did: that as good as I was, I should have been better. But in '61, for the first time, the old-time Yankee fans began to feel that Roger was stealing my glory, and it seemed they resented him for that, as dumb as it sounds. When Roger was surly to reporters, you guys would write about it, and people were under the false impression I was the nice guy. A year before, I was getting booed like I had killed someone. The next year I got cheers every time I came to bat. What pissed me off was that Roger was getting booed, which I held you and your buddies responsible for.

We were just reporting what he was saying.

Some of the writers were making shit up about Roger. They started writing articles saying that Roger was jealous of me. Total bullshit. Roger wasn't jealous of anyone. He couldn't have cared less who finished the season with more home runs. He couldn't have cared less about beating the Babe. His one goal—my goal—was to win the pennant. And at the end of the day both of us wanted to be left alone.

When September began, I had fifty homers and he had forty-nine. Whitey already had twenty-two wins. You know how many games ahead of the Tigers we were with thirty games left? One and a half! They had Norm Cash and Al Kaline, and they didn't lose much either.

We finished them off the first week in September. They came into the

Stadium for three games. Moose singled up the middle to win the first game, 1–0. The Tigers led late in the second game when Roger, in a slump because he was swinging at bad pitches, homered, and then he homered again in a 7–2 win. I hurt myself that game, pulling a muscle in my left arm swinging the bat.

Ralph wanted to rest me the next day, but I wouldn't let him. I got to the Stadium early, took a whirlpool, had my arm taped, and when I swung under the grandstands, I was stiff but I could play. I told Ralph to play me, and he did.

Jim Bunning, the best of the Tiger pitchers, started. He threw me an inside fastball, and I felt the pain when I swung, but I managed to pull the ball into the lower grandstands for my fifty-first home run. Later in the game Bunning hit a long fly deep into Death Valley, and I was able to run it down and make an over-the-shoulder catch. We still trailed by a run in the ninth.

I was the first batter up for the Yankees. Gerry Staley, a right-hander, was on the mound. He got a pitch up too high, and I pulled that one 450 feet into the right-field stands. I'll never forget the cheers. Like I said, that year I really felt loved by the Yankee fans for the first time.

After my home run, the rest of the guys did the rest. Ellie finished them off with a three-run home run to win it. The Tigers left town four and a half games back. Ten days later our lead was twelve and a half games, and it was over.

With the pennant race decided, the fans could concentrate on you and Roger trying to catch the Babe.

I really loved coming to the park to play. I doubt if any athlete who ever played in Yankee Stadium was ever treated so wonderfully. It was as though everyone was making up for how lousy they had treated me before.

On September 10, I hit my fifty-third home run off Jim Perry in the first inning. I had a terrible head cold, plus my right shoulder was killing me, and so was my right leg, but I played because I was really excited by the challenge of trying to beat the Babe, since the pennant already was sewn up, and I knew I wouldn't be hurting our chances by playing.

We had a day off the next day. My cold had gotten worse, and our radio and TV announcer, Mel Allen, suggested I get a penicillin shot. I asked him who I should go to, and he recommended his personal doctor near his home in Greenwich, Connecticut.

You took medical advice from the team's announcer? Geez, Mick, how about using a little common sense?

Yeah, not one of my brightest moves. The doc gave me a shot in the ass, and I went on a long road trip west. The doc, it turned out, had used a needle that wasn't sterile, and I developed an infection where he had given me the shot.

For the next week I felt like shit. I didn't hit a single home run, while Roger kept hitting them, one after another, until he reached fifty-seven. Roger caught a break in a game against the Tigers when Moose made an error to send the game into extra innings. Roger hit number fifty-eight off Terry Fox to win the game.

Gus Mauch, the Yankees trainer, examined me, and he saw I had an open wound that was leaking pus. I was too weak to play. My chance of catching Ruth had ended, because that day commissioner Ford Frick ruled that it would be an official record only if we did it in 154 games, which was how many games Babe played in 1927, which I thought was fucking stupid. We had exactly three games left to break the record. Roger needed to hit three in three days. That's hard to do.

Did you know that Frick once had ghosted a book for the Babe and that he was trying to keep you from breaking the record any way he could?

I heard that, but it never affected me, because I wasn't going to be able to play for at least a week. Frick's ruling put all the pressure on Roger, who must have had to answer that one question, "Are you going to do it?" maybe five hundred thousand times. Before and after every game the reporters, from as far away as Japan and Australia, lined up to ask him that one question. Nowadays there would have been a press conference or something. If Roger was sick of talking to the reporters he knew, he really hated getting grilled by guys he had never seen before. No one could understand that breaking that record wasn't that important to him, and no amount of media and public attention was going to get him to change his mind.

Roger was the story in all of sports. Did he think we were going to ignore what he was doing?

Rog just didn't think anyone should care what he ate for breakfast or whether he was sleeping well at night or whether he'd break the Babe's record. Rog had no idea whether he could break the record. He was trying hard to hold back his contempt for what was going on, but he didn't always succeed. And after you guys jumped all over him and wrote what a prick he was, the fans started to get on him, and he was living in hell while he was trying to break the greatest record in all of sports. Roger was getting booed, and he wasn't used to getting booed. He said he was sorry he ever left Kansas City, where he had once been in a terrible slump but never once was booed.

Roger Maris silently slips into Toots Shor's. He still wears his recognizable crew cut, grown in a bit more now. He grabs a chair and walks over to the growing circle of men and women listening to Mickey talk. He sits down and listens intently to what Mickey has to say.

When we played on the road, the opposing fans picked up on how sensitive Roger was, and they began to target Roger for abuse. They threw bottles at him, garbage, anything handy. After a game in Detroit he was very upset—mad that the fans were treating him so badly, but even angrier that the Yankee organization wasn't doing anything to protect him. After the game he hid in the trainer's room for an hour to get away. He made all the writers miss their deadlines, and they abused Roger even more.

We flew to Baltimore to play the Orioles for the last three games to 154. I still couldn't play. Memorial Stadium was not an easy park to hit a home run in. When the first game of a Sunday doubleheader began, a strong wind was blowing in from right field. I thought, *Rog is in trouble now.* That day he didn't hit one. Paul Richards threw not one knuckleball pitcher, but two, Hoyt Wilhelm and Skinny Brown.

One game to 154. I thought Roger was going to have a nervous breakdown. I doubt he slept all night. When he arrived at the ballpark, tears were streaming down his face. He was shaking.

"I need help," he said to me.

I told him to go see Ralph, that he'd know what to do.

My heart went out to Roger. He didn't have the emotional makeup to survive under the strain. I doubt that anyone did. Ralph told him if he could stick it out for just a couple more days, the season would be over. Ralph got him a brown paper bag, and he had him breathe into it to calm himself. You were one of the reasons he couldn't breathe, Lenny. You and your buddies were heartless bastards.

I'm sorry, Mick. I guess I took his insolence personally, and I shouldn't have. I really am sorry. If we could have talked then the way we're talking now, I'm sure it would have been different. But Roger was a tough nut to crack. Every day he wore the red ass, and even when guys tried to be nice to him, he brushed them off.

He wanted to see one crummy article about the pressure he was under, just one writer to cut the guy some slack. You're damn lucky they don't let the players go back to the paper with you and stand behind you and criticize as you write your goddamn stories. It would get old real quick.

I suppose it would. The nice thing was that Roger did it, even with all that pressure.

Which is why the guy deserves to be in the Hall of Fame, hands down. How could you idiots not have voted him in?

Maybe one day, Mick. Maybe one day. Tell me about Game 154.

The first time up that day I thought Roger had hit one, but it was caught by the right fielder. The next at-bat, against Milt Pappas, Roger lined the ball on a line into the right-field bleachers. You should have seen the madhouse in the bleachers by the fans trying to collect the ball. The scramble for the ball looked like a war. It was home run number fifty-nine, one short of the Babe.

Rog got to bat one more time. Paul Richards sent in Hoyt Wilhelm, who told me later Richards had warned him if he threw anything but knuckleballs, he'd fine him $5,000. Which was about half his salary. Roger took a half-assed swing and grounded out weakly to the pitcher.

That win was the pennant clincher, and we celebrated in the locker room by getting snockered on champagne. Everyone, that is, except Roger, who had to sit on his stool answering question after question. He kept saying, "I tried. I really tried." Every one of us walked over and shook his hand. I can't remember admiring a ballplayer more.

There were still nine more games to play.

Which Frick said wouldn't count against the record. Dumbest thing he could have done, and I'll tell you why in a minute. In the Baltimore finale he went 0 for 4, and after the game Roger and I were drinking beer, watching TV in our hotel room, when he came over and showed me a clump of blond hair in his fist.

"Look at this, Mick," he said, "my fucking hair is falling out." He went to find Doc Gaynor, who told him it was because of nerves. The tension had really gotten to him.

We returned to the Stadium with five games left in the '61 season, two against Baltimore, and three against the Red Sox. Frick had made a ruling he had to do it in 154 games, but we didn't pay any attention to it. Of course, what Frick's ruling did more than anything else was kill the attendance at those last games. The Yankees should have had full houses of sixty thousand. Instead, we had half that, with most of them sitting in the right field bleachers to catch any home runs Roger might hit. If anyone should have been apeshit furious at Frick, it should have been Topping and Webb. Probably cost them half a million bucks.

Believe it or not, most of the writers didn't take Frick's ruling seriously either. We were rooting for Roger as much as anyone. We may not have liked him, but we certainly admired the way he was hitting and appreciated how momentous a feat he was accomplishing. Talk about the last couple of games.

Roger hit number sixty against Jack Fisher of Baltimore, and then Ralph let him sit out a game and watch in peace from the bench. My infection, meanwhile, was getting worse, not better, and I stayed home. Roger was shut out the first two games against the Sox. One game remained.

We won that day 1–0. People remember Roger's home run off Tracy Stallard in the fourth inning, but they don't remember it was the only run of the game. When Roger hit it, you'd never have thought it was anything special for him. As with every other home run, he put his head down, ran around the bases, and headed for the dugout. There were no theatrics, no showboating.

This time, the guys wouldn't let him in the dugout. They pushed him back out four times so he could hear the roar from the crowd. The last time, Roger waved his cap. He even smiled. I loved hearing those cheers for Roger. He deserved them. What he did was very special. And it turned out that Frick never did put an asterisk by Roger's record.

I finished the season with fifty-four home runs. Considering I had fifty-three on September 10 and had more than three weeks left in the season, I have to admit I was very disappointed in myself. I didn't have it in my heart to blame Mel or his doctor. They were only trying to help me. But if I had stayed healthy, the way I was going, I might have hit sixty-five home runs that year. And then McGwire, Sosa, and Bonds all would have had to break my record.

Did you ever use steroids, Mick? Sorry, but I have to ask.

Nope. All we needed to keep us in tip-top shape was a case of Ballantine beer, breakfast of champions.

Sixty-one was another year when you didn't get to play much in the World Series.

I ended up in the hospital during the final week of the 1961 season because of the abscess in my thigh, and when I got out, I was listless and weak. I really didn't see how I could play in the Series against the Cincinnati Reds. A large piece of gauze covered the wound, which was about a foot square. When I ran all-out, it would ooze blood.

I didn't play in the first two games. Whitey didn't need me in the opener, as he pitched his third World Series shutout in a row. We lost the second game on a chickenshit passed ball and a single by their catcher Edwards, who I had never even heard of. None of us thought the Reds could beat us even one game.

We flew to Cincinnati for three games. The Reds played in Crosley Field, a bandbox that had been built at the turn of the century. Like Forbes Field, it was perfect for us.

The Reds led Game 3 by 2–1 with two outs in the eighth. Ralph called Johnny Blanchard in from the bullpen to pinch-hit. When he walked into the dugout, he asked me what their pitcher, Bob Purkey, was throwing. I told him the first pitch would be a slider to get ahead, and then all knuckleballs. I told him to jump on the first pitch.

Just like I told him, Johnny swung at the first pitch and hit the ball into the right-field bleachers to tie the game. He came back to the bench grinning.

Roger faced Purkey in the top of the ninth. The Reds fans started booing him. Rog really gave them something to boo about when he hit the ball twenty rows deep into the stands to give us the run that won it. When he came into the dugout, he was as serious as death. He had stopped smiling weeks before.

Whitey did it again in Game 4, his fourth shutout in a row going back to the Pirates Series the year before. We buried the Reds 7–0. Whitey ran his World Series scoreless streak to 32, beating Babe Ruth's pitching record when the Babe was with the Red Sox. As Whitey said, 1961 wasn't a very good year for the Babe.

In the fourth inning I lined a shot to left center off the scoreboard. Normally, I'd have had a double, but I still couldn't run. I could only limp to first. Ralph sent in a runner, and as I came off the field, I was crying like a baby. Here was another World Series I had to leave early. But the blood was oozing from my open wound, and since I couldn't run, there was no point staying in the game.

While I sat on the bench and watched, we closed it out the next day in a rout. Ralph Terry again couldn't get anyone out, but Bud Daley, one of those quiet, unappreciated lefties who Weiss had gotten from Kansas City, came in to shut them down. Johnny Blanchard hit another home run, and Hector Lopez, who took my place, also hit one. He also hit a long triple to score a run. Moose drove in a few. We were so good that year, it was a shame the season ever had to end. Maybe the '27 Yankees could have given us a run for it, but no one else, not before or after. In '61, we may well have been the best baseball team ever assembled.

A bear and a bunny are sitting in a forest taking a shit. The bear leans over to the bunny and says, "Do you ever have a problem of shit sticking to your fur?" The bunny says no. So the bear grabs the bunny and wipes his ass.

The Yankees were always accused of being like U.S. Steel, but over the years we had a bunch of players who could have just as easily played the circus or the vaudeville circuit. In 1962 one of the greatest characters ever to play baseball came up to the Yankees. His name: Joe Pepitone. I can talk about him, because Pepi will tell you all these stories himself. If you ever get a chance to ask him, he'll tell you everything. There is only one Pepi. He's a beauty.

Pepi almost didn't make it to the majors because he was shot in the stomach in high school by a kid with a zip gun. Pepi liked to walk around the clubhouse showing everyone his scar.

In '62, Pepi's rookie year, Ralph assigned Moose the task of keeping an eye on Pepi and getting him to go to bed at a decent hour. Pepi's reputation had preceded him. The first night Pepi came in late, Moose put the chain on the hotel room door and told him he would have to spend the night sleeping in the hall. Pepi, pissed, kicked the door down. He told Moose, who was a big guy, that if he ever did something like that again, he'd be sorry he did.

When the half-clothed Moose got out of bed, for the first time Pepi saw just what a moose Moose really was. Pepi ran out of there, deciding to find a less intimidating roommate. When the Yankees traveling secretary told him he couldn't switch rooms, Pepi treated Moose with more deference. Pepi also found someone to take him in on the nights he came in late—me. Moose never could rein him in. After a while Moose couldn't take it anymore, and Pepi moved in with another rookie, Phil Linz.

One time Pepi had a date with a stripper. We were in Detroit, and he had arranged to meet her after she got off work—about three in the morning. He decided he'd go down to the strip club and watch her perform first. Around one, he got up and dressed, tiptoed out of his room, and when the elevator came up, who was standing there but Ralph Houk, who asked him where he was going.

Pepi, who was maybe twenty-two years old, didn't know what to say. He was all dressed up, smelling of cologne, and the first thing that came out of his mouth was, "I'm going out to look for Phil," meaning his roommate, Linz. Houk ordered him back in his room, and when they walked in, there was Phil sound asleep. Pepi looked at Linz and said, "Phil, how did you get there? Where the hell were you, man?"

The next day Ralph shipped Pepi's ass back to Richmond!

But Pepi was too good to stay there long. He came back, and once again we were playing in Detroit. Whitey and I were having a few drinks at the bar of one of Detroit's better restaurants when Pepi and Linz came by to say hello. I loved those guys. Pepi and Linz added a lot of life and fun to the team.

Whitey told them, "Joe, Phil, later this evening we're going to the Flame Lounge for a few drinks. We'll meet you over there after we have dinner." Whitey wrote out the address for them. "Grab a cab," Whitey said. "It'll only cost a few bucks."

Pepi and Linz did as Whitey told them. "The Flame Lounge," Pepi said, handing the cabbie the address.

Pepi and Phil didn't know it, but the Flame Lounge was miles from our hotel, in the heart of the black section of Detroit. How Whitey had found out about it, I have no idea, but the cab ride out there must have cost them a good fifteen bucks. When the cab stopped in front of the place, Pepi and Linz couldn't believe the kind of joint they were walking into. It had big, round windows and you could see the strippers dancing looking in from the outside. They paid the cabbie and went in.

They were the only two white guys in the place!

The bartender asked if he could help them.

"Mickey Mantle's table," Pepi said.

The bartender let out a laugh. "You kiddin'?" he said. "Mickey Mantle sure don't come in here."

It cost them another fifteen bucks to get back to our hotel.

The next day on the team bus going to Tiger Stadium, Pepi came over to Whitey and me and said, "Hey, Mick, sorry about last night. We just weren't able to meet you guys."

"You went, didn't you?" I asked.

Pepi tried to look all innocent. "No why? Didn't you go?"

"Oh yeah, Pepi," I said. "We were there."

Pep started to laugh. "Why, you no good son of a bitch," he said to Whitey.

Whitey and I laughed like crazy.

Pepi was a player in every way. He once was married to a former Playboy bunny. Before her, he was married to another beauty. They had a game they played: they'd each get all dolled up and go to a bar separately. She'd arrive first, drinking at the bar, and he'd come in a few minutes later and pretend he didn't know her. He'd buy her a drink, and then they'd dance, and then he'd ask her how much she charged, and she'd say, "Fifty dollars," and he'd take out the money and lay it on the bar. She'd take it, and he'd take her home, and they'd make love.

The first time I saw Pepi do this, I didn't know she was his wife. I thought he was picking up a call girl. The transaction really turned me on. Later when I asked Pepi if I could have her phone number, he got all fake-pissed, the way he could get. He wouldn't give me her number no matter how hard I pushed for it. The next night I watched him pick her up a second time, and I asked the bartender what was going on. He clued me in that she was Pepi's wife.

Pepi and I were a lot alike, guys who didn't keep our marriage vows very well. In fact, one time we discussed it. I told Pepi that there wasn't a girl, no matter what she looked like, who I wouldn't fuck. Pepi looked me right in the eye, and he said, "Me, neither." I'm not proud of this, but one time we made a bet as to which of us could sleep with the ugliest girl we could find that night. We were in Chicago, playing a day game, so we had all evening. We were rooming next door to each other, so we wouldn't have any trouble introducing our dates to each other.

Now if you think that's an easy bet to win, you'd be wrong. First of all, the really plug-ugly girls don't hang around bars. They tend to stay home. You can see them at the ballpark, but it's hard to hook up with them there. And a lot of ugly girls have a terrible self-image, and they'd freak at the idea of a ballplayer or a movie star wanting to go out with them. Like I said, this was going to be harder than it sounded.

The women's movement would have you strung up a tree if they'd ever heard about this. You're lucky you're not around any more.

Like I said, I'm not proud of this, but it happened, so I'm telling you the story. It's not always easy finding ways to make recreational sex interesting. Let's go to the videotape, as Warner Wolf used to say. C'mon, I'll show you what I mean.

The lights dim in the restaurant as Mickey and Lenny turn in their seats. The fifty or so other patrons of Toots Shor's who have gathered around and have been listening in on the conversation turn in their seats as well, not quite sure what's going to happen.

It is now 1962, and Mickey and Joe Pepitone walk in to the main dining area at the Pump Room, one of Chicago's premier restaurants. The décor is sophisticated and timeless; the clientele is famous, moneyed, or on expense accounts. This is where the movie stars go when they're in town, and where regular folks go for special occasions. The waitstaff is a mix of older, professional career waiters, and young, attractive men and women—some of them college kids from the University of Chicago to the south, or Northwestern to the north. A moon-faced blonde with a pert button nose, a spray of freckles, and a pair of corn-fed Midwestern 36Ds walks by carrying a tray of drinks. She recognizes Mickey and flashes him a big smile.

Mickey, despite his "aw shucks" way about him, has benefited from his ten-plus years in New York. His suit is expensive and well-cut, his shirt and tie well chosen, and his shoes the top of the line and highly polished. No one is mistaking this guy for a dumb hick.

Pepi, on the other hand, looks like he's just graduated from gangster school. He's decked out in a gray sharkskin suit that seems to shimmer when the light hits it at the right angle. His freshly shaved face is already showing a five o'clock shadow—like Richard Nixon, Pepi needs to shave twice a day to control his heavy beard.

They scan the room, looking for likely candidates to participate—unknowingly—in their bizarre bet. They are seated by the maître d', order a round of drinks, and when no likely candidates appear, they figure what the heck and order a couple of steaks with all the trimmings. Just as they are finishing their meal and are about to ask for the bill, their quarry walks in.

The maître d' seats a group at the next table—eight dowdy women. The women stick out as if someone were shining a spotlight on them. They seem as uncomfortable in the posh surroundings as they are awed by them.

As the women are handed their menus, Pepi gets up from his table and introduces himself.

"Good evening, ladies," Pepi says, oozing charm. "I don't know if any of you happen to be baseball fans, but my name is Joseph Pepitone, and I play for the New York Yankees. We're in town for a three-game series against the White Sox. Have you ladies come to the Windy City for business or for pleasure?"

The women giggle nervously, but the spokeswoman for the group, a thin, long-faced, plain-looking woman in her late thirties, who is actually wearing glasses on a silver chain around her neck, answers. "Good evening, Mr. Pepitone. We are indeed here on business—for the American Library Association conference. And while I do know a little about baseball—we librarians must know about a great deal of subjects—I can't say that I've heard of you. You seem awfully young. Are you new to the Yankees?"

Pep smiles. "Why, yes, as a matter of fact, this is my rookie season. That's most astute of you. I myself have always been in awe of librarians. There was many a day back in Brooklyn when the librarian had to call the po—I don't wish to bore you with stories of my youth. I'm here with one of my friends and teammates. I'm sure you'll recognize him." He waves at Mickey to come over and join him. Mickey, fortified with three vodka collinses, saunters over.

"Hiya ladies," he drawls. "Mickey Mantle. Pleased to meet ya." Mickey goes around the table shaking hands. The librarians are in awe of meeting a real celebrity—the cover of one of their periodicals come to life.

Pepi turns to the spokeswoman and asks, "Excuse me, but I didn't catch your name."

"It's Irma."

Mickey stifles a laugh while Pepi elbows him out of sight of the librarians.

"Irma—now that's an exotic name! What is that, French? Irma, would you do me the honor of joining me at the bar for a drink?" Pepi puts on his most dazzling smile—guaranteed irresistible to women, dogs, and small babies.

Irma looks up, and says, "Why yes, Mr. Pepitone . . . Joseph . . . I'd be delighted. She gets up, unfolding her angular body to a height of five foot eleven, takes Pepi's elbow, and together they walk to the bar, leaving Mickey behind with seven shocked, openmouthed librarians. The most shocked of all is Mickey. Now the pressure is on not to lose the bet. He's down by a run and it's only the top of the first.

Mickey looks out at the vast sea of librarians. Each one is as plain as the next—bony, severe, pale. All wear glasses or squint. He is having a hard time imagining any of them without their clothes on. He takes a deep breath, mentally preparing himself for the task at hand, as if going up to bat against Camilo Pascual when he has his good stuff going.

"So you ladies are librarians? Huh. I never could figure out that Dewey Decimal System." This is the best Mick can come up with—a weak swing at a high hard one.

"Well, Mr. Mantle, I'd be glad to explain it to you." Mickey's weak swing connects, sending a Texas League double into short left field. "My name is Winifred, and I'm a big fan of yours. Well, I should say my younger brother is—I'm from right here in Chicago, and you know your teammate, Moose Skowron, is from Chicago, too, so we've always followed his career, from the time he was in high school. Come on, let's join Irma and your friend Mr. Pepitone."

Before Mick knew what hit him, he was being guided by the forward Winifred while waving good-bye to the other ladies over his shoulder.

She wore a charcoal wool sack dress, light gray kneesocks, and Mary Jane shoes. With her horn-rimmed glasses, she looked like a refugee from a poetry reading at some dingy coffeehouse.

Mickey and Winifred and Pepi and Irma sat at the bar and had a couple more rounds of drinks. Winifred prattles on about the usefulness of the Dewey Decimal System and how it made finding books a snap at any library in the entire country. It was painfully boring, but Mickey stuck in a few "you don't says" and "is that sos" to make it appear that he was interested. Pepi and Irma seemed to actually be hitting it off—Pepi actually getting the severe-looking woman who had to be at least fifteen years his senior to laugh—at one time slapping the bar.

"Hey, Winifred . . ." Mickey starts.

"Please, call me Winnie."

"Okay, Winnie, I just wanted to say how much I've enjoyed meeting you and talking to you. Joe and I have to check in for a team meeting in a few minutes, but if you want to meet later on and continue where we left off, well, uh . . ."

Mickey scrawls his hotel room number on a napkin, folds it, and places it into Winnie's hand. Winnie looks at his hand touching hers.

"I sure do hope you can come on by . . ."

"Oh yes," Winnie promises. "I'd like that very much." Mickey glances over and sees Pepi doing the same with Irma, who also promises to show up.

It was a sucker bet, Len. I knew he'd lose. There was no way those women would show up.

I can't believe you actually went through with it.
Just wait till you see what happened.

At about ten-thirty, there is a polite knock on the door of Mickey's hotel room. He's been lying in bed, watching TV, his suit jacket and tie draped over a chair, his shirt unbuttoned at the neck. He figures it's Pepi, coming to call the bet off, or to admit defeat. He opens the door, and there is Winnie standing in the hall.

"Uh, hi, Winnie. C'mon in." Mickey closes the door behind him as she walks in. "Hello, Mr. Mantle. I hope your team meeting went well."

"What meet—oh, yeah, we just went over the other team's lineup for tomorrow's game. You know—what so-and-so likes to hit, where to play him, what their pitcher likes to throw, that sort of stuff. Can I offer you a vodka collins?"

"Why yes, that would be lovely." She looks around the room as Mickey calls the bar downstairs to bring up a couple more vodka collinses. She looks out the window at the bustling street scene down below.

An awkward silence hangs over the room, the only sound the gunshots and war whoops of the cowboy movie playing on the TV. At last, room service shows up with the drinks. Mickey signs for them. He hands one to Winnie and pulls over the chair. As he sits on the edge of the bed, she turns off the television.

"Cheers," Mickey says, and tips his glass at her. He downs the drink in one gulp, while she demurely sips hers. Mickey smiles at her. She smiles back. Thank God her teeth are all right, Mickey thinks.

Len, I didn't want to just start taking off her clothes. I was afraid she'd freak out and call the police.

•　　•　　•

The awkward silence continues. Winnie finishes her drink, reaches behind her, and unties the scarf holding her ponytail. "You know," she says quietly, "I've always had fantasies about going to bed with you." She slips off her shoes, and unrolls her kneesocks, revealing shapely calves.

Mickey tries to hide his surprise. Instead, he slips off his belt.

Winnie starts to slowly, seductively unzip her dress. Mickey unbuttons his shirt and flings it on the bed. Little Mick is at full attention now.

Winnie's dress slides to the carpeted floor. She steps out of the dress, wearing only a bra and panties. Her legs are her best feature, although no one ever would know it from the way she dresses. Her hips are a little wider than her shoulders, and her stomach is even flatter than her chest. She walks over to Mickey and unbuttons his pants for him. She slides the zipper down, surprised but pleased that he's not wearing any boxers or briefs. He kicks off his pants. Mick reaches behind her and undoes the bra hooks. It gets flung, coming to rest on the lampshade. Mickey turns off the lamp—the only light now coming from the street lamps and neon signs and car headlights of the Chicago night.

She shrugs off her panties, and they come together, slowly sinking onto the bed. Winnie's mouth is on Mickey's—they kiss deeply. She takes his hand and guides it inside her, letting Mickey know she is already wet and ready for action. This is a woman Joe D would have loved—no need for foreplay. She grabs Little Mick and makes sure he's ready, too.

This is a woman who hasn't gotten out much, but she's up-to-date in her reading. She's read Henry Miller's *Tropic of Cancer*, published in the United States the previous year, and followed the obscenity trial here in Illinois. Winnie knows what to do, and she has no reservations about doing any of it. And she knows what she wants. When she's sure Mick is ready, she mounts him. He is still wearing his socks.

"Oh God, oh yes, oh, oh, oh, fuck me harder!!! Now! Yes!!! Oh God, yess!!"

The prim, proper librarian is not shy about letting the world know that she's having an orgasm.

Mickey has a fleeting thought about the bet and Pepi in the adjoining room, but then he gets caught up in Winnie's obvious enthusiasm for sex and forgets everything else. He is existing totally in the moment. He is in the zone, as athletes say. Yeah, the puss zone.

After a bathroom break and another round of drinks, they get ready for the second inning. Winnie passes her oral exam and gets Little Mick to pay attention again. This time, Mick is on top, his socks now gone. Winnie gets going again, and begins urging Mickey on as if she were Frankie Crosetti over in the coaching box.

"That's the way, Mick. Come on. Keep on going. Yeah, that's it. Oh, that's good. You're rounding third now, Mick. Bring it on home. Oh yes, yes, *yessss*!! It's a home run!"

Then they do it doggie style, and then once more in the shower before they both collapse in a wet, exhausted heap on top of the king-sized bed. Mickey is sure he'll never walk again, much less run. Winnie knows that she has a story that none of her friends will ever believe. They both fall asleep with smiles on their faces.

Len, we had a really great time in the sack. She was a lot better in bed than the really good-looking girls I had been with. I always thought that most of the real pretty ones didn't like sex all that much but just wanted to be with someone famous.

What did Pepi have to say?

He was bragging about the great time he had, too. They had even made a second date. So when people talk about librarians, I can tell you that just because a woman is into books, that doesn't mean it's all she's into.

Geez, Mickey, I think I need a vodka collins right about now.

Pepi was the only player I knew who had sex in the middle of a major league baseball game he was playing in. He did this for the whole time we played together. Even as a rookie Pepi was real close with the grounds crew, and when he saw a girl in the stands he wanted to meet, he'd send Frankie or Bobby or one of the other guys over to ask if she wanted to meet him up close and personal. If the girl agreed, she'd be taken under the stands to the grounds crew's toolshed, which was out in right field. If we were up, and Pepi wasn't scheduled to hit real soon, he would head back into the clubhouse and race in his spikes on the concrete under the stands to the toolshed, where he'd meet his girl of the game. Pepi told me some of the girls would pull their pants down and fuck him right then and there, but he said a lot of them would only let him feel her up. A few would give him a blow job. If the girl was someone he wanted to have sex with again, he would arrange to go out with her that night. Every once in a while, if we had a big inning going, Pepi's turn in the batting order would come up. He would be next to bat and there'd be no one in the on-deck circle. We'd be sitting on the bench snickering as we waited for him, huffing and puffing, stuffing his uniform top back in his pants, to grab a bat and run out there.

In addition to all these other girls, Pepi also had a regular girl who would routinely visit him in the toolshed during the game. She was married, she loved the Yankees, and she loved giving Pepi a quickie or a blow job between innings. Pepi would come back to the dugout singing arias from Italian operas, "O Solo Mio," and we'd know what he'd been up to.

When I think back on it, Pepi was the closest thing to Billy the Yankees had in those days, except he wasn't a fighter like Billy. If ever there was a fight, Pepi would run the other way. But like Billy, Pepi would do some crazy-assed things sometimes just to see if he could get away with them. He liked having sex with mothers and daughters, with sisters, with married women, with women about to get married. Pepi didn't care who it was, and he never considered the risk involved. I know there were at least two husbands who threatened to kill him. Pepi'd say, "Fuck 'em if they can't take a joke." It's a miracle Joe Pep made it past the age of thirty.

Pepi wasn't the only character on that team. We had a pitcher by the name of Marshall Bridges. So what do you do when you have a guy on your team whose name is Marshall? You call him The Sheriff, of course. Not very original, but what the fuck. The Sheriff was afraid of snakes and bugs and mice. One time Whitey and I went out and bought a rubber snake, and we put it in our refrigerator to make it cold and slimy, and we hit it inside Sheriff's uniform pants leg. He put his pants on, and we watched him rip 'em to shreds to get it off.

Another time the grounds crew guys showed me a couple of dead field mice they had found in the bowels of the Stadium. I took them and put them inside Sheriff's wing-tip shoes. After the game he wore paper shower shoes out to his car. He wouldn't go near those dead mice.

That year, 1962, you and Roger again had great seasons.

I got off to a great start, until mid-May when I ripped a muscle high inside my left thigh. I was the last batter in a game against the Minnesota Twins. I grounded to the infield and raced down the line. When I got ten feet from the bag, I collapsed in a heap. I was contorted in pain. I didn't play again until mid-June. Three days later Whitey suffered a muscle strain in his arm. He didn't come back until the day before I did. If the Tigers hadn't also had some injuries, they'd have probably won the pennant. But Frank Lary was out, and so were Al Kaline and Billy Bruton, and they slogged along just like we did.

What happened after you returned?

I came back in early July, and I hit six home runs in four games, and once I began hitting, opposing teams could no longer pitch around Roger like they'd been doing, and he hit a bunch of home runs as well. We won ten games in a row, and though there were teams who thought they could catch us, we knew that none of them could. Every team had a weakness, except us. We were a team of All-Stars: Skowron, Richardson, Kubek, Boyer, rookie Tom Tresh in left, me, and Roger. Plus Ellie, Yogi, and Whitey. Plus, we had a bunch of young pitchers including Ralph Terry, who won 23 games that year. The rest of the '62 season we were pretty much invincible.

Despite missing six weeks of the season, you finished the year hitting .321, second in the league, hit thirty home runs, and drove in eighty-nine runs. You were named the American League Most Valuable Player for the third time.

I really didn't deserve it in '62. Roger did. He hit thirty-three home runs that year, played the best right field I ever saw except for maybe Roberto Clemente. He was a great base runner, a great team player, and a great clutch-hitter. Despite all that, the writers voted him The Flop of the Year. After Roger drove in a hundred runs. Like I said, he should have been the MVP.

You played the San Francisco Giants in the World Series. What do you recall about that Series?

There were two things memorable about that Series: It rained a lot in San Francisco. And the final out.

We led the Series three games to two when we flew to the West Coast. It was raining when we got there, and it rained for four more days straight, leaving us to get drunk, play high-stakes poker, and hunt puss. I thought about Marilyn the whole time I was there—it was nearly ten years since our get-together—she had died that summer of a drug overdose. She was only thirty-six.

As I said, she was dating Bobby Kennedy, a guy with ten kids, at the time of her death. Now there was a pussy chaser.

I liked Bobby Kennedy. He had to have been a good guy, because Joe DiMaggio hated him. Kennedy came to Old Timers' Day during the summer of '62. It was after Marilyn had died, and when DiMaggio saw that Kennedy was there, he turned white. If looks could have killed, Kennedy'd have been dead right there on the infield. Joe knew they had been having an affair and blamed him for Marilyn's death.

After the rain delay, you won Game 6, tying the Series at three games each.

The rain allowed Ralph Terry to start Game 7. Ralph had gotten creamed in '60 and '61 in the postseason, but in '62 he blossomed as a pitcher. He was the best in the league that year, and against the Giants he was a gamer. Jack Sanford, the Giants' ace, was their starter. We scored a run in the fifth when Kubek grounded into a double play with the bases loaded. It was the only run of the game going into the bottom of the ninth.

Matty Alou led off with a bunt single. The next two hitters also tried to bunt, but Ralph struck them both out. Willie Mays, the guy Giants fans always compared me to, was up next. Willie took two balls and then lined a hard shot toward right, where the ground was slick and treacherous because it was still so wet out there. If the ball had gotten past Roger, Alou would have scored, but Roger raced over, cut it off, and quickly threw it back in as the Giants wisely held Alou at third. It was a big defensive play, something Roger did every week. Ralph Terry, running to back up the play behind the plate, slipped in the mud and fell. With runners on second and third and two outs, Ralph Houk came over to see if he was okay and ask him whether he preferred to pitch to Willie McCovey or to Orlando Cepeda.

I wouldn't have wanted to pitch to either of them. McCovey was about six foot four and could hit the ball 500 feet, and Cepeda wasn't called the Baby Bull for nothing. McCovey batted left-handed, Cepeda right. But if we walked McCovey to load the bases, another walk would tie it. Either way, all of a sudden we went from having the Series sewn up to being one pitch away from losing it. One base hit, and we were done for.

To Houk's credit, he didn't take Terry out, even though Ralph had given up Bill Mazeroski's home run to lose the '60 Series against the Pirates, and even though he wasn't so good against the Reds in '61. Ralph could have relieved him, but back then managers didn't overmanage the way they do now, bringing in a lefty pitcher to face a lefty hitter, or a righty pitcher to face a righty batter. Rather, Ralph figured that Terry had gotten us this far, it was his game to win, and so he left him in there to finish it win or lose.

Terry said he'd rather face McCovey. He figured he would pitch him tight, not let him get his arms out, work real carefully to him, and if he walked him, no harm done. Another reason Terry didn't want to have to face Cepeda with the bases loaded was that two weeks earlier he had watched the final National League playoff game on TV when Dodger pitcher Stan Williams walked in the deciding run with the bases loaded to give the Giants the pennant.

McCovey, who wore size seventeen shoes, stood up at the plate. Terry threw him a slow curve, and McCovey pulled a shot—foul down the right-field line into the seats. Ralph came back with an inside fastball. McCovey swung, and he sent a low bullet toward right center field that I started racing after. I didn't run more than three strides when second baseman Bobby Richardson caught it chest high. He didn't have to move a step. Two feet to either side, the Giants win.

The best part of winning was the redemption for Ralph Terry. After being the goat in '60, two years later he was the Series hero. That's one of the great things about baseball. If you play long enough, you often get a second chance.

What I remember most about spring training in '63 was that Marshall Bridges almost got himself killed.

He was drinking at a bar in Fort Lauderdale, where we had moved our spring training headquarters because hotels in St. Petersburg wouldn't let Ellie, Marshall, or any other black players stay with the team, and Dan Topping finally blew his stack. Fort Lauderdale was a much more tolerant town and a much better town for chasing puss. It's where all the college kids came during spring break. I must have watched that movie *Where the Boys Are* ten times, and I was hoping to run into Connie Francis or Suzanne Pleshette, but no such luck. God, Suzanne Pleshette had the sexiest voice. I would watch her on the *Bob Newhart Show* years later just to hear her talk. I often thought about having phone sex with her.

Back to what happened to Marshall Bridges, Mick.

Bridges didn't have very good luck. He tried to pick up a girl, and she pulled out a pistol and shot him in the knee. I can't imagine what he said.

But that was the risk black guys took back then when they wanted to go out with white women.

Some of them white girls were cra-zee. It was almost as dangerous as black guys trying to swim in a St. Petersburg hotel pool.

Did Marshall ever try to swim in the hotel pool?

He was crazy, Len, but he wasn't stupid.

When Marshall returned a few weeks later, we started calling him "Bang Bang." I asked him, "Sheriff, after she shot you, did you ask her to have sex with you?" He said, "That's *why* she shot me." We laughed for about ten minutes, until he showed me the bullet hole in his leg.

Joe Pep opened the season by hitting two home runs, and his fielding was as good as anything I had ever seen at first base. Pepi had a lot of range, which allowed Richardson to play closer to the bag at second, and Kubek to play deeper in the hole, and with Clete Boyer catching everything hit his way, nothing—and I mean nothing—ever got through that infield.

Another kid who did real well in '63 was your *Ball Four* buddy, Jim Bouton. He had a good fastball and one of the best curves I had ever seen a young pitcher throw, and he had a fierce determination that I loved. As I told you, I gave him the nickname, Bulldog. With Whitey, Terry, and Bouton, we had a very strong rotation.

You got hurt pretty badly in June.

I suffered one of the worst injuries of my career. We were in Baltimore. Whitey was pitching. Brooks Robinson, their young third baseman, hit a shot toward the right center-field fence. I raced after it. The ball, the wire mesh fence, and I all arrived at the same time. I ran into it running at full speed and caught my left spike in the wire mesh. As I fell, I could hear my ankle make a loud "snap." I was in so much pain that I was in tears. While I lay on the ground, I could hear the Orioles fans cheering. The fuckers were celebrating that I had broken my ankle.

Bobby and Roger were the first to reach me. I told them the ankle was broken. The next week Roger smashed a ball off his toe, and he had to miss some time as well. That summer he also needed rectal surgery, and for a period Tom Tresh was hurt, and so none of the starting outfielders played.

Rectal surgery might be more than I wanted to know. But it didn't matter. You kept winning anyway.

That's how good our reserves were. Your favorite, Hector Lopez filled in. Johnny Blanchard, who you guys called "Roger's caddy," drove in a ton of runs in '63.

As Casey always said, you win with pitching and defense, and our pitching was awesome.

Whitey, the best pitcher I ever saw, and that includes Koufax and Bob Gibson, was 24–7 that year. Bouton won twenty-one, Terry seventeen, and a young kid by the name of Al Downing won thirteen after coming up in June.

When I first saw him, I thought Al had a chance of being as good as Koufax. He was that impressive. He was a lefty like Koufax, with a beautiful, overhand motion, and he had a rising fastball that even the best hitters had trouble catching up with.

Despite my missing sixty games, we tore the American League apart in '63. By August the race was all but over. But the two months I had to sit out were the longest two months of my life. I'd go to the ballpark, but because my foot was broken, I couldn't run, couldn't work out. And because I couldn't play, I felt totally worthless, like I was invisible. I was sitting there with the guys, but feeling like an impostor. They'd go out onto the field and take ground balls or batting practice, while I sat in the dugout keeping out of the way. By the beginning of August I knew that if I didn't come back and play soon, I would go out of my mind.

You finally got to play in early August.

It was a doubleheader against Baltimore at the Stadium. For a couple of weeks the fans had been shouting, "We want Mickey. We want Mickey," and I'd sit there on the bench and I'd say to whoever was sitting next to me, "I want Mickey more than they do."

I didn't play in the first game, and Ralph wasn't intending to play me in the nightcap either. But we were losing 10–9 in the bottom of the seventh with our pitcher coming to bat. New York fans know the game, and they were aware it was a perfect spot for Ralph to send me up as a pinch-hitter. The player they wanted to see was me. I was hoping for the same thing, and just in case Ralph was thinking of sending up someone else, I got up and went over to the bat rack and grabbed a couple of bats.

I remember that game, Mick.

The lights dim and Toots Shor's recedes into the background. By now, all the hangers-on and listeners know what to do—and everyone turns in their seat to be brought back to Yankee Stadium on a steamy August afternoon in 1963.

Mickey is at the bat rack, rummaging around for some good wood. He wasn't picky about his bats the way some players were—like Cobb or Williams, or some of the guys playing today. He is purposefully avoiding looking over at the manager.

The fans across the field can see into the dugout and start to go wild when they see Mickey at the rack. Finally, as if playing his part in this elaborate ritual, Ralph Houk yells, "Go up and hit, Mick." Before Mickey leaves the dugout, before he is even announced into the game, a roar arises from the stands, the likes of which hadn't been heard in the House that Ruth Built in a long time. Mickey gets goose bumps. When he walks up the five steps from the dugout and onto the field, the entire crowd stands and cheers. Love and adoration flood the stadium. Even the Baltimore players in the dugout are standing to see what all the noise is about.

Journeyman George Brunet, a lefty with a half-assed slider who can't break a pane of glass, is on the mound—one of only sixteen games he will play with Baltimore in a season that will see him have an 0–4 record with a 6.06 ERA.

Mickey is announced and strolls slowly to the right-hand side of the plate, savoring the applause. He is batting righty against Brunet, and he digs his right shoe deep in the batter's box. Brunet rocks and deals—the first pitch is a fastball, low, ball one. The fans boo because they think Brunet is going to take the chickenshit way out and walk him since the bases are empty.

Mickey steps out, takes a few practice cuts, trying to get loose. It's been a long time since he was in a game. Brunet winds up and lets go with his next pitch, an inside slider. Mickey's batting eye is still sharp, and he follows the pitch, waiting, and then unleashing an overeager swing. He pulls it high and deep to left field. Boog Powell, still a year away from becoming a full-time first baseman, is playing left field. He lumbers back for the ball.

The fans hold their collective breath, wondering whether or not he's going to catch it. But just as soon as he starts, he stops running. The fans in the left-field bleachers stand and begin clapping and cheering.

The ball drops over the fence, out of reach of Powell. Mickey runs the bases slowly, more slowly than usual. Not because he wants to show up the Orioles, not because he isn't sure how the ankle would hold up, but because he wants to prolong the feeling, to experience the physical effort of running around the bases and the emotions of being back in the game and of having all these people loving him.

When Mickey at last steps on home plate, he takes off his cap and raises it a couple of inches in a salute to the fans.

The lights come back up and the stadium scene fades away.

Gosh, Mick, says Toots, that was a hell of a return. I remember it like it was yesterday.

If ever there was a moment that defined your role as the elder statesman of the Yankees, that was it, Mick. It was one of the most memorable home runs I ever saw.

I may not have wanted to be around the fans individually, but I sure loved them as a group that day. They had missed me, Lenny. I grinned and grinned. If I could have hugged every one of them, I would have. In the tenth inning Yogi pinch-hit with a runner on third and hit a long sacrifice fly to give us a very satisfying win.

You clinched the pennant in mid-September.

Bouton won his twentieth game of the season, shutting out Minnesota. The only negative note came a few days later when Ralph Terry's slider mysteriously disappeared, along with his effectiveness. We worried about him. Ralph was in a state of panic. He had been so good, and suddenly he became very hittable.

I continued to pinch-hit when my ankle didn't come around like it was supposed to. And because I wasn't playing regularly, sometimes I would spend most of the night drinking and partying with lady friends.

We were in Baltimore the last day of August, and this was one of those nights. I never expected to play the next day. When I woke up the next morning, my head hurt so badly I couldn't get out of bed. By the time I arrived at the ballpark, I didn't feel a lot better. I needed some sleep and a stiff drink.

We were losing 4–1 in the eighth. Clete singled. Our pitcher was up next. I sat on the bench, not moving much, because my head felt like a watermelon. I was feeling shitty, if you want to know the truth. In my haze I could hear Ralph Houk's voice: "Hey, Mick, grab a bat."

I didn't really want to go up there, but I had no choice. I walked out into the blinding sun toward the on-deck circle. The last time I was in Baltimore, I had broken my ankle and was mocked by their fans. The thought of that sobered me up some.

Mike McCormick, who once had a real great fastball when he was a kid, was on the mound. He was a left-hander, and he figured he would throw the first pitch over the plate, and I would take it for a strike. I knew I'd better hit the first good pitch thrown my way, because I was in no condition to hit.

McCormick threw, and I hit that son of a bitch nine miles deep into the left-field stands. As I circled the bases, I listened for the fans. There was only silence. And when I trotted into the dugout, that's when I made that famous line, "They don't have any idea how hard that really was." Everyone laughed when I said it, but I wasn't kidding.

No sooner had I sat down when Bobby Richardson singled. Dick Hall replaced McCormick, and Tom Tresh, a switch-hitter like me, hit a pitch into the right-field grandstands for another Yankee victory. Tom, a quiet kid, hit 25 home runs that year.

Three days later we were playing in Washington. The Senators led by a run in the ninth, when Roger got up with a man on and hit a long home run off Claude Osteen. Roger missed seventy games that year, but he still hit twenty-three home runs. Again, we won the pennant in a cakewalk, Ralph Houk's third in a row.

Your injuries caught up with you in the World Series in '63.

We played the L.A. Dodgers, with Koufax and Drysdale. They also had Maury Wills, who had stolen over a hundred bases the year before. Wills changed the game with his speed. Wills and Roger are the two guys not in the Hall of Fame who belong there more than anyone else.

Going into the Series, we weren't impressed by the Dodgers, though we should have been. We hadn't faced them since they'd left Brooklyn, we didn't read about 'em in the papers anymore, and they were a very different team. We figured—wrongly—Koufax was hittable and that our pitching staff would shut down L.A. Well, we only allowed them to score twelve runs. Unfortunately, we scored exactly four. We got swept. Koufax struck out fifteen in the opener. He threw a fastball I only heard. He beat Whitey 5–2. In the next game Johnny Podres, yes, the same Johnny Podres, allowed us one run in a 4–1 loss.

The last two games were classics, but we lost them both. Jim Bouton allowed just four singles and a cheap run in the first inning, but Drysdale shut us out. And in the finale it was Whitey against Koufax, the two best pitchers in baseball. Whitey pitched a two-hitter—and lost. Frank Howard hit a home run in the upper deck in Chavez Ravine, and I finally got a hit off Koufax. I caught a fastball and hit it out to tie the game in the seventh.

It was your fifteenth World Series home run, tying Babe Ruth.

We lost the game in the bottom of the seventh when Clete Boyer threw over to first from third, and Pepi lost the ball in the white shirt-sleeves of the crowd. Junior Gilliam, who hit the ball, ran all the way to third. Willie Davis then hit a long fly ball to me in center. There was no way I could throw Gilliam out. I threw a perfect one-hopper home, but he was already on the way back to the dugout with the winning run. Koufax finished us off no sweat.

In the clubhouse after the game Pepi was in tears. Whitey walked over, put his arm around him, and said, "You really blew that son of a bitch, didn't you, Pepi?" Pepi looked at him horrified, then saw Whitey was kidding, and he started to laugh, and Whitey was laughing, and so was I. I told Whitey, "I don't care if the Dodgers had beaten us ten games in a row. I know we still have a better team."

I didn't know it then, but that was the last carefree moment I would ever have on a baseball diamond. We would win one more pennant, but that last one would be a struggle. After that, the champion New York Yankees would self-destruct. The owners sold us out.

For the last years of my playing career, I would become a drawing card. My value to the team would be solely to draw people into the park to make money for the owners. To do that, the Yankees paid me $100,000 a year. If we could have just gone back to our winning ways, I would have played for nothing.

You still had one more great year and one more pennant left, in 1964.

By then owner Dan Topping was in a panic over the new National League team in town, the New York Mets, and it was his own damn fault. We were American League champs, but the Mets were the darlings of New York City because of their manager—Casey Stengel. In three years, Yankee attendance had dropped like a rock, and so Topping decided to do something designed to give the Mets a run for their money.

Topping, who had fired Casey after the 1960 World Series, never figured that the Old Man would come back to haunt him. As manager of the Mets, a really shitty team, Casey, the most colorful figure in the history of baseball next to Babe Ruth, was drawing fans like crazy. Topping, who didn't know as much about baseball as he thought he did, decided that for the Yankees to compete with the Mets for the hearts and minds of New York's fans, he would hire a similarly colorful and lovable manager for the 1964 season.

Topping promoted Houk, who had been a really fine manager for us, to the position of general manager, a job he had no business taking, and he hired as manager Yogi Berra. After all, wasn't Yogi the inventor of all those Yogiisms, like the time he was thrown a day, and he said, "I want to thank you for making this day necessary," and who once looked at his piano and asked his wife, "How does this thing work?"

As much as I loved and admired Yogi, I really wondered what ole Dan, who loved the sauce as much as I did, could have been thinking. I guess he didn't know Yogi that well. Yogi had been one of the best clutch-hitters who ever lived, but he was a guy who normally never said two words from one day to the next. Joe Garagiola, Yogi's neighbor in St. Louis, had made up a lot of the funny stories about Yogi and put them in Yogi's mouth. If Topping wanted a comic, he should have hired Garagiola. But Yogi wasn't funny at all. If you snapped him in the ass with a towel, he would smile, but as a person Yogi was very, very quiet. He was actually uncomfortable with the press. And as a player whenever he was asked a question, his answer often would come out in the form of a grunt.

Making Yogi's job as manager more difficult was the undeniable fact that a lot of us were getting old, and injuries took their toll. Roger and I kept pulling hamstring muscles and missing games, and in 1964 most of our starting pitchers, Whitey, Bouton, and Al Downing, all suffered arm injuries. Yogi, who had no managerial experience, didn't know squat about using his pitching staff even though he was a catcher. His relievers were in a constant state of rebellion.

By the beginning of July we trailed the Baltimore Orioles, and the players were streaming into Ralph Houk's office begging for him to come back and manage. Ralph, who people said had been jealous of Yogi his whole career—it was Yogi, after all, who had relegated Houk to a career as bullpen catcher—should have kicked the players out of his office and told them to be loyal to Yogi. Instead, he sat and listened to all their complaints.

By the end of July, Topping decided he had made a mistake and that Yogi should be fired at the end of the season no matter what happened. Yogi, they saw, wasn't respected by the players and seemingly had lost control of the team.

The worst incident came on a bus ride in Chicago from Comiskey

Park to O'Hare airport. We had just lost our fourth game in a row to the Sox, and Yogi was really pissed. He knew his job was on the line and that a lot of guys were second-guessing him, and he was pretty sure Houk was going to stab him in the back at the first opportunity. Yogi was feeling the pressure.

In the back of the bus Phil Linz, Joe Pep's partner in crime, pulled a small piece of sheet music from his pocket and placed it behind Ellie Howard's head right in front of him. Pepi asked Phil, "What's that for?"

"I'm learning to play the harmonica," Linz said, not innocently. Linz pulled a harmonica from his pocket.

"What are you going to do with that thing?" Pepi asked him.

"I'm going to play it," Linz said.

This was a perfect situation for Pepi, who enjoyed stirring things up when they got too quiet. But even Pepi knew that Phil was asking for trouble when he started playing "Mary Had a Little Lamb."

When Yogi heard the annoying tootling from the back of the bus, he got up and yelled at Phil, "Shove that thing up your ass." And he sat down.

Phil turned to me and said, "What did he say?"

I couldn't help myself. I told him, "Yogi said to play it louder."

"Hey man, put that thing away," Pepi warned Phil. But Phil was pissed at Yogi. He had been one of the players complaining to Ralph. A week before Yogi had put Phil's name on the lineup card that hung in the dugout, but he had written Tony Kubek's name on the card he gave to the umpires. Linz ran out onto the field to start the game, only to discover he wasn't starting. Phil was one of the few guys who had been playing well. He was still mad. Basically, he didn't give a shit what Yogi wanted.

When the tune "Mary Had a Little Lamb" filled the bus again, Yogi blew a gasket. He ran back down the aisle and swatted the harmonica out of Linz's hand. The harmonica flew off and struck Pepi in the leg. Pepi started screaming, "Mayday, mayday, I need a medic. My leg. My leg." Phil and Yogi, meanwhile, were screaming at each other.

"What are you getting on me for?" Phil shouted to Yogi. "I'm on the bench. Why don't you yell at the guys who are playing?" Phil was pissed, but the scene was so comical the rest of us couldn't decide whether to laugh or what.

I picked up the harmonica from the floor of the bus. I said to Whitey, "It looks like I'm going to be managing this club pretty soon. Will you be my third base coach?" Then I said, "Here are my signals. One toot," and I tooted the harmonica, "that means bunt. Two toots," and I tooted twice, "that means hit and run." Everyone in the back of the bus started to giggle.

Didn't Linz get fined?

Yogi fined him something like two hundred bucks, and Phil did apologize, because Phil genuinely did like Yogi. Because of the publicity, Phil got five grand from the Hohner Harmonica company. The next day in the clubhouse I decided the club needed a shake-up, and I set off a cherry bomb. That sure woke everybody up!

To his credit, the only person who wasn't counting us out for the pennant was Yogi. He saw that Baltimore and the White Sox had a bunch of games against each other, and he predicted that after they knocked each other off, we'd be back in the driver's seat. Yogi was famous for his saying, "It ain't over till it's over," and that's what he kept saying, only no one was paying any attention to him.

I got hot in September.

You finished the '64 season with 35 homers and 111 RBIs.

Ellie and Roger also hit well, and both Whitey and Bouton had great Septembers. We got back into first in mid-September, and just as Yogi predicted, Baltimore and Chicago knocked each other off, and we snuck in. Joy returned to our clubhouse. Pepi kept having sex in the middle of games, and I was getting off on the idea he was doing it. Hey, I loved Pepi. He was separated from his second wife, and he didn't have a lot of money, and so he stayed with me in my suite at the St. Moritz for a month.

Sometimes Pepi and I would go out for dinner, and Pepi would pretend to be my bodyguard. We'd be eating at a corner table, and a fan would start to come over to us, and Pepi would growl, "Hey you, get away. He don't want to be bothered. Capeesh?"

And the guy would leave us alone.

You won the '64 pennant with two days to go.

We were saved by a young kid by the name of Mel Stottlemyre. He came up from Richmond and won game after game, nine in all.

That was also the year the Phillies blew the National League pennant. They had it locked up with a month to go, but blew it when Gene Mauch panicked and overworked his starting pitchers. The Cardinals came on in the end under Johnny Keane and won. No one knew it, but the Yankees had hired Keane to manage the Yankees in '65 in a secret deal with Ralph Houk. When Gussie Busch tried to rehire Keane, Keane said no, 'cause he knew he was going to the Yankees.

Why Houk thought so highly of Keane I'll never know. But when the Yankees played the Cardinals in the Series, Houk and Keane both knew he was moving to the Yankees the next season. Yogi, of course, figured he was due a big raise, only to find he was the odd man out.

The Series went seven games. Bob Gibson beat you in the finale.

You have to give Gibson credit. The son of a bitch could really pitch. The highlight of the Series for me came in Game 3 at the Stadium. Bouton was pitching against Curt Simmons. The score was 1–1 going into the ninth. Keane had pinch-hit for Simmons in the ninth, and in the bottom of the inning had to send in a reliever, an old knuckleballer by the name of Barney Schultz.

I was the first batter up in the ninth. While Schultz was completing his warm-ups, I said to Ellie Howard, "If he throws the first ball over, I'm going to hit it out."

Schultz did throw the first ball over, knee high, a knuckleball that didn't do much, and I hit it into the right-field stands. It was the last great moment of my career. I can still hear the seventy thousand fans cheering and hollering and yelling for me. I can still feel the pump of adrenaline go through my body. I can still feel the slaps on the back as my teammates greeted me at home plate.

It was your sixteenth World Series home run, breaking Babe's record.

And I hit two more, including one in the final game against Gibson.

You had forty World Series RBIs, a record, and you scored forty-two runs, also a record.

Those numbers I cherish. I also finished with fifty-nine World Series hits, but that was still way short of Yogi's amazing record of seventy-one. I played in twelve World Series. That's what I'm most proud of. Every Series was special to me.

After hitting that home run to beat the Cards, my emotions were tempered when I learned that Whitey had a sore arm and wouldn't be able to pitch again in the Series. We made up a story to try to hide the truth, but everyone knew what was going on. Whitey and I both were at the end of our productive years. We couldn't hide that. You can't fool Mother Nature.

After we lost that final game, Yogi called us together and told us, "We'll get 'em next year," but there was no next year, not for Yogi, and not for us.

Yogi was fired as manager by the Yankees—and it wouldn't be the last time—even though he brought us within one game of winning the World Championship. Ralph brought in Johnny Keane. As might have been expected, the Mets hired Yogi as a coach. Now the Mets had Casey and Yogi both, and it wouldn't be long before we were bad—or worse—than the Mets were. Yogi would go on to win a second pennant as a manager with the Mets.

Johnny Keane didn't turn out very well.

Keane might have been a good manager in the National League, but he sure was the wrong guy for us. We had a veteran team, and we were used to being left alone by the manager. We didn't need anyone telling us when to come in or tell us how to play.

About two weeks into spring training, we had gone something like

1 and 8, and Keane decided he'd hang around our hotel and see what time we were coming in. At midnight, he checked, and no one had come back. We were all in the bars drunk, staggering around the hotel, and we'd come to practice soaked in alcohol.

John held a meeting. He said, "Fellas, I told you the first day I had seen just about everything in all my years in baseball. But men, I was wrong. There are about five of you who have gotten into some careless habits. You are acting very carelessly. And I would like to see a stop to it."

For the rest of the spring, when we'd be sitting in the bar, one of the guys would say, "Should we have another round?" Another guy would say, "I don't know. It's awful careless of us. Should we be doing something so careless?" "Shit yeah, let's."

A couple weeks later John held another meeting. This time he said fifteen of us had gotten careless. None of us gave a damn what he thought. We had never needed spring training before. We were the championship Yankees. We had never kept hours in the past. I mean, Casey was out late with us, and Ralph and Yogi never cared. But Johnny Keane took our behavior personally. Keane wanted us to win in the spring. By the end of spring training, everyone but Bobby Richardson and Tony Kubek were being accused of being careless. And while he was berating us, we were sitting there giggling, not giving a shit what he felt.

Once the season began, Keane began getting pissed off at us. As I said, he took our behavior personally. John was a religious guy, and our drinking and carousing offended him morally. So he was just the absolute wrong guy for the Yankees manager job. And once the season began, he decided to crack down, and some of the guys really suffered because of the way he treated us. I know Pepi wasn't the same ballplayer. He and Keane hated each other. One time Keane ordered Pepi onto the field to take ground balls, and Pepi got so mad he ripped off his uniform, sending his buttons flying all over the room. He told Keane, "You can take this uniform and shove it up your ass." Pepi got dressed and left the ballpark.

I wasn't spared. One day in spring training Keane waited for me to come in hungover, and he sent me out to center field to practice field-ing fly balls. He grabbed a fungo, and he hit me one ball after another, running me left and then right. I suspect he was trying to get me to throw up.

After what seemed like an hour, he hit me a ball that went real short. I picked it up and threw it as hard as I could right at him. Good thing he ducked. As soon as I did it, I regretted it, but that's how mad he made me.

In 1965 my right leg was so bad I couldn't play anymore. Both knees were bad, and everyone knew it, including me. I was thirty-three years old—a very old thirty-three, and I was still convinced I was going to die at age forty like my father and uncle. And in '65 the Yankees team had grown old and infirm along with me. We were a bad team. I knew early on we weren't going to win, that our day had come and gone. But even though I was hurting, Keane wanted me in the game, and most of the time I obliged him.

Keane tried to use his psychology on me to get me to play. Before games Jim Bouton and I would have made-up conversations where Jim pretended he was Keane. Jim was funny. He made me laugh so hard. He'd say, "How is your leg today, Mick?" I'd play along. I'd say, "Not too good, Skip. It's broken in four places." Jim'd say, "But Mick, can you set the bones in time for the game? We sure could use you." I'd say, "If I can set the bones, I can play, Skip." He'd say, "Good, how is your back?" "Skip, my back fell clean off." "Can you get another back, Mick? We can proba-bly find one for you before the game starts." "That will be fine, Skip. If you can get me another back, I guess I can play." "Good Mick, I knew you would."

Jim could have been a stand-up comic.

In June I went into a bad slump. The team was losing, and I felt it was my fault. In the middle of a game, my lack of productivity really got to me. After striking out, I went down to the dugout john, and I began to sob. I was inconsolable. Pepi found me, and he tried to comfort me, but I knew it was over, both for the Yankees and for me. Pepi also started to cry, and there were the two of us, famous professional athletes, bawling like babies.

The Yankees finished sixth in 1965. You hit .255 with 19 home runs, and you only drove in 46 runs.

I wasn't the only one who had broken down. Early in May Roger came sliding home, and he caught his fingers on the umpire's cleats and broke his hand. The Yankees had it x-rayed but never told Roger it was broken. Houk wanted him out there, drawing fans, so he kept the medical report from Roger all year long.

When Roger found out the truth at the end of the season, he was furious with Houk, who he felt really made him look bad, because his batting average was down near the Mendoza line. He was so mad he quit. He told Houk he was retiring, but Ralph asked him if he'd hold off making the announcement until the spring so the Yankees could still use him to sell season tickets. Roger, always a team player, said okay, but then during the winter Ralph traded him to the Cardinals and put Roger in a terrible position. He played in St. Louis because he was afraid people would think badly of him if he quit after the trade. All Roger did was help the Cardinals win two pennants! Like I said, it's a joke Roger wasn't voted into the Hall of Fame on the first ballot. But Roger never forgave Ralph for not telling him about the broken hand or for trading him after he told Ralph he wanted to retire. It was a long time before Roger would agree to come back to the Yankees Old Timers' game.

At the end of 1965 I was also thinking of retiring. In November I was playing touch football with my brothers Roy and Ray when I was blindsided running out for a pass. My throwing shoulder was killing me. The Yankees sent me to the Mayo Clinic and had it operated on. Houk told me I'd be fine. When February rolled around I felt okay. The Yankees paid me my usual hundred, and I signed on for another dismal year.

After the '64 season Topping and Webb sold the Yankees to CBS, which didn't realize they had bought an empty shell. Topping and Webb had stripped the club bare of every asset except the players already on the Yankee roster.

They knew they were selling, and for five years they stopped signing prospects and pocketed the money. You finished dead last in '66.

It was the worst Yankees team since the Babe joined the team. You'd have to go back to the dead ball era—maybe even to when the team was called the Highlanders—to find a worse team. We began the season 4–16, and Houk, forced to admit his mistake in hiring Johnny Keane, fired him and took over. Eight months later Johnny Keane had a heart attack and died. I have always felt bad that I never had the chance to tell John how sorry I was for the way we had treated him.

Maybe you can do it now that you're up here, but somehow I don't think we'll ever see Johnny walk into Toots Shor's.

I hope I get that chance, Len, because Johnny wasn't a bad guy at all. He was just out of his element. He should have swallowed his pride and stayed in St. Louis and never have gotten involved with Ralph Houk. He'd have won those pennants in '67 and '68 for the Cardinals.

You had Horace Clarke at second base.

Horace replaced Bobby Richardson.

Why did Bobby retire? He wasn't that old, his stats weren't that bad, and he wasn't injured. He played the entire '66 season.

But Bobby wasn't used to losing, and he wanted to spend more time with his family, and so he retired, and we ended up with Horace—a good guy, but a mediocre player. He came to represent the sorry-ass CBS Yankees between 1964 and 1973, when George Steinbrenner bought the team. By 1967 Mel Stottlemyre, Pepi, and I were the only players left from the Dynasty teams. Whitey, Roger, Tony, Bobby, and Clete had all been traded or retired. The guys who replaced them weren't scrubs, but they weren't very good either. Our infield had me at first because I just couldn't cover any ground in the outfield anymore, Horace at second, Ruben Amaro at short, and Charlie Smith, who the Yankees got for Roger, at third. Our outfield had an unhappy Pepi, a crippled Tom Tresh, and Steve Whitaker. We finished tenth—last. Even the Mets finished higher than we did—they were ninth.

Your numbers stunk. You hit .245, hit 22 homers, and drove in 55 runs.

And I was lucky to get those. I was the only home run hitter on the team, and I got walked one time out of four. I was surprised anyone ever pitched to me. But as horseshit as I was, I got cheered like never before. I found it wonderful but at the same time confusing. When I was young, I had been the best player in baseball, won the Triple Crown, and I got booed. Once the fans saw how horseshit I was, they cheered me like crazy. I loved every minute of it, but I never did understand it.

Why did you hang on?

Fear. I was afraid to hang it up. Playing baseball was the only thing I knew how to do, the only thing I've ever done since I was a boy. Baseball had been my family. I loved putting on the uniform, sitting with the guys in the clubhouse and in the bars. I loved going out to shag balls in the outfield. I loved everything about the game.

The other reason I stayed on is I pretty much pissed away most of my money. Hell, I wasn't making all that much anyway, well, not compared to what players make today. But drinking costs money, and I always tipped big and traveled first class. A hundred grand wasn't bad, but I had a lifestyle that didn't leave much at the end of the year. I couldn't afford to quit. And yet, I knew the day was coming. I had been scared most of my playing career, but looking ahead to when my career was over, that scared me a whole lot worse. It petrified me.

Your final season was 1968.

I never should have played that year. All my career I prided myself on the fact that my lifetime batting average was over .300. But in 1968 I hit a pathetic .237, and by the end of the year my lifetime average had dropped to .298. I beat myself up emotionally just to think about it. But by playing in '68, I was able to pass Ted Williams in home runs with 521, and I went past Jimmy Foxx at 534. I'll never forget the home run that let me pass him. Denny McLain of the Tigers, the best pitcher in the American League that year, was pitching. He told me later he had always been a big fan of mine; it was toward the end of the game, and we were getting beat bad, and so Denny walked toward the plate and said to his catcher, a guy named Price, loud enough for me to hear, "I'm gonna let him hit one." Denny would win thirty-one games that year. He was as good as they came. When he said that, I didn't believe him. He threw me a medium-speed pitch waist high, and I was so shocked, I let it go by.

"Is he shitting me?" I said to Price.

"No, Mick, he wants you to hit one," he said.

The next pitch was like the first one, batting practice speed down the middle, and swung from my heels, and I fouled it off.

McLain whispered to me, "Where do you want it?"

I held my left hand belt-high over the plate and inside.

"Here comes another one," said Price.

This time I hit it deep into the upper deck of Tiger Stadium.

The crowd went wild. The Tiger fans had always hated the Yankees, but on this day they cheered and cheered.

The next batter was Pepi. Pepi held his hand waist-high, signaling for McLain to throw him the same sort of cripple he threw me. McLain threw him a pea that almost hit him in the head!

When I think of the '60s, I always think of Pepi. He was hip, and he took full advantage of the sexual revolution, which as far as I was concerned ended a few years later when two Yankee pitchers took their experimenting a little too far. They did what Billy and I dreamed of doing but couldn't quite talk ourselves into doing: they wife swapped. Fritz Peterson and Mike Kekich were two left-handers—maybe that explains it, but one day they decided it might be exciting to have sex with each other's wives. Or maybe their wives decided it might be exciting to have sex with their husband's friend. And then they took it a step further, and pretty soon Mike was living with Fritz's wife and family and dog and driving Fritz's car, and Fritz was living with Mike's wife and family and dog and driving Mike's car. Eventually, the press found out, and everyone was outraged and fascinated. Fritz was traded to the White Sox. Kekich got released. I can't imagine what happened to their families after that.

Didn't Fritz and Susanne Kekich get married?

Yeah, and they're still together as far as I know. But Mike and Marilyn Peterson didn't last very long. Mike went to Mexico to study to become a doctor. I think he lives in New Mexico somewhere.

Do you remember your final home run?

Not really. I hit it in late September, number 536. A week later, I batted in the first inning, limped to first base, and was replaced by a young kid by the name of Andy Kosko. I went into the dugout, walked through the runway to the clubhouse, got dressed, and left the ballpark, never to return.

I died when I quit at age thirty-six. That was back in '68, the year Bobby Kennedy and Martin Luther King were murdered. Looking back, I'd have to say they were the lucky ones. They never grew bitter and depressed. They never grew old.

I don't know why, but none of the so-called experts ever wrote about how much I loved the game and loved to play the game. I guess it's because writers almost never write about things that matter to us players. Toward the end of my career, I would be standing out in the field, looking out into the bleachers of Yankee Stadium, and I'd be thinking how lucky I was to still be out there and how much I'd miss it, and how sorry I was that I hadn't taken better care of myself so I could have played longer.

We came over and asked you, Mick. I know I did, but you would never give us a straight answer.

'Cause at the time I felt it was none of your damn business, that's why. I was too suspicious. If a writer asked me how I was feeling, I'd just say, "Talk to Skip," and leave it at that. When there's so much attention coming your way, it's hard to know who's for you and who's agin you, so it's just easier to blow everyone off. I can see now it was a big mistake on my part.

So like I said, I hung on even after I became a shadow of my old self, because I knew the day I quit, my life would be as good as over like Joe D and Ty Cobb and all the rest of the old timers I met at the Old Timers' game.

In the spring of 1969 I officially retired. I stood in front of reporters at the Yankee Clipper Hotel in Fort Lauderdale. I told them, "I just can't play anymore. I don't hit the ball when I need to. I can't steal when I need to."

I had the rest of my life ahead of me. The only question I kept asking myself was, "What the hell am I going to do with myself day after day after day after fucking day?"

In June 1969 the Yankees held a day for you to retire your number. What do you remember about that?

The day was a blur. I gave a little speech, was presented with a big Chrysler and a hundred-pound salami, and I rode around the perimeter of the Stadium in a little cart, waving to everyone. I never wanted that ride to end, but of course, like everything else, it did.

After I retired I was haunted by the fact I was no longer a Yankee. That's when my nightmares began. I would have the same dream I told you about over and over and over—I would be standing outside Yankee Stadium, and I could hear Bob Sheppard, the public address announcer, saying my name and announcing my place in the lineup and my uniform number 7, and I would be standing outside the high walls of Yankee Stadium listening to my name being called, but in my dream I couldn't find the entrance to get inside. I would walk around and around and around, and then I'd be running, trying to find my way in, pounding on the walls until my hands would bleed, then I would jerk myself awake to find myself in bed in a cold sweat, screaming.

Why didn't you go see a psychiatrist? You needed help.

Plenty of times I thought about it, but I came from a generation that believed in handling your problems yourself. My mother, who was a weak woman, would be sobbing, and my dad would always tell her, "Handle it, woman. It's nobody else's goddamn business." For my dad, getting help, even medical help, was a sign of weakness. To him it meant a lack of manhood. Also, whenever I thought about getting help, I thought about that senator from Missouri, Eagleton, who wanted to run for president when the press found out he had gone to a psychiatrist for depression. It was the end of his political career. So I never did go, until I ended up in AA many years later. I was afraid of what people might say about me if it ever got out in the papers I was seeing a shrink.

Besides, all those years I had my personal shrink: Jack Daniel's. And a damn fine job Dr. Daniel's did, too. Except that eventually my liver belonged in a museum, as Casey used to say.

What did you do after you retired?

After I retired I was stuck in a living hell. There were some highs, for sure. In August 1974 I was inducted into the Baseball Hall of Fame in Cooperstown along with the best pitcher in New York Yankees history, my friend Whitey Ford. Casey was sitting in the audience staring out at us. It was the proudest day of my life. I was only sorry my father wasn't there to see it.

I didn't live long enough to see that. I died on January 19, 1974.

I knew you had died, Lenny. I didn't know when or how.

I got sick in 1972. I didn't tell anyone I had leukemia. My wife Ginny knew, and Stan Isaacs knew. I didn't even tell Jim Bouton. I didn't want people feeling sorry for me. I really thought I was going to beat it. I went to the hospital once, had my radiation treatments, and it went into remission. Then it came back with a vengeance. The last time I saw Jim he kissed me on the forehead.

"Get better, Lenny," he said, but I didn't. I died a few days later. In January. It was cold in New York. So I never got to attend your Hall of Fame ceremony, which was too bad, because I wouldn't have missed it.

You were lucky, Lenny. You got to do the thing you loved to do until the day you died.

I was lucky in other ways, Mickey. Unlike you, I had a father who gave me unquestioned love. I never had to perform or show him anything for him to love me. One of my fondest memories is just walking down the street with him holding his hand. I really loved my father. And I really loved my wife, Ginny. And more important, she loved me. Can I confide in you, Mickey?

I'd be an awful heel if I said no, wouldn't I? Sure. Go ahead.

In my time I wasn't so different from you. I had girlfriends. Not as many as you, but a few women found me attractive. But the difference between you and me was that I never stopped loving Ginny. And she always forgave me and looked the other way. And you're right, I was lucky I never had to stop being a journalist. Until I got sick, I looked forward to getting up and going to work every single day.

When I got up in the morning, I didn't look forward to anything. The first ten years of my retirement were particularly difficult. That's because it took that long before autograph collecting became a craze, enabling me and all the other famous retired athletes to get paid sacks of money for signing our names. Before that happened, I was just scraping along, getting my name involved in various business schemes, none of which seemed to work very well. Mickey Mantle Country Fried Chicken seemed the most promising. It was a turkey—no pun intended.

There was Namath Girls and Mantle Men, an employment agency. Joe and I were old drinking buddies, and we were approached to use our names. Other people used our names and made money. Like everything else I got involved in, these schemes went belly-up. It seems that if you don't really care all that much about making money, you don't make very much.

How did you pay the bills?

By attending every dinner, golf tournament, and department store or business function that would pay me for an appearance. I even attended a bar mitzvah or two. L'chaim, you all.

If I got paid, I went. As a side benefit, I'd have all the booze I could drink, and every once in a while I'd find a lady host or guest or a waitress to take back to my hotel room with me for an hour or two. I really do love waitresses. They never seem to have enough excitement or happiness in their lives, and I am always very happy to provide a little of both.

There's a great line that works all the time with waitresses. A waitress usually has her name pinned on her right breast. When I call her over, I say to her, "Honey, what's the name of the other one?" Often, she will get all flustered and giggly. I then write my room number on her arm or a piece of paper, and I was never surprised when the gal came to see me after her shift was over.

I had moved from Oklahoma to Dallas, Texas, in 1957 to open a bowling alley. Wouldn't you know it, the bowling craze was ending right about that time. Yogi made a killing with his bowling alley. I lost my shirt.

Didn't you play a lot of golf?

Ten years after I moved to Dallas, with my career nearing an end, I joined the Preston Trail Golf Club so I'd have a place to go during the day where I could hoist a few and hit golf balls. For the rest of my life playing golf became the sole release for my competitive juices, one way I could compete at sports and have fun. But because my legs were so bad, it got harder and harder to go out on the course, and so the clubhouse bar became my refuge.

Couldn't you sit home and drink?

I hated to stay at home. I was like that all my life. At home I felt caged and worthless. At the clubhouse bar I could sit with the guys and flirt with the waitresses. Sometimes I'd drink myself into oblivion. Too many mornings I'd awaken in the clubhouse of Preston Trail, still dressed in my clothes from the day before.

It wasn't long after I retired that my marriage was pretty well over. I had met this little ole gal in a bar, and we got talking, and we started seeing each other, and I thought it might be a good idea for her to become my "personal assistant." We tried to keep it quiet, but one time she and I were on a boat, got drunk, and got into a pissing match over her wanting me to divorce my wife, which I told her I never would do. When she threatened to expose me, I got so mad I pushed her out of the boat into the water.

My wife found out about this, but like I told you before, nothing I did moved her to divorce me. All I had left was being Mickey Mantle, and all she had left was her being Mrs. Mickey Mantle.

You didn't love her anymore?

The sad truth was I was incapable of giving love. I'm not sure I was *ever* in love. I had more sex than anyone except maybe Wilt Chamberlain, who said he slept with twenty thousand women. But I really can't say I was in love with any of them.

Your wife still loved you, didn't she?

She never stopped loving me, and just knowing that made me very sad, until I was at the point where I was drinking myself to death. For a time I even thought about suicide. I'd sit on the john at home reading old clippings hundreds of fans had sent me over the years. I really felt my life was over. I was no longer a baseball player. I was no longer anybody at all. Two reasons I didn't kill myself: One, I'm a coward; two, I kept my gun in my car and I was usually too messed up to go to the trouble to get it.

What happened to your affair?

My affair with this woman ended when she started showing up at parties unannounced at my home in Dallas. She pushed me to divorce Merlyn and marry her, but I wouldn't do it. At the same time Merlyn's anger with me was growing.

A woman is wearing a full-length mink coat. An animal rights activist walks up to her and says, "Do you know how many animals had to die for that coat?"

The lady says, "Mister, do you know how many animals I had to fuck for this coat?"

The person who saved my life is a woman named Greer Johnson. I met her in 1983 at the Claridge Hotel and Casino in Atlantic City, which had hired me to be a greeter for $100,000 a year. The biggest reason I took the job was that my son Billy had gotten Hodgkin's, and I needed the money for medical bills.

It was the best job I ever had. Basically, I was supposed to work there five days a month. My job had nothing to do with gambling. I shook hands, signed autographs, and hung around the guests. For two years, Bowie Kuhn banned me and Willie Mays from baseball because we were working for a casino, but baseball hadn't hired me to do anything, and Claridge's did, so what did Kuhn expect me to do? Starve to death because he didn't approve of an association with gambling? Christ, George Steinbrenner owns race horses. Isn't that gambling? Why was he allowed to be in baseball? Bowie's idiotic ruling was no skin off my butt, except that as long as I was banned, I couldn't go to any baseball events including Old Timers' Day, which I really enjoyed because I really loved to visit with my old teammates.

I met Greer, a divorcée who had come from Georgia with friends, that first year when I was working at Claridge's. She was fun to be with and, what I liked most, she didn't know shit about my career in baseball. She liked me because she thought I was funny. She was one of the few women who weren't offended by my dirty jokes. About this same time my celebrity—and the autograph craze—started paying off. I was amazed when I'd get offers to spend a weekend at a card show to sign my name over and over for $20,000. The collector-card hobby quickly became so big that I could have spent every weekend for the rest of my life signing my name for anywhere from $50,000 to $200,000 a weekend. I couldn't believe it. For years I had hated when someone came up and asked for an autograph. But once they started paying me ten, then twenty, then thirty, then forty bucks a pop or more—I no longer cared *why* they wanted the thing. It got so crazy these people started paying me more money to sign my name than the Yankees ever paid me to play ball! The offers were coming in so hot and heavy that I needed someone to run my business.

Greer was smart and very sharp, and I decided she should be the one to do it. And I'm glad I did. After we started working together, we were together almost twelve years. She did such a good job, she also handled some of my former teammates including Moose Skowron, Hank Bauer, and Yogi.

You said that Greer saved your life. How did she do that?

Greer made me see a lot of things about myself. As I told you, sometimes when I got drunk, I'd treat people badly. Here I was in some town where I didn't want to be, going to a sports dinner I didn't want to attend, and these men would be hanging around me—and so when one of them would come up to me and ask for an autograph or tell me how much he'd admire me, I would get so angry I'd tell him to "get the fuck away from me," and I would watch the guy slink away. For some reason I would get some real pleasure when that happened, and Greer made me understand I had to stop doing that. Other times, people would come up to me to shake my hand or get an autograph, and if I was in hurry, I'd be rude, and she would drill it into my thick skull that these people loved me and just wanted to meet me. She impressed upon me the need for me to be polite and not to fly off the handle if something upset me. Looking back, I'm sure I hurt a lot of people's feelings, and I deeply regret that now. Whenever she'd scold me for being a prick, I'd feel so bad I'd almost want to cry.

Because of Greer I became a much better me.

Hey, what's the best thing about a blow job?
Ten minutes of peace and quiet.

I was tortured by the fact that no matter how hard I tried, I could not control my drinking. I had started out as a kid, having a few drinks to lose my inhibitions, to overcome my natural shyness, so I could talk to girls. But as the years went by, I *needed* to drink. I needed it badly. My body craved it. And my mind did, too. But if I didn't realize what my drinking did to me, I certainly was aware of what it had done to my podner, poor Billy Martin, may he rest in peace.

Billy died because of puss and booze. Remember way back when my high school coach warned me about A & P—alcohol and pussy? Too bad he didn't warn Billy. In the end, make no mistake, that's what killed my friend Billy: A & P.

Billy led a soap-opera existence.

You have no idea. His last ten years were crazier than any soap opera ever put on TV. The insanity began when Billy was manager of the Oakland A's in 1980.

He had met this teenage girl Heather when he was managing the Yankees. She couldn't have been much over sixteen when they met, but he was crazy about her. They began living together, and she was with him in Oakland, after the first time Steinbrenner fired him. Then, when he was managing the A's, the team went to L.A. to play the Angels, and he met this other very sexy girl named Jill, who said she was a photographer, but who, many felt, was using her camera to meet ballplayers.

Billy, the crazy motherfucker, decided to carry on two long-term relationships at one time. During the same time Billy was living with Heather in Oakland, he paid for a house for Jill to live in near L.A., and for a year he shuttled back and forth between the two women without letting either of them know about the other! Billy told me he was also boffing the younger sister of a friend of Heather's. Talk about having your puss and eating it too! It didn't take long for all of Billy's friends to come to the same conclusion: Jill was the devil.

Sounds more to me that Billy was the devil.

No. Never. The only person Billy really ever hurt was Billy.

Mickey, that's bullshit and you know it.

Well, maybe so, but Jill ended up hurting everyone who ever cared for Billy. By plotting and scheming she separated Billy one by one from almost all his friends—all but Billy Reedy—including me. Looking back, I regret letting her do that to us, though I'm not sure any of us could have acted any different, because she was so good at fucking with people's minds.

Heather was the first to go. The end for Heather came, ironically enough, when the *Daily News* took a picture of Billy and Jill together at a local nightclub and put it in the paper. All of Heather's friends called her wanting to know why Billy was on the back page of the *Daily News* escorting some other woman. Billy, cornered, did the only thing he could think of: he asked Heather to marry him! To attend his own wedding, which was held in New Orleans, Billy had to lie to Jill about where he was going that weekend! I'm sure Billy knew on some level that once Jill found out about Heather that Jill would figure out a way to end that relationship. He told all of us, "If Jill ever finds out about Heather, whatever you do, don't give her my telephone number at home." By "home," he meant his Oakland home.

Well, of course, Jill found out about Heather. And eventually she succeeded in getting Heather's phone number. Then the calls to Heather began: "He doesn't love you. He loves me. He's going to divorce you. He's going to marry me."

Billy kept telling Heather that Jill didn't mean all that much to him, that she was a delusional stalker. He got away with this for more than four years!

Then Billy and Jill got into a fight at their home in Del Mar that ended up in the newspapers. Jill wanted an air-conditioned trailer for her horse, and Billy didn't want to pay for one. He figured her fucking horse could breathe fresh air.

When Billy left the house and headed off for the local bar, Jill locked him out. When he returned, Billy, who was dead drunk, put his fist through a window, and Jill called the police. It made all the newspapers, and that's how Heather found out that Billy hadn't been telling her the truth about his relationship with Jill.

A couple goes to a masquerade party dressed as a cow. The guy is the front half, and the wife is the back half. The party gets boring, so they decide to go for a walk in a field. All of a sudden they hear something snorting. The wife says, "Honey, there's a bull over there. I think he's going to charge. What are we going to do?"

The husband says, "I'm going to eat some grass. You better brace yourself."

Billy tried to break it off with Jill so he could stay married to Heather, but Jill wouldn't let go. She threatened him with a palimony suit. When Billy agreed to pay her off, it was supposed to be the end of their relationship. But Jill kept calling him, and Billy was addicted to her puss, and so they got back together again. It was only a matter of time before Jill found a way to get Billy to leave Heather. She told Billy that Heather was cheating on him with the bartender at the local country club. It was a lie. Heather was not that type of person. But she told that to Billy over and over until Billy began believing it, and it wasn't long before Billy divorced Heather and made plans to marry Jill.

You mean, this was going on at the same time Billy was managing the Yankees and getting hired and fired by Steinbrenner over and over?

Oh yeah. Billy was addicted to managing the Yankees as much as he was addicted to Jill's puss. They were a perfect pair. George was a sadist, and Billy was a masochist. I learned all about that in AA. One guy is the addict, and the other guy is what they call an enabler.

Actually, George was a lot more than that. George was a big reason Billy drank more than ever. Billy always wanted to be in charge, and George never let him forget for one moment that George was the boss. Every minute Billy was Yankees manager was a minute taken off his life.

After George fired Billy the first time, he never should have gone back to the Yankees because Steinbrenner tortured him and drove him to a constant state of drunkenness. After Billy was fired the first time, he was hired by the Oakland A's. He did so well in Oakland that they called his brand of hustling baseball "Billyball." He could have kept that job for the rest of his life, and if he had, maybe he'd still be alive. But Billy said bye-

bye to the A's after George called him and told him he could get his old job back if he could get fired. A few days later Billy tore up his office, called the A's owner a "Jew bastard," got himself fired. All so he could be abused by George again.

By July 1985, his fourth tour with the Yankees, Billy was drunk every day. It was the season when Steinbrenner tortured Billy by firing Art Fowler, his pitching coach. The pitchers, including Ed Whitson, were fond of Art, and Whitson took out his anger on Billy. The team was in Baltimore when Whitson got drunk and got in a fight in the bar with a fan who was heckling him. Billy started as the peacemaker, but Whitson, who hated him, called Billy a "motherfucker." When Whitson said the magic word, Billy slugged Whitson in the face, splitting his lip. Whitson, a big guy who was a black belt, karate-kicked him with his cowboy boots, breaking Billy's arm and cracking his ribs. Billy was still coughing up blood a week later.

At the end of the season George fired Billy, again, I guess because of the Whitson fight. Billy became a member of the Yankees broadcasting team in 1986. It was a calm period for Billy. George left him alone, and he was pretty happy, except when he was fighting with Jill.

I was with the Yankees in Fort Lauderdale for spring training in 1987 when Billy and Jill got into one of their classic fights. She locked him out of their motel room, and he kicked the door in. After Jill snapped off the heads of his golf clubs, he began throwing the shafts at her like spears. Jill ran out of the room, scared to death. All of Billy's friends were hoping against hope that Billy would either kill her or dump her, but every time I saw Billy, he would go on about how great she was in bed. He'd have this look in his eye, and all I could do was shake my head. I told him he was a lot better off with hookers. A blow job is a blow job, and he'd have known exactly what it was going to cost him.

In January 1988 Billy called me to say he was getting married to Jill. He wanted me to come to the wedding. Greer and I flew to northern California to be there for him. When we got there, every one of Billy's closest friends kept asking the same thing, "Why is he marrying this bitch?" No one had a good answer.

Billy and Jill never agreed on anything. Billy wanted a small wedding. Jill wanted hundreds of guests, a limo to take them, pomp and ceremony, and two weeks in Hawaii. Billy wanted to make a short trip to Las Vegas in front of a justice of the peace. But Billy never got his way with Jill. What she wanted, she got. The tough-guy Billy Martin was mush in her hands.

The whole weekend I was in California, Billy complained to me about how much money "this fucking wedding" was costing him. He didn't do anything about it. He was totally under her control. This was *her* wedding. Billy was just a spectator. I was so upset he was marrying her that I spent the whole time drinking heavily.

More than Billy, if you can imagine that!

As we waited for the ceremony Billy's friends and I made a bet as to how long the marriage would last. We drew slips of paper. Mine said, "One hour." *That sounds about right*, I thought.

I took another drink. Billy marched down the aisle. I followed behind him, but I can't really remember making it to the altar. My job was to put the ring on her finger. I couldn't get the damn ring on. I confess I didn't want to. I was too drunk anyway. They had to help me do it.

As the bride and groom walked off the altar after the ceremony, a waiter lost his footing, dropped a couple of glasses, and broke them. Jill hissed at him, "You stupid son of a bitch."

Billy, who had wanted a simple wedding, said to her something like, "I suppose the champagne and this shit was your idea, you cocksucker."

"Keep it up. I have an hour in the pool," I said to them.

Jill went off, and Billy and I spent the rest of the evening reminiscing about some of the women we had had, including the Heavenly Twins, and we talked about how we used to sneak into each other's hotel rooms to watch each other having sex with our wives.

Before the night was over, I got so upset thinking that Billy would have to live with that bitch that I passed out cold on the floor of the club-house lawn before the end of the evening. I awoke around midnight and went to my hotel room with Greer.

Billy and Jill had the room next to ours. All night long they shouted at each other, calling each other the vilest names. I feared for Billy's life. He was so addicted to her puss that I was afraid she'd drive him so crazy that he would kill himself.

In mid-February 1988 Billy and Jill came to New York to join me for the grand opening of Mickey Mantle's Restaurant. It was a lifelong dream of mine to open a place just like this one, where a ballplayer could come in and not be hassled, and the food would be good, and there'd be plenty to drink. My restaurant is still there on Central Park South, and I'm real proud of it. I can't be there, but it keeps my name alive in New York.

The next time I saw Billy was in Dallas in May, when the Yankees were in to play the Texas Rangers. Billy was still manager. After the game, which the Yankees lost in the ninth inning on a bad call, my son Mickey Jr. and I hopped in a cab and went to meet Billy at Lace, a cowboy bar not far from the ballpark. The batting practice pitcher, Tony Ferrara, also went with us.

I was drinking and talking to this sweet little ole gal, a stripper, and we were hitting it off, and these two big goons, motorcycle guys, one who might have been her boyfriend, started giving me a hard time. Billy and Ferrara decided I ought to leave, and so Ferrara and I took a cab back to the hotel where the Yankees were staying, where I had left my car before the game. Ferrara was supposed to go back and get Billy, but apparently he never did. He should have, because the two guys waited for Billy in the bathroom, dragged and kicked him down a flight of stairs, before they fin-ished with him, they almost tore his ear off and darn near killed him.

Lace, which should have taken Billy to the hospital, put him in a cab and sent him to the hotel where the team was staying.

He was lucky—and he was unlucky. When he arrived, the players and team personnel including George Steinbrenner, were standing outside because someone had pulled the fire alarm, emptying the building. So when Billy arrived, all the guests were outside the hotel, and everyone couldn't help but notice he was covered in blood. The team trainer took one look and rushed him to the hospital. If they hadn't gotten him there when they did, he might have bled to death.

Billy needed eighty stitches to close his wounds. It was worse than the beating he took from Ed Whitson. Because someone rang the fire alarm, the reporters saw him too, bleeding like a stuck pig, and so the story was in all the papers the next day. For the rest of the season Billy was afraid Steinbrenner was going to fire him. I told Billy that he didn't need the Yankees and didn't need Jill, that the combination was going to kill him. He didn't listen to me. He wouldn't listen to anyone. He was as addicted to George as he was to her.

Billy's mom had abused him pretty bad when he was a kid, and I guess Billy was used to being treated like that. Or needed to be treated like that—that's what he equated with love. Heather had treated him kindly, and look what he did to her. The blue jeans guy who owned the Oakland A's loved Billy, and look what Billy did to him.

Billy lasted another month. It was the fifth and last time he managed the Yankees. If Steinbrenner had kept Billy, they would have won the 1988 pennant. But goofy George was as self-destructive as Billy, and it marked the end of an era. Billy had been a Yankee—on and off—since 1950. That's a long time, pardner.

Billy ended up living in Binghamton, New York. How did that happen? What was he doing there of all places? I mean . . . Binghamton?

When Billy was fired, the first person I called was my friend, Mike Klepfer, who lived in Binghamton, in upstate New York. Mike owned a trucking company. He had once invited Billy, Whitey, and me to speak at one of his company dinners, and we had become close friends. When I called Mike, he suggested that Billy and Jill come up and live with them in their big house overlooking a pond and a stable. They had built an entire suite of rooms in their basement for guests.

Even before I could call Billy, he was on the phone to Klepfer, who invited him up. Billy accepted immediately. By five in the afternoon Billy and Jill were in Binghamton living with the Klepfers.

Out of a job, Billy discovered that Jill was incredibly pissed that he was no longer Yankees manager, blamed him for getting fired, and bitched about it to him constantly. To get away from her, Billy would get Mike to drive him to town, where he would call me or his friend Bill Reedy or one of his many girlfriends.

What Billy, a city kid, was doing living in the country in upstate New York in the middle of nowhere was a real mystery, except that it was a way for Jill to keep an eye on him. Every day they fought. During one fight she told him, "Look what you've put us into," and she began telling him how much money his firing had cost them. She told Billy, "You're a loser." Billy pushed Jill so hard she hit her head against the wall. Then he got in his car and drove off.

The next day he told her he was getting a divorce, that he wasn't coming back. All of us, Klepfer, Reedy, and I were jumping for joy, praying he would be good to his word, but we all knew he'd be back for more.

Billy was away three weeks when he returned. Klepfer and his wife were pissed because they were stuck having to entertain Jill that whole time. Klepfer's wife finally ran out of patience.

Against Jill's will, she packed Jill's belongings and moved her into an apartment in Binghamton. Jill never talked to her again. Jill got her revenge. She told Billy that Klepfer had been hitting on her. It was a lie, of course, but Billy dropped Klepfer like he had leprosy. See, Jill had done the same thing to me. She wrote me a letter saying Klepfer was carrying on an affair with Greer. I should have known better than to believe her. The letter almost ended Mike's and my friendship. I stopped calling Mike, and I was also pissed at Billy. That's how devious Jill was. How could he have married that bitch? I hated to be with Jill more than I loved being with Billy, so Billy and I stopped seeing each other. It broke my heart.

It took a while, but Bill Reedy got us back together again. Billy sneaked away from Jill, and Reedy, Billy, and I got together in my restaurant for dinner and acted like nothing was wrong. We agreed to put all the foolishness behind us. Unfortunately, Billy didn't have long to live.

Billy died on Christmas Day 1989.

On that day a part of me died too. Billy and Bill Reedy had gone out to a local bar, which opened just for them, and on the way home Billy got within a hundred feet of the front gate of his house when he crashed his truck into a culvert and was killed.

Billy had been driving, but after the accident Reedy, who was injured badly, was afraid the police would arrest Billy for drunk driving, so he pulled himself over from the passenger seat to the driver's side. When the police came, he basically lied, saying he was the driver, not Billy. Reedy was the best friend any person could have ever had. Reedy was also sure if Billy was caught driving drunk, Steinbrenner wouldn't ever take him back as Yankees manager. What Reedy didn't know was that poor Billy had broken his neck in the crash and had died.

Jill got even with Reedy for being Billy's best friend and trying to protect Billy by suing Reedy for wrongful death.

Why Reedy if Billy was driving?

Because Reedy told the cops he had been the driver, and she held him to his word. How's that for sick?

At the time he died, Billy had made about $800,000 a year for the past five or six years. That's about four million dollars. When Jill distributed his estate, she paid his two kids $8.82 each. She was a better magician than David Copperfield. She made all that money disappear without a trace.

I went by myself to Billy's funeral. The service was held at St. Patrick's Cathedral. Billy would have been impressed by how many people showed up. Billy'd told me he wanted to be buried in Berkeley next to his mother, and Billy also told his two sisters he wanted to be buried there, but the widow makes the decision, and Jill hated Billy's sisters and she certainly hated his mother, and she and Steinbrenner had him buried in a cemetery in Valhalla, New York, not far from the Babe.

I remember standing with Whitey during the burial service. It was colder than a motherfucker. A priest started to read, and all of a sudden it started to snow. Whitey whispered to me, "Jesus Christ, right to the very end he had to pull something like this, the little bastard."

I couldn't imagine having to spend the rest of my life without him.

19

After Billy died, I felt a loneliness I had never known before. Billy and I had been like brothers for almost forty years. Even his witch of a wife hadn't been able to keep us apart for long, hard as she tried. Without Billy, I was lost. Nowhere. If it hadn't been for Greer, I probably would have gotten a rubber hose, attached one end to the tail pipe of my car, and put the other end inside the car. And I would have turned on the engine and happily gone to join Billy.

The year before Billy's death, Merlyn and I had separated. Our road to separate paths began three years earlier, a few weeks after Roger Maris died on December 14, 1985. As with Billy's death, I was devastated when Roger died of cancer. Rog was another teammate I loved dearly. He was the salt of the earth, a great person as well as a great ballplayer. When he died, I sobbed and sobbed.

Despite my being away from home a lot of the time, like I told you, I always came home for Christmas. After attending the memorial service for Roger in New York City, I flew to our second home in Joplin, Missouri. I guess Merlyn couldn't take the way I had been treating her any longer. One night she started yelling at me about my relationship with the woman I had left before Greer. She ended up throwing a wine bottle at my head.

"Dammit, Merlyn," I said, "there's already someone else, and you're still fighting with me about the last one."

I got in my car and left, and I didn't come back for several days.

It wasn't long after that that Merlyn suffered a mild stroke. I was in the middle of a book tour, and as soon as I heard, I flew right home. But Merlyn wasn't about to forgive me, and we continued to fight all the time.

The end came in January 1988. Looking back, some of the things I did were truly unforgivable. People who made excuses for me blamed it on my drinking. The truth was I couldn't help myself. The doctors at Betty Ford said I had both an alcohol and a sex addiction. I thought they were nuts, but maybe the one with the screw loose was me.

The whole Mantle family, Merlyn, myself, and three of my boys, were at my fantasy baseball camp in Orlando at Disney World, and during dinner we had a real cute waitress, and all I could think about the whole meal was what she looked like naked.

I asked her for her phone number. Had I been alone, there wouldn't have been any trouble, but unknown to me, she had to go and tell Merlyn. When we got back to our hotel room, Merlyn picked up a bar stool and threw it at me. Good thing she missed, or I'd have really gotten hurt.

I had had a few drinks too many, and I fell back onto the bed and just lay there. In a furor, Merlyn jumped on top of me and began slapping my face, over and over. When I covered up, she began punching me with her fists. She was hurting me, and I was yelling for her to stop. We made such a ruckus, the police had to come and break it up. Afterward, she said she was sorry, but for me it was the end. It was time for us to separate.

I announced I was leaving. I told her one thing: she would always be my wife. Which didn't sit too well with Greer. Greer and I fought about that a lot. Whenever I would return to Dallas, I'd call and invite Merlyn to join me, but she would refuse. I had abused her emotionally once too often.

We had four sons, Mickey Jr., David, Billy, and Danny. They were all wonderful boys. Mickey Jr., they said, was the most like me, quiet and not very forthcoming. David was the business brains in the family. Billy was a loner. Danny was the most outgoing. The biggest regret of my life was that I was never there for any of them. Makes me want to break down and cry. What I did to them . . . the only places I ever took them were bars and strip joints. When I think of what happened to my son Billy . . .

What happened to him?

When Billy was a young boy, he was just adorable. When he became a teenager, he raised all kinds of hell. When he was nineteen, he woke up one morning with a lump in the lymph node under his ear. The lump was malignant—Hodgkin's disease, the same disease that killed my dad and uncle. After treatment, the disease went into remission, but Billy felt he was doomed.

I always thought I was going to die young, but I never thought it would happen to one of my children. After Billy was diagnosed, my guilt was immense. I was the one who was supposed to die from it, not my son.

After a remission, his Hodgkin's returned. It had spread to his liver and bone marrow. He underwent six months of chemo. We took him to Houston, where he underwent experimental treatment. He was supposed to die, but Billy was a brave kid. After the first treatment, he vomited all night, but he recovered.

What we didn't know was that he had gotten hooked on Dilaudid, which is a synthetic heroin. Billy would crush the pills, dilute them in water, and inject it into the catheter in his chest with a syringe.

I freaked over the idea that a son of mine was a junkie. We checked Billy into a psychiatric hospital for treatment, but after he got out, his drug use got worse. He started smoking crack, and his new friends were so scary, we feared for his life. He would disappear for weeks at a time.

Merlyn was living alone in our house on Watson Circle. We had owned that house for thirty-six years. I was living in a condo with my youngest son Danny. One night when Merlyn came home, she drove into the garage. All the lights were out, and as she came in the front door, she could hear footsteps of someone running out the back. In the living room were a pile of pillow cases the crooks had taken from the beds, and my gun, which had jammed. Perhaps if it hadn't jammed, they wouldn't have left so quickly, and maybe they'd have killed her. Merlyn was sure the thieves were some of Billy's druggie friends. She felt like a sitting duck because she was sure they'd come back, and so she decided to sell our home and move into a high-rise condo.

I didn't want Billy living with Merlyn, doing drugs, putting her in danger, so we bought Billy his own place. The stress on Merlyn took its toll. After she sold the house, she was packing up, getting ready to move, when she had a heart attack. When Billy followed the ambulance to the hospital in her car, Merlyn lay in the hospital bed worried Billy might hock the car or take off with it. I was doing an appearance for Upper Deck baseball cards, and I came home as soon as I heard. Merlyn had double bypass heart surgery. When I saw her, I started sobbing.

I sent her flowers every day. I have always hated hospitals, and so I would visit for a few minutes each day and then leave.

While Merlyn was still in the hospital, Billy, who had disappeared, was rushed to another hospital for a heart operation of his own. He suffered a stroke on the operating table that left him paralyzed on one side.

My God, Mick, that's awful. I'm really sorry.

My drinking became worse than ever. I think, subconsciously, I was trying to kill myself. I was totally out of control, unable to stop drinking. Unable to control my behavior. Sometimes I would tell Danny to lock me in my room to keep from getting behind the wheel in my condition. I didn't want people to see me wandering the streets like a homeless bum, though many a time I would go out, drink all night, and then call David or Danny and ask them to pick me up. The problem was most of the time I didn't know where I was or couldn't tell them. Somehow, though, they were able to find me.

I began having blackouts. I'd be sitting in a meeting with Roy True, my business manager, and he'd be talking about something, and I'd suddenly realize I hadn't heard a word he said. Sometimes I'd forget what month it was, or even where I was. I really thought I had Alzheimer's disease.

Why didn't you get help?

I was still too afraid to check myself into a rehabilitation clinic. I was still worried what the autograph seekers might think if they found out I was in a nuthouse.

Who did you drink with?

Often, I drank alone. While I was still in Dallas, Danny, Mickey Jr., and David would go out with me to the bars at night. If I had a woman join us, that was our little secret.

Did all your boys end up with drinking problems, too?

Please understand: I never pushed my sons to drink. They were grown men. They were on their own. But yes, all of us, it turned out, had serious drinking problems. It's the nature of alcoholism—it is passed down from generation to generation. I didn't know that then. If I had known, maybe I wouldn't have taken them to the bars. Maybe I would have gotten them help. Maybe I would have gotten myself help to protect them. But I didn't know, and I needed to drink, and they wanted to be with me. The bottom line was: I was not able to admit to myself that I was an alcoholic.

So what happened?

Danny was the first one to do something about it. It was October 1993. Danny was with me at a card show, and the second day he disappeared on a drinking binge, and I didn't see him again for a month. He had gone out with a friend and had gotten very sick. Instead of going home, he checked into Betty Ford. And then he checked his wife Kay in.

After Danny went to rehab, he was afraid of how I was going to react to his sobriety. He wanted to get well, but he was afraid I would respect him less for it. How fucked up is that?

He shouldn't have been concerned. Yeah, I hated to drink alone, but it was just beginning to sink in that my drinking had turned me into a drunken bum. I'd go out in public, not remember anything I did, and find out later I had felt up the wife of the president of the chamber of commerce or made an indecent proposal to my waitress or somebody's wife in front of the whole table or I'd be at a banquet and pass out.

After Danny and his wife Kay came home from Betty Ford, we went out to dinner together, and I found myself crying, quietly so no one else could see, wondering if I could do what they had just done.

Why were you crying?

Fear. Fear of change. I had been afraid of one thing or another my whole life, starting when I was a boy. I had feared not pleasing my dad and feared getting a beating from my mama. I had feared not measuring up to Dad's high standards, then after I made the Yankees, I feared getting traded or doing badly. I feared what people would think of me, what Casey would think of me, what my teammates would think of me, and finally I feared being fearful. From the moment I woke up to the time I put my head back down on the pillow, I was so consumed by fear that if I didn't get some booze down me, I was certain I was going to die. Then I would drink until the fear went away, but the older I got, the more fearful I became, until I got so drunk I'd be in a state of paralysis. You want to hear irony—I never feared death. I only feared the pain. And the fear itself.

So Franklin Roosevelt was right.

Franklin Roosevelt has nothing to do with this. It's not a good idea to mention Franklin Roosevelt in front of a Texan, Len.

Sorry, Mick. This is bad. We all knew you drank, but nothing like this. This is way beyond "low self-esteem" or any of that pop psychology crap you get at parties and on TV. So what did you do?

Greer, who lives in Greensboro, Georgia, did everything she could do to get me to stop drinking, but being with her caused me pain, too. Often, when I was with her, I felt horribly guilty about not being home in Dallas with Merlyn and the boys. That pain kept me drinking. The other person who tried to help me was Pat Summerall, the ex-Giants football player and football announcer on TV who almost drank himself to death. Pat and I had many long discussions about how therapy had helped him. Yet I was still afraid to go get help.

Danny pleaded with me to go to Betty Ford. I told Danny I would go if I didn't have to hear about religion.

Didn't you believe in God?

I believed in God. It's preachers I hated. I didn't believe people should go around calling themselves messengers of God. Especially when all you have to do is hang out a shingle, and you too can be in the God business. It's also my experience that these so-called messengers of God never talk about love thy neighbor, forgiveness, or understanding. What they know best is hatred and bigotry. Oh, and puss. When they caught Jimmy Swaggart in a motel with a hooker, I wasn't surprised. He was Jerry Lee Lewis's cousin, and the apple doesn't fall far from the tree. Whenever I saw a preacher, I ran, not walked. I always believed true Christians shouldn't have to advertise.

I also didn't want to go to rehab, because I was afraid I would have to talk to a group of total strangers about the shit going on in my head. I could just see them going home and telling their friends, "I was hanging out with Mickey Mantle at Betty Ford, and you know, that guy is a fucking fall-down drunk."

But you ended up going to Betty Ford.

I did.

When?

I remember the date: January 7, 1994. And I hated the place. I wanted out of there so bad I thought I was going to lose my mind. Greer came out to see me, and that helped, but most of the time I was miserable.

The most emotional day I spent came when they asked me to write a letter to my father. I sobbed the whole time I was writing it. At the same time I knew dad would have been real pissed to learn I had gone for help at the Betty Ford Clinic. He always believed you had to stand on your own two feet. He'd have called me a pansy or a girl. I could hear him mocking me the whole time I was there. When I told the counselor that, he told me I had long been the victim of his child abuse and that eventually I would learn to forgive him. But I wasn't interested in forgiving him. I wanted him to forgive me.

Forgive you? For what?

When I wrote that letter I told him I had tried to be everything he had wanted me to be: tough, strong, and standing on my own two feet. But I admitted to him that living that way hadn't worked very well for me, that his boy was going to have to try something different. I told him I would have to stop living for him and stop putting his limits on my behavior.

In rehab they taught me to live one day at a time. And they said I couldn't do it alone. If I felt panic or fear, I was to call somebody, my life partner. His job was to talk to me until my fear subsided. A day without fear, they said, meant a day without drinking.

What did you do when you got out?

After I got out of rehab, the first thing I did was to try and apologize to as many of the people I had hurt over the years as I could think of. Every single one said the same thing, that they had never held my behavior against me because they knew I couldn't help myself. I was sure my family wouldn't be as forgiving. And you don't have to ask, I'll show you what happened.

The restaurant fades into darkness. As Mickey and Lenny turn in their seats, they hear the unmistakable sound of hundreds of chair legs and shoes scraping on the floor as the gathered watchers and listeners turn around to view the scene.

Mickey is seated in a kitchen chair he has brought into the living room of his house. He faces Merlyn, who sits dead center on the sofa, flanked by Danny and David. Mickey Jr. sits in an armchair. Mickey's house doesn't really look lived in, as if someone had gone to a furniture store and ordered the set of furniture off the showroom floor. The personal touches that would make it recognizable as the place Mickey Mantle lives—the MVP awards, the milestone home run balls in a glass case, the actual Triple Crown—aren't there.

"I know you're wondering why I wanted y'all here today," Mickey says. "You know that I resisted the idea of going to Betty Ford, to any kind of rehab, and that I really didn't enjoy being there. So I thank you—especially Danny—for not listening to me whine and for getting my ass in there. It was probably the toughest thing I ever had to do—taking a real hard look at myself and all. And when I looked in the mirror, I didn't like what I saw."

Mickey pauses and sniffs. The boys glance at Merlyn for her reaction, but they can't read the look on her face.

"Sorry. This is real hard for me. I want to apologize to y'all. No, I need to apologize." He coughs, buying a few seconds to try to figure out how to put it. "I'm going to say some unpleasant things, and I only ask that you just let me talk myself out before y'all say anything. Let me just get this out." He takes a deep breath.

"I've pretty much been a liar and a cheat my entire life. Merlyn, I'm sorry. You've known there were other women for a long time. But there weren't just a few here or there. There were women in every city, sometimes a different one every night, and that goes back to before I came up to the Yankees. And that means right from the start of when we met. I was awful in the way I completely ignored you and our marriage vows. I just didn't care. I'll understand if you don't forgive me. Hell, I wouldn't forgive me. I can understand a guy who tries to stay faithful but strays—maybe once, maybe twice. But I never even tried.

"It's not like I loved any of those women. I didn't really give a shit about them, and I'm sure none of 'em gave a shit about me either. But for the time that passed while I was getting laid, well, that was time I wasn't afraid of living, of being Mickey Mantle, of playing ball, of failing, of letting my teammates down. I'm sorry. I never even thought that I was letting you down.

"Mickey, David, Danny . . . I'm sorry too. You boys mean more to me than you'll ever know. I only wish Billy was here too. What I'm sorry for is that I was never around. Yeah, I had to be gone from March through October, but I should have been around November through February. And I should have moved y'all up to New York, so I could have been with you during the season—well, while we were playing at home, anyway. But I was so selfish. If I had a nice home to go home to—you boys, and your mother—it would have made it so much harder to drink and fuck like I did all season long. But even worse, when the season ended and I came home to y'all—I still found excuses to get the hell out of the house. Maybe I made a couple bucks attending some banquet or making a TV commercial, but they were just excuses to get out of the house. And drink and fuck. With a young man in his twenties, they call it sowing your wild oats. By the time a man hits forty, I call it pathetic. I was pathetic.

"I missed your childhoods. I was never there for your own ball games. I was never there for anything—schoolwork, clubs, church, teaching you how to fish or ride a bicycle or drive a car. Maybe you were better off without me being there. I don't know. All I know is I missed out on so much. And I'll never get that time back. I hated myself for that, but I learned at Betty Ford to forgive myself. Because I was sick—I had an addiction. To booze. To sex. And I really, honestly, couldn't have helped myself without getting help first. If a place like this had existed thirty, forty years earlier, it could have really helped me.

"So I'm sorry. I'm sorry for everything. I'm not sorry for living, though, or for bringing you boys into the world. Your mother is a saint, and she did a great job of raising you. I hope y'all can grow up into the kind of men I never could be—honest, responsible, and sober.

"I know that I screwed up the past. I can't go back there and make it all better. But I promise you, in the future, I will be there for you. Starting today, starting right now.

"I gotta tell you something. I've never done this before, and I can't believe that I never have. My dad never said it, but I'm gonna. Merlyn, I love you." Merlyn starts to sob. Tears well up in Mickey's eyes.

"Mickey, I love you. David, I love you. Danny, I love you. And Billy, even though you're not here, I love you, too." Now all the boys are sniffling. Tears are streaming down Mickey's cheeks. "I love you all. I always have. I just didn't know it."

The boys watch as Merlyn rises and goes over to Mickey. Mickey's head is in his hands, his broad shoulders heaving with sobs. It is as if he is crying out a lifetime's worth of pain, of self-hatred, of insecurity. Merlyn's hand touches Mickey's shoulder, and he looks up. Merlyn's makeup is running down her cheeks, and she is smiling through her tears. "Mickey," she says, "I love you, too."

Mickey stands and hugs her. It is a desperate hug. Merlyn is a life preserver in an ocean of tears. The boys stand and join in for a group hug. They are all crying now. Mickey feels as if his knees will buckle, yet he also feels light as a feather. He reaches out and touches Mickey Jr. on the cheek, then musses David's hair, and grabs Danny by the shoulder. The boys all say that they love him.

The lights come up in the restaurant. The chairs are shuffled back around to face Mickey and Lenny, accompanied by the sound of sniffling, tissues and handkerchiefs being produced, and noses being blown.

Lenny turns back to face Mickey.

So did you stay sober?

After I got out, I surprised my friends—hell, I surprised myself, by staying sober. Was that way for almost two years, though I have to admit I wasn't nearly as much fun as I used to be. Or as I thought I used to be. I drank soda water. I drank Diet Coke. I stayed out of bars. I stayed home more with Danny and Kay. I didn't feel the need always to be out on the town anymore. I went to baseball shows and signed my name, over and over and over. Mickey Mantle, number 7. Mickey Mantle, 536 home runs. Mickey Mantle, Hall of Fame. I didn't like doing it, but at forty dollars a signature, I didn't dislike it nearly as much as when I was doing it for nothing.

I would like to say I liked myself a whole lot better sober, but I really can't. I'd be lying if I told you that sobriety brought peace. I still felt fear, but instead of drinking it away, I tried to recognize it, admit it, and then most of the time it would go away by itself. When it didn't, I made a phone call to one of my AA buddies. I was just sorry it took me forty years to realize I had a problem I had to do something about.

Getting sober allowed me to become closer to Merlyn and my boys. Merlyn and I became friends again. We were too far gone to get back together, but we had long talks on the phone, which both of us enjoyed. We talked about my plans to get involved in programs to warn kids against drugs and alcohol. I was feeling pretty good about the way things were going when in March 1994 I got a call that my son Billy had been arrested for DUI and was in the Dallas jail. This time we didn't bail him out, and in the middle of the night he suffered chest pains. He was taken to the hospital; and as he was being taken to the cafeteria for lunch, he suffered a fatal heart attack. I was at the Preston Trail golf course when I got the news. I was the one who had to tell Merlyn.

As Merlyn sobbed, I held her, and that night I stayed with her for the last time.

Around this time I started having panic attacks and premonitions about death. I suffered from a deep depression I couldn't shake, and I became short-tempered and angry, lashing out at my sons or whoever else happened to be around. I had physical pain, a pain I didn't want to admit I had. I figured my ulcers were acting up, or I had stomach cramps. I chomped a lot of Rolaids, let me tell you.

Early in 1995 I felt something inside me, something bad, a deep pain that didn't allow me to eat. I didn't think much about it, because all my life I had had aches and pains, and always they had gone away. But this pain was stubborn, persistent, like termites eating away my insides, and when I went to see a doctor, I was told I had stomach problems. *Stomach problems, my ass.* I had lost thirty pounds. I looked like a fucking skeleton.

In May 1995, Merlyn, Danny, his wife Kay, and their two kids drove from Dallas to South Dakota to visit Kay's parents. They were away five days, and I spent the whole time in bed. The pain never went away the whole time I lay there.

When they returned and found me still in bed, they called the family doctor, and he checked me into the Baylor University Medical Center. I wouldn't let anyone go in with me. I didn't want my family to see me wasting away. A week later I learned I had cancer of the liver. The docs said my liver was "hard, lumpy, and swollen." The bile duct was blocked, and they had to drain the pus before they could replace it. I was given forty-eight hours to live if I didn't get a new liver. Thank God I had been sober. The rule was that you had to be sober for six months to be eligible for a new liver. I was sober a full eighteen months. When my plight became known, I made every newspaper in the country. I still don't understand why. I hadn't played in more than twenty-five years. But they put it in the papers that I needed a liver, and I got one. And quickly. I wonder if I'd have had one so fast if I hadn't been Mickey Mantle, though the docs swore to me it didn't matter, that I had been the only one in the area on the list and I'd have gotten one even if my name had been Melvin Oppenheimer.

When I found out I was getting a liver, I was relieved. I was given new life. And I used my operation as an opportunity to tell others about the organ donor program, and maybe my life ended up having some meaning after all. When you go for your driver's license, please check the box that allows your organs to be donated if you die in a car crash. Tell 'em Mickey sent you.

The transplant operation was a success?

But the patient didn't make it. I was feeling okay for a couple of weeks and then the pain returned. I had more tests, and the docs told me they found spots on my lungs. The cancer had spread to the rest of my body, and I started shrinking fast. As I said before, I knew how Babe Ruth felt during the last days of his life.

You should also know that I had not forgotten my responsibilities to America's memorabilia collectors. After the doctors performed a rectal exam, I told them I wanted them to save the plastic glove they used with the shit smudge still on it. The doc looked at me kind of funny, but he left it on the nightstand. I had a nurse get me a small cardboard box, and put it in the box and mailed it to Barry Halper, my baseball collector friend from New Jersey. I wrote him a note, "Dear Barry, They just pulled this out of my asshole. Best wishes, Mickey Mantle." Let's see them put that on display in the Hall of Fame!

It was May, and Danny's wife Kay was expecting in December. I was told that they were having a boy, William Charles, and I had a deep regret that he would never get to know his grandfather, the same way my first son, Mickey Jr., never got to meet my dad, his grandfather.

But hey, I never wanted anyone to feel sorry for me. I had more fun in my life than anyone had a right to have, although it came at a great cost to my family. I hope Bob Costas and Billy Crystal aren't mad because I wrote this book. I like them, and the work they've done, but like *Ball Four*, this book isn't for them. They should stick to reading Joe Garagiola, or that four-eyed political gasbag, George Will, or The Hardy Boys. Bob and Billy are into the myth of the game. I will always be part of that myth, it seems. In this book I'm giving everybody the final score. My reality. And the fun. My fun. And not everyone's gonna want to hear it.

Bowie Kuhn isn't going to like it, either.

No, but he had his own problems. He went bankrupt and buried all his money into a house in Florida and his creditors couldn't touch him. Bowie wasn't a total saint. And I doubt that Bud Selig is either. This book is for all the bar-hopping, beer-drinking guys who've drunk too much and who've fooled around on the side and maybe who've gotten caught and who have really fucked up because of it. There are more of us out there than people think. I know that because I've met a lot of you. You guys should know you aren't alone.

A guy says to his friend, "I was talking to my wife's doctor last night, and I can't remember if he said she had AIDS or Alzheimer's.

His friend says, "That's no problem. Drive her to the other side of town and let her out. If she finds her way home, don't fuck her."

That's about the best advice I have to give, I'm afraid to say. That and live life to the fullest, because life is so short.

I can remember what I was thinking as I lay in Baylor Memorial waiting to die. I thought, *Tell the Babe I'm looking forward to meeting him soon. And you can tell that prick Joe D to his face that his piece-of-ass trophy wife was a lousy lay.* And to Merlyn and the kids, I'm sorry I wasn't there for you like I should have been. I may have been a hero to many, but not to those who loved me most. I hope you will find it in your heart to forgive me.

I'm sure they will, Mick.

Have you forgiven me, Lenny?

I forgave you hours ago. I had resented you because you resented me. You never tried to understand what I was doing. As a reporter, what was important to me was the truth. I didn't want to be an extension of the Yankee PR department, like some of the guys. I wanted my readers to know what was really going on.

And now you've had your chance.

And I have you to thank for that. This has been one memorable experience.

So you've forgiven me?

You've been forgiven, Mick. Isn't it obvious everyone's forgiven you. It's probably why you've ended up in heaven.

I no longer have to run from my demons. And I'm glad.

There's only one thing that still puzzles me. I hate to bring it up again now that we've become . . . well . . . friends. You've explained your alcoholism. But I haven't quite figured out your craving for all those women, all that sex. You said the people at Betty Ford said you were a sex addict. There had to be something that triggered it. Usually, it's child abuse. You hinted at it earlier. What happened to you, Mick? I know you'll feel better if you tell me. You have to tell me. You promised me you'd tell me anything I wanted to know.

Lenny, you SOB, I was hoping you had forgotten. I was abused as a child, but I still feel so ashamed to talk about it. It's one of the last things I told Merlyn before I passed away. I waited until I was on my deathbed to tell her, because I hoped she would understand me better after I told it to her. I hoped she would stop hating me for all the rotten things I did to her.

What happened, Mick?

It happened when I was a boy, and even after so many years, I am almost too embarrassed to reveal it. It started when I was little, maybe five, maybe six, and it went on for several years. I had a half sister by the name of Anna Bea—the daughter of my father's first wife—who was almost ten years older than I was. A couple of her girlfriends would come over to the house, and in front of them she would grab me, pull down my pants, pin me down, and play with me, while her friends looked on and laughed.

Why didn't you tell your mom or dad?

She said if I did, my parents wouldn't love me anymore.

How often did this happen?

This went on for a quite a while, until she and her brother moved away. All my life whenever I thought about that, I felt such shame. I never could shake that overwhelming feeling of shame, of how she made me feel it was my fault. But at the same time I also felt aroused, and I came to really enjoy that feeling. I never stopped wanting to feel that way.

You were a little boy, Mick. She molested you. Maybe it explains why you loved having sex with women but never could respect them.

I never thought of it exactly in those terms, but maybe you're right. And now you know everything. I'd say we're done? Seems about time to stick a fork in it.

I guess so.

There is really nothing more to say except that for all my fans who loved me, I hope you can forgive me for not always loving you back. For all of you who adored me, please forgive me for not being appreciative. I wish I could have felt satisfaction in the things I accomplished the way they did, but I never could. As I said, I felt that nothing I did was ever good enough. I should have taken better care of myself. I would have played better. Been injured less. Had a longer career. I just wish I had been a better husband and father. When Merlyn and my boys read this book, maybe they'll understand that fathers can be heroes, but heroes can't always be fathers. And for that, I'm sorry. For eternity, I'll be praying for their forgiveness. And yours.

There is a smattering of polite applause that slowly grows into a loud, raucous standing ovation. Mickey looks up, startled. Unnoticed and silent in rapture while he was talking, the crowd surrounding his table had grown until the entire restaurant had become a crush of humanity. Hundreds of people are standing and clapping—men, women, waiters, busboys, bartenders, chefs. All have tears in their eyes.

Mickey gets up from his seat and walks to greet them one by one. He shakes their hands and accepts their hugs. Among the throng are common fans, the men and women who had loved him while he played, memorabilia collectors like Barry Halper and George Lyons, but also in the crowd are some famous faces. Casey Stengel winks and embraces him like the son he never had, as does Roger Maris, still tall and erect; Ellie Howard, who had died too young of an enlarged heart; Johnny Keane to everyone's great surprise, to whom Mickey finally is able to express his sorrow for treating him the way he did; and other former teammates he cherished, including Gene Woodling, Joe Collins, Johnny Lindell, and Joe Page, who knew a thing or two about women in his day. After hugging them, two young men come over. They appear to be younger versions of Mickey himself. Billy Mantle and Mickey Mantle Jr., his two sons whom he hadn't seen in such a long, long time, entangle their arms around his neck. He is surprised to see Mickey Jr., not knowing that he too had passed away. Mickey Jr., a ballplayer and alcoholic like his dad, had died of cancer at the age of forty-seven in December 2000, five years after his father's death. The three embrace. Tears are flowing. Bearhugs. Kisses. All Mickey can say is, "I love you all."

From inside the room comes a chorus in response.

"We love you too, Mick."

ACKNOWLEDGMENTS

Ever since I first met Mickey Mantle back in 1975 when I interviewed him for my very first book, *Dynasty*, I wanted to write the story of his life. But every time I sat down to write a proposal to do it, I was stopped by the knowledge that his life was far more ribald and interesting than anything that would appear in a straight biography. After Mickey died, his story kept nagging at me, only I couldn't figure out how to do it until it hit me like a thunderclap: write the story he would have written had he had the sobriety and the self-awareness to do it.

I did that, and I sent the manuscript to Robert Lipsyte, a friend and a mentor, though he would blush if I said that to his face. He was enthusiastic, but he thought that Mickey, the cancer fighter, deserved more acclaim at the end. He suggested that Mickey write this book from heaven and that I invent someone for him to tell his story to. When he said that, I knew just who that should be: Lenny Shecter, and almost immediately I phoned Jim Bouton, Lenny's coauthor of *Ball Four*, to learn more about him. Jim, my friend and neighbor in Englewood, New Jersey, before both of us moved away too many years ago, was happy to oblige.

Over the years countless people have told me stories about Mickey. Among them were Mickey himself, a delightful raconteur when he was among friends; Billy Martin, who loved him like a brother; Bill Reedy, the best friend a person could have; and Yankee teammates including Joe Pepitone, Tom Sturdivant, Jim Bouton, Hank Bauer, Whitey Ford, and Joe Collins. Then there were the magic moments like when I attended a dinner at Eckerd College in St. Pete, where I met a woman who told me she had dated Mantle when he was young, and he had used the alias

Melvin Oppenheimer. Bill Mastry regaled me one day about the time Billy came into his bar and bragged about the young girl he had impregnated. I couldn't make this stuff up, though a lot of times I do have to fill in the blanks.

I want to thank Judith Regan and Doug Grad for getting behind the book, and thank Neil and Dawn Reshen for selling it to them. Thanks also go to Burton Hersh, Bob Lipsyte, Shaun Kelly at Greenwich Country Day, and Bill Reedy for making suggestions and giving me blurbs, and to Dr. Irv Kolin, an expert on drug and alcohol abuse who made suggestions and gave me advice, all of which I took gratefully. I also want to thank Gene Brissie and Scott Watrous of The Lyons Press for having the cojones to publish this book. And finally, here's to you, Mick, for being such an important part of my childhood. You touched them—and us—all.